TECHNOLOGY TRANSFER

TECHNOLOGY TRANSFER

Geographic, Economic, Cultural, and Technical Dimensions

Edited by
A. COSKUN SAMLI

Q

Quorum Books
Westport, Connecticut • London, England

Library of Congress Cataloging in Publication Data

Main entry under title:

Technology transfer.

Bibliography: p.
Includes index.
1. Technology transfer.   I. Samli, A. Coskun.
T174.3.T384 1985   338.9   84-16113
ISBN 0-89930-057-X (lib. bdg.)

Library of Congress Catalog Card Number: 84-16113
ISBN: 0-89930-057-X

First published in 1985 by Quorum Books

Greenwood Press
A division of Congressional Information Service, Inc.
88 Post Road West, Westport, Connecticut 06881

Printed in the United States of America

10 9 8 7 6 5 4 3 2 1

To the memory of my father, Suleyman Seref Samli, who so aptly explained to me the importance of technology transfer when I was a very young man.

Contents

Illustrations

Tables

Preface

Technology transfer represents the single most important hope of alleviating the ever widening gap between the haves and have-nots in the world. It may provide an accelerated and long-lasting growth for the world's poor nations. Similarly, by encouraging technology transfer among the rich nations, mutual understanding and peaceful co-existence among nations may result. It is hoped that this book will make a significant contribution in both of these extremely critical issues.

However important the present status of technology is, it will be far more crucial in the future. During the coming two decades or so, the nations of the world will experience tremendous amounts of technology transfer. If these transfer processes are successful, the world will become a better place to live in and a safer place than before. Thus, technology transfer is the viable alternative to war and poverty, and we all must do our part to sustain it and to make it more successful.

I am grateful to Lynn Taylor, the Quorum Books editor at Greenwood Press, for suggesting that I put this book together. We called it a handbook because by exploring the lesser known aspects of technology transfer, it will facilitate successful transfer of technology throughout the world.

Many people were extremely helpful in this project. First and foremost to the contributors to this volume go my deepest gratitude. They worked extremely diligently and produced chapters that will make a considerable contribution to the theory and practice of technology transfer.

My assistants, David Randall and Jennifer Helm, were very helpful in searching for basic information and key references. Our secretaries Becky Glick, Wanda Belcher, and Janice Blevins were always available and rose to the challenge of reading my sometimes totally illegible handwriting. My colleagues in the Department of Marketing, through their reactions to my seminars relating to technology transfer, made a profound impact on my thinking.

Thanks are due to my brother Osman Samli who took time off from his busy schedule and spent literally hundreds of hours with me in the streets of Istanbul interviewing numerous small and large businesses to provide me with the appropriate practical background about technology transfer in Third World countries.

My friend and colleague, M. Joseph Sirgy, contributed not only directly to this book, but also indirectly by always being there to react to my way of thinking. My wife Jane and my children Ayla, Evan, Susan, and Gena were patient and understanding.

My students in my graduate course in international marketing, presented at the University of Hawaii in conjunction with the total offerings of the Pacific Asian Management Institute (PAMI), were very perceptive and helped me immeasurably to clarify my ideas and concepts.

To these people and many others whose names are not mentioned go my deep gratitude. Needless to say I am solely responsible for the organization and contents of this book. I fully agree and support the ideas and positions taken by all the contributors in this book.

Introduction

Emmanual (1983) maintains that technology transfer is a shortcut to Third World development. He posits that regardless of whether the technology is transferred directly as it is purchased by the less developed country (LDC) or indirectly through perhaps a multinational company or foreign investments in the country, superior capital-intensive technology is necessary for this shortcut. He argues that underdeveloped technology in an underdeveloped country simply accelerates the problems of underdevelopment, rather than eliminating them.

This book offers two major propositions. First, technology transfer is a shortcut not only for the Third World countries, but also for all the countries in the world. Technology transfer is as important to developed countries (DCs) as it is to LDCs. It is important not only for world understanding, but also for taking advantage of progress in different parts of the world in applying modern science to economic activity. Second, success in technology transfer is related to its appropriateness. If the transferred technology is not appropriate for the needs and conditions prevailing in the receiving country, no matter how superior or efficient that technology may be it will be rejected. Here appropriateness, unlike what Emmanual implies, does not mean the most up-to-date technology, but it is most likely to be transferred successfully.

In order to identify the appropriate technology and transfer it effectively, the geographic, economic, cultural, and technical dimensions of technology transfer must be examined carefully. This book aims to accomplish just that. Its chapters deal with these specific dimensions of technology transfer with the hope that it may facilitate this all-important international activity.

Before some of the highlights of the book are described, an important issue must be clarified. Although hundreds of studies have been published relating to the diffusion process (Rogers, 1976) as it analyzes how new products are diffused within societies, this process has not been carefully distinguished from technology transfer (or diffusion between societies). In this book, we propose that technology transfer and international diffusion process are much the same thing. This distinction between diffusion within societies and technology transfer is important because international diffusion (or technology transfer) has to cope with diverse cultures prevailing in many parts of the world.

Technology transfer, as discussed in this book, therefore emphasizes cultural barriers as the greatest challenge to a successful transfer of technology. Penetrating through the cultural barrier implies the senders' perceptions as to the receivers' needs. It also implies the appropriateness of the technology for the recipient. This book addresses a principle which is all-important in the technology transfer process, namely, congruence among the sender, technology, and the receiver. If a high degree of congruence among these three is not present, the technology will not be transferred effectively.

In this book a serious attempt was made to answer the following questions:

What strategies do senders use to transfer technologies successfully?

What technologies should have higher priorities and how is the prioritization done?

What are some of the key aspects of cultural barriers to technology transfer?

What are the key institutional instruments of technology transfer and how do they proceed in the transfer activities?

What are the key influences of technology transfer and how do people respond to them?

How should the process of technology transfer and its aftermath be monitored?

The chapters in this book delve into one or more of these questions. Both scholars and practitioners will find some very specific answers to these questions.

The sixteen chapters were written by scientists, economists, and marketing specialists. Technology transfer is predominantly a commercial undertaking and involves the general areas of international or industrial marketing. Therefore, the role of marketing scholars in this book was particularly important.

The book briefly covers the following important aspects of technology transfer.

Chapter 1 explores the characteristics and constraints of a general technology transfer model. It reflects the general philosophy of the book and this author's position in bringing the components of the book together.

Since the greatest challenge faced by the technology transfer process is its successful application to Third World countries, this issue is addressed at a very early stage in the book, in chapter 2. Perhaps the greatest hope of these countries is to break away from chronic poverty through proper technology.

Chapter 3 examines the specific issues encompassing the food distribution technology transfer problems of LDCs. Food is, of course, critical in achieving successful economic gains. Its effective distribution is likely to make a very significant contribution in the economic development of Third World countries.

Utilizing human resources more effectively can contribute substantially to the economic development process. Any type of technology transfer that can improve human resource utilization is likely to be critical for the world's future. Women are perhaps the most underutilized resource in most parts of the Third World. If women are to bolster a country's economic well-being they must be relieved of their primary activity of struggling for food. Chapter 4, therefore, deals with improving the food supply in Third World countries by transferring special techologies to women.

In addition to a country's economic status, its political structure is also very important in successful transfer of technology, Chapter 5 explores the complex problems of transferring technology to East European countries. The socialist governments of these countries are crucial to the success or failure of the transfer process. Since many LDCs have socialistic tendencies, this chapter contributes an additional dimension to the general knowledge of successful technology transfer in general and successful technology transfer to Third World countries in particular.

Chapter 6 discusses technology transfer activities among East European countries. The dealings of socialist governments with each other shed special light on the subject matter of the book.

China as the largest less developed country in the world is a special subject of study in any attempt to gain better knowledge of successful technology transfer. Chapter 7 explores some of the special problems in transferring technology to the world's largest potential market, China.

As noted earlier, technology transfer is as important to developed as to less developed nations. However, most of the technology transfer information to developed countries is related to technology being transferred from one developed country to another. Reversed technology transfer, as it is termed in this book, is a neglected area. Chapter 8 introduces this new concept and explores the diffusion of ideas relating to managing scarce resources as they are exercised in less developed countries.

Japan has been extremely successful in transferring technology, particularly in Southeast Asia. The Japanese type of technology transfer activity is particularly important in regards to improving the technology transfer process regardless of the source or destination of technology. Chapter 9 explores some of the key factors behind Japan's success in this area.

The technology transfer process needs to be modified according to other factors, including the culture prevailing in the receiving country. Geographically and culturally, a country such as Turkey presents a very different set of perspectives from Southeast Asia or other parts of the world where LDCs are located. Hence, chapter 10 makes a special attempt to explore the special case of Turkey in order to understand the technology process and how to make it more effective.

Technology transfer cannot be successful unless the transferred technology is accepted. The psychological dimension in technology transfer needs to be explored carefully, an issue covered in chapter 11. This chapter explores how preferences are prioritized through cultural pressures and values so that the imported technology is accepted.

Chapter 12 examines another psychological dimension in the technology transfer process: achievement motivation. If people do not in general strive to achieve, they will not accept the newly imported technology.

Much of the technology transfer discussion in chapters 1 through 12 does not specifically imply the vehicle through which the transfer process takes place. Multinational corporations are extremely important in this process. They transfer technology and manage the process carefully. Chapter 13 examines companies' involvement in technology transfer.

On the receiving end of technology transfer there are large and small companies. The recipients' managerial capabilities are seldom explored. Entrepreneurs are particularly important in either receiving technologies or starting domestic ones. Thus, another vehicle of technology transfer is entrepreneurship. Chapter 14 examines this particular dimension.

Chapters 15 and 16 together cover a very important aspect of technology transfer, namely, progress. Chapter 15 sets forth the discussion of technology transfer measurement. Chapter 16 presents various approaches to monitoring the process in the interest of evaluating its effectiveness.

This book should be viewed as an ongoing source rather than as the last word on this all-important topic. It is hoped that this work will contribute to progress in technology transfer theory and practice.

REFERENCES

Emmanual, Arghiri. *Appropriate or Underdeveloped Technology?* New York: John Wiley and Sons, 1982.

Rogers, Everett M. "New Product Adoption and Diffusion." *Journal of Consumer Research* (March 1976).

TECHNOLOGY TRANSFER

1
Technology Transfer: The General Model

A. C. SAMLI

Technology, the application of science and scientific progress to solving economic problems with all its ramifications, perhaps offers the single most important hope for the future of all nations, providing it is used to enhance the human condition rather than contributing to warlike activity.

Just because nations are not endowed equally in terms of natural resources as well as people's temperaments or talents, technological advances have been uneven. This unevenness of technological progress throughout the world provides the basis for technology transfer. This does not necessarily mean that there should be no gap at all, technologically speaking, among nations; rather, it means that technology transfer must take place to narrow the gap among them. If all nations, through technology transfer, benefit from technological advances, first, the gap among the rich and the poor will narrow. Second, all nations, rich and poor, will learn to be more efficient and therefore there will be less waste in the world's industrial endeavors. More knowledge, better utilization of resources, fast industrial progress, and, therefore, elimination of economic underdevelopment are all feasible outcomes of successful technology transfer.

This chapter attempts to construct a model that will facilitate international technology transfer. Despite its high desirability, technology transfer across the national boundaries is at present an extremely critical and difficult activity. Thus, a model must be constructed to illustrate the problems of technology transfer across the national boundaries.

THE NEED FOR A MODEL

The technology transfer process is extremely complex, encompassing many dimensions. Some of these dimensions may work against each other.

For instance, while the economic development process calls for certain technology, the people of the country may have very strong objections to using this new technology. Thus, people's attitudes or the culture may work against the country's best economic interests.

The complexity of the technology transfer process coupled with its desirability necessitates modeling this process. Such a model can help explain not only the process itself but also the hurdles or hindrances it has to overcome. There is perhaps no one best way of transferring technology. This is so because, first, technology does not exist in a social vacuum. It is "embodied in products, processes and people" (Goulet, 1978, p. 31). Second, technology circulates only through very diverse institutional channels or mechanisms (Goulet, 1978). Thus, social values and cultures become an integral part of the technology and its transfer. Third, the channels through which technology circulates are diverse, and there is no best channel to be used for successful transfer. Developing an effective technology transfer model, therefore, is extremely important to find better ways of transferring the total knowledge and processes that technology commands. Two key aspects of technology transfer are particularly emphasized in this chapter. These are the dimensions of technology transfer and the components of the transfer model.

THE MODEL CONSIDERATIONS: KEY DIMENSIONS OF TECHNOLOGY

Where the technology is developed, how it is utilized, who uses it for what purpose—all these aspects must be explored in any study of technology transfer. Six dimensions of technology relate to these specific aspects, namely, geography, culture, economy, people, business, and government.

Geography

With different parts of the world endowed differently in both natural resources and population, different countries or geographic regions have developed differently. Thanks to international communications and trade, these differences are not as drastic as they might have been a few centuries ago. Even so, as a result, there are different levels of technological development as well as perceptions of different needs for technology.

Because of geography, some technologies cannot be transferred. If, for instance, it is either unfeasible or impossible to grow sugar beets in Iraq, then the technology to convert sugar beets into sugar will not be needed.

Thus, all things being the same, geography influences technology transfer in at least two distinct ways. First, if the natural resources or new materials needed to produce certain products by applying the new technology do not exist because of geographic conditions, this will directly affect the applicable technology. If the country cannot grow cotton, technology to produce cotton textiles cannot be transferred. However, even if the country has the raw materials, it may still lack a certain key ingredient to make the technology transferable. For instance, the technological process may require plentiful water, which the country may lack, even though it may have all the other necessary raw materials. This is the second way in which geography influences technology transfer.

Culture

According to one school of thought, culture is the way the people live. According to another, it is the sum total of the values, beliefs, and mores that condition life in general and behavior in particular. Whatever definition is used, it is clear that culture plays an essential role as to the need for and acceptability of specific technologies.

Some cultures are more tradition-oriented. They may, therefore, be more closed to new technologies, and they may resist the development and adoption of these technologies. Other cultures are more futuristic, thriving on new developments. They, therefore, are very open to new technologies; they adopt them quickly, and they constantly encourage technological advances and breakthroughs.

Economy

Since the beginning of humankind, it seems that the world has been composed of haves and have-nots. Some countries or some people at any given time in history have been economically more advanced than others. The economic dichotomy of haves and have-nots implies at least three key situations regarding technology transfer.

Situation 1. The poor countries' needs far exceed their capability of absorbing the transferred technology.

Situation 2. Economically advanced countries, by generating, adopting, and most of all by properly utilizing the most up-to-date technology, expand the economic gap between themselves and less developed countries (LDCs).

Situation 3. Regardless of the degree of economic development, the economy dictates, to a substantial extent, the appropriateness of the technology to be transferred.

With regard to the first situation, the LDCs that need technology the most so that they will break the vicious cycle of economic underdevelopment are limited by their economies as to what technology they can transfer. Some of the special high technologies which require know-how, resources, and infrastructure cannot be adopted because of the deficiencies in these requirements. A country may, for instance, lack water or energy, or it may have widespread illiteracy. Hence, it cannot adopt and utilize effectively those technologies that require abundant water or energy (Coates, 1977) and a high degree of know-how on the part of the populace.

Economically advanced countries, on the other hand, generally enjoy a momentum in the development and transfer of technologies (situation 2). This momentum further enhances their economic status and creates a greater gap between them and LDCs.

Finally, as suggested in situation 3, there are economic limits to technology transfer regardless of the degree of poverty or richness. Many rich but small countries, for instance, Switzerland, cannot successfully adopt high technological, extensive farming which is geared to large-size farms in the United States.

People

It is difficult to talk about people separately from culture and economy. However, regardless of whether the causes can be traced to the culture or to the economic conditions, people's behavior and openness are likely to hinder technology transfer. If we adopt Riesman's (1953) classification of inner-directed, other-directed, and tradition-directed as indicators of their approach to technology developed elsewhere, three distinct types of behavior can be described.

The inner-directed people may not be closed to new technologies, but they like to develop these technologies themselves rather than adopting transferred technology. The other-directed people will be most prone to adopt transferred technology since they are quite open to other people's behaviors. And finally, tradition-directed people are perhaps most closed to the transfer of technologies developed elsewhere. They will not condone development of technology domestically either. They adopt this attitude because they believe the technologies are radical deviations from the tradition and the tradition is the most important guiding factor of the society.

Business

Business is perhaps the most important vehicle of technology transfer. In both developed and less developed countries, multinational corporations are major vehicles of transfer and diffusion of technology (Rugman, 1983). While multinationals pursue profitable returns for their efforts, they make an effort to improve operational efficiency or produce certain technical products. In either case the multinational companies transfer technology through their multinational production networks. Their direct positive impact has been enumerated by Aggarwal (1982):

1. They may supplement the local capital which is needed in the LDC's economic development.
2. Additional national income generated by the multinational's technology transfer efforts may encourage the development of ancillary industries and create jobs in the LDC.
3. Additional revenues may be generated for government expenditures.
4. Technology transfer by multinationals may develop the LDC's export potential by the adoption of highly sophisticated technology which would not have come without the multinational company.
5. The LDC's foreign exchange gap may be reduced or the country's foreign exchange reserves may increase.
6. The multinationals may sell technology at a marginal cost that does not include a large portion of the fixed costs which would have been incurred if the technology had been developed indigenously.

Multinationals may also generate negative impact (Aggarwal, 1982).

1. Outflow of dividends or profits, management and royalty fees, and interest on loans and other remittances can be too costly to LDCs.
2. Too much technology transfer may destroy the local "infant" industries.
3. The multinational firm may use scarce local capital and make it scarcer for local industries.
4. Similarly, other scarce resources, such as trained manpower and raw materials, may also be used excessively by the multinational.
5. Because of the technology transfer through multinationals, certain parallel industry which is totally unconnected to the rest of the LDC's economy may not develop.
6. A "halo effect" may be created by the multinational being an example and local industry's developing inappropriate methods.
7. For a number of reasons, the transferred technology may not be appropriate.

Thus, technology transfer by multinational companies cannot be allowed without close scrutiny. The recipient country often has a lot at stake. A wrong move may significantly widen the gap between the upper economic (capital-intensive technologies) and lower economic level (local labor-intensive technologies) (Aggarwal, 1982).

Government

Governments, directly or indirectly, play a vital role in technology transfer. Among the direct roles of the government of the recipient country are (1) specifications of national needs or approval of the technology; (2) coercion of the domestic industry or political forces to import the technology; (3) involvement in direct importing of the technology; and (4) participation in direct negotiations about the mechanics of importing the technology. The indirect role governments play in the technology transfer process is, at least, equally important. In this context, first, instead of importing the technology itself, the government may provide special incentives so that certain specified technologies will be given higher priority by the private sector that will take over the responsibility of importing. Second, the government can assist in the process of making the imported technology successful. For instance, many Third World countries will provide protection to aid the imported infant industry. Finally, the government has the authority to allow, approve, or reject joint ventures that can be instrumental in transferring the technology (Kindra, 1983).

A BASIC MODEL

No one all-inclusive and perfectly functional model of technology transfer is applicable to all related situations. However, the model presented here, however broad, provides insights into the key components of technology transfer. The way these components interact would facilitate or hinder the successful transfer of technology in question.

Five key components are considered in this model: the sender, the technology, the receiver, the aftermath, and the assessment (Figure 1.1).

The Sender

In addition to being capable of developing the technology to be transferred, the sender must have certain other qualities. First and foremost, the sender must have enough knowledge and sensitivity as to the receiver's background and needs. Second, the sender must have the willingness to send the technology. The sender's needs must coincide with the receiver's needs in such a way that the technology transfer would be a mutually advantageous transaction. Thus, the sender plays a very critical role in the whole process.

The Technology

Technology means a variety of things. Many people think of it as only the technical heavy equipment aspect of applying modern science to economic activity. It is basically more than just the heavy equipment, however: it is the capability of applying science to economic activity or production. Hence, it includes all the hardware, software, and other supporting activity.

Determining the appropriate technology that the receiver needs and transferring it effectively are most difficult tasks. The appropriateness of the technology must be assessed on the basis of numerous factors. Of all of the multitudinous factors, five are considered in this chapter: (1) market, (2)

Figure 1.1
The Basic Model of Technology Transfer

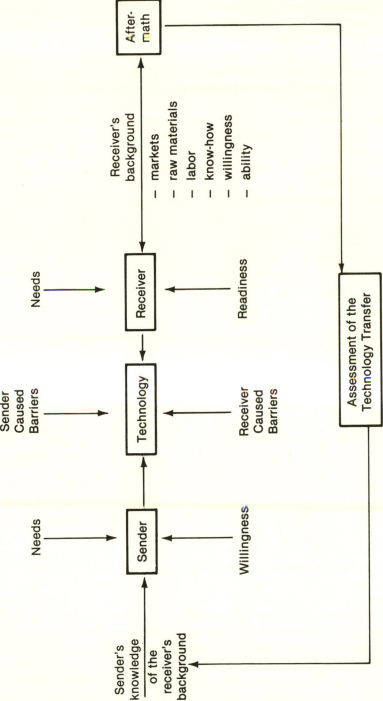

raw materials, (3) economies of scale, (4) labor, and (5) machinery (Teitel, 1978).

Market

Since market conditions are different in all countries, it is logical that the technology and pursuant industrial products must meet different preferences and specifications that prevail in each individual market. Quality is the first subfactor that needs to be considered within the context of the market. Quality perception and requirement vary significantly. The diesel engines in India, for instance, were found to be of higher quality standards than those found in industrialized countries. The major reason for this condition is that repair/services and parts are harder to find. Unfavorable conditions of maintenance would have made this product very undesirable in the Indian market (Teitel, 1978).

Similar considerations are applicable to durability. Razor blades, light bulbs, and similar products have been found to have longer lives in Latin America (Teitel, 1978). This is perhaps because the monopolies producing these products do not wish to lose their market positions. Furthermore, once again the markets are not rich enough to accept excessive planned obsolescence which will shorten the lives of these products.

Raw Materials

Raw material requirements in the production of the products is another critical variable in determining the appropriateness of the technology.

Three specific considerations relate to raw materials. First, will the technology make use of the raw materials already available in the recipient country? If it does not, then the technology can be a permanent burden on the national economy. Second, and closely related to the first point, does the product need heavy importation of raw materials? If excessive amounts of raw materials need to be imported, then the appropriateness of the technology becomes quite questionable. Particularly in LDCs where foreign exchange is limited or scarce, this point becomes critical. Third, does the product call for the use of rare materials or scarce resources? Even though these materials may be domestically available in the recipient country, the fact that they are needed for other and more important products makes the particular technology quite undesirable.

Economies of Scale

Economies of scale are a common factor in manufacturing processing. With regard to this factor, the assessment of the specific technology can be concentrated on at least three points. First, can the technology be utilized in the receiving country with the full benefits of economies of scale? The receiving country may or may not have a large market for this particular industry. If the domestic market for the output of this technology is rather small and if the technology requires a large volume to be produced before it reaches the optimum economies of scales level, then the technology may not be very appropriate for the recipient. Second, the flexibility of the technology regarding the economies of scale can be critical. If the demand for the products that this industry will produce is not well known or if the receiver's domestic market is undergoing substantial changes, the flexibility of the industry becomes particularly important. If the industry is not flexible, economies of scale may never be materialized. The steel industry, for instance, has had this kind of experience in Latin America. The inflexibility of the industry made it difficult, if not impossible, to reach the desired level of efficiency. Third, if the industry provides flexibility in terms not only of size but also of multiple new products, then it will be particularly attractive for the recipient. If the receiving country is going through significant economic changes, the demand for various products including some new products may be changing sharply. If the industry can experience economies of scale and accommodate to suddenly changing demands through the new technology, that technology becomes very appropriate.

Labor

Three aspects of labor are particularly important in ascertaining the value of the proposed technology. First, the labor or capital intensity must be decided upon. For instance, if a technology is to be considered appropriate for Third World countries, it must provide substantial employment for the labor which is plentiful in these countries. The opposite may be considered as the standard case for the developed countries. Labor is somewhat more scarce and usually quite expensive, and hence a capital-intensive technology may be more appropriate. Second, cost considerations regarding the labor must be carefully examined. Particularly in LDCs, if the new technology creates disproportional ratios between capital and labor to the point that it distorts the existing cost ratios between the two key factors of production, then the new technology may be deemed to be inappropriate. In Latin America, for example, experts have suggested that the technology that raises the cost of labor may be strongly objectionable (Teitel, 1978). Finally, the new technology must be assessed on the basis of the available skilled labor. The problem of availability is not necessarily unique to LDCs. Many developed countries, particularly in the present age of hi-tech, are finding themselves short of qualified labor, with inadequate resources to retrain the labor force. Naturally, each case and each country situation must be considered according to its own unique conditions and peculiarities.

Machinery

The machinery and equipment portions of the new technology must be scrutinized with great care before they can be transferred. Many experts agree that the machinery used in LDCs is usually not properly adapted to the needs and prevailing conditions of these countries (Teitel, 1978). This situation is not necessarily unique to LDCs.

Because of the uniqueness of its resource supply and prevailing economic conditions, each country must consider the proper adaptation of the technology to its particular needs. If the machinery and equipment that come with the new proposed technology cannot be adapted to the prevailing conditions, that technology may be judged inappropriate for that country. Lack of adaptability may be due to numerous factors, including difficult repairability, obsolescence, lack of adaptation to climate, lack of sturdiness, and incompatibility with other equipment (Teitel, 1978).

The Receiver

The third component of the basic model is the receiver. Each receiving country has different needs, resources, values, and culture. Thus, successful technology transfer implies congruence among the sender's needs and understanding of the recipient's needs, the nature of the technology, and the receiver's priority ordering as to the immediate economic needs. Without this three-way congruence it is impossible to expect a smooth and successful transfer of the technology.

In dealing with the receiver so that a congruence among the sender, technology, and receiver is achieved, at least three factors must be considered: the receiver's needs, its readiness, and its background.

Receiver's Needs

Every receiver has different needs. There are probably no definite criteria that would indicate perfectly the priority ordering of the recipient's needs. Some recipients may be long-run oriented, while others may be short-range oriented. Similarly, some recipients may opt for import substitution as opposed to export stimulation. If the receiver does not understand its needs and opts for the technology that is not appropriate, numerous problems may result varying from economic to political.

Readiness

Regardless of how anxious the country may be in terms of importing the technology, it is necessary to raise the question of whether or not it is ready for that technology. If the country is not ready for the proposed technology, it will have extreme difficulty in absorbing it and using it successfully. The readiness factor is above all related to the barriers that may be created partially by the sender and partially by the receiver. The sender may insist on very high royalty returns or very high licensing fees. The receiver may insist on majority ownership of a joint venture to name just two of the many possible technical barriers. Readiness partially implies having cleared these barriers and the country is now ready to receive the technology. However, a more important aspect of readiness is related to the receiver's having achieved the required level of sophistication or know-how. It simply implies that the receiver is in a proper position to make good use of the imported technology.

Background

The receiver's background is a significant factor in a smooth transfer of technology. This factor is not necessarily separate from the receiver's needs and readiness. In fact, the receiver's needs and readiness may be viewed as closely related to its background. The background is reflected by the prevailing values and attitudes toward new developments and deviation from traditions—in short, the culture. If the recipient does not have the appropriate background, it is impossible to transfer the technology because the country and its people will not adopt it.

The Aftermath

While the technology itself, the transfer-related issues, and the actual transfer process have been the focal point of many studies, the aftermath of technology transfer has been neglected. However, the direct and indirect impact of the transferred technology must be singled out and evaluated so that future attempts will be more successful. Furthermore, if the aftermath cannot be identified, the overall assessment of the technology transfer cannot take place.

Two steps are involved in the total outcome of technology transfer. The first is the *aftermath* and the second is the *assessment*. While the aftermath is related to the immediate and mostly the direct impact, the overall assessment is related to longer-run and far-reaching outcomes.

It is necessary to establish the criteria for the aftermath. As Hetman (1978) states, "each separate technology creates opportunities for constant innovation" (p. 304). Perhaps the first criterion in aftermath analysis is the degree to which the newly imported technology stimulates constant innovation. The second criterion is simply whether or not the newly acquired technology is working. The third is related to the objectives of the particular technology transfer in question. If the newly acquired technology is fulfilling its original objectives, then the aftermath is positive. These three criteria are suggestive rather than exhaustive. For example, the objectives criterion can be broken into numerous factors which need to be dealt with on the basis of the particularities of each case.

The Assessment

The importance of the assessment process of technology transfer as stated by Hetman stems primarily from a belief that "while technology is advancing at an accelerated pace, human adaptability and social structures in general are stagnating if not actually regressing. . . . [This way of thinking reinforces the thesis of] . . . human, social and ethical phenomena lag behind technological developments [which] implies that social problems tend to derive from technological change (p. 304)."

Thus, it is particularly important to assess the outcomes of the transferred technology. Its social impact is so far-reaching that some scholars call the process "social assessment of technology" (Hetman, 1978). The six main areas identified as the key criteria for technology assessment studies (Hetman, 1978) are technology, economy, society, the individual, the environment, and the value system. Others approach technology assessment studies through two broad categories, technology-initiated and problem-initiated. If the assessment is done from the technologist's point of view, it is technology-initiated. However, the assessment from the social engineer's point of view provides completely different perspectives. This approach is coined problem-initiated. The latter types of assessment are particularly scarce (Hetman, 1978). More emphasis is necessary on the development of appropriate constructs for social assessment of technology. Without significant progress in this area, total effectiveness of technology transfer cannot fully materialize.

SUMMARY AND CONCLUSIONS

There is a need for a general model of technology transfer, and the development of such a model is quite possible. The model presented in this chapter has five key components: the sender, the technology, the receiver, the aftermath, and the assessment.

Before such a model can be successfully implemented, it is necessary to understand the specific dimensions of technology. These dimensions must also be accounted for if a successful transfer of the technology is expected. Six such dimensions are identified: geography, culture, economy, people, business, and government.

There is a need to evaluate the outcome of technology transfer. In this process there are two stages: the aftermath and the assessment. This total evaluation process is still in its infancy. The future success of technology transfer depends primarily on this evaluation process which will function as feedback for improving future technology transfer attempts.

REFERENCES

Aggarwal, Raj. "The Role of Foreign Direct Investment and Technology Transfer in India." *Proceedings of AIB Conference.* University of Hawaii, 1982, pp. 252-259.

Coates, Joseph F. "Technological Change and Future Growth: Issues and Opportunities." *Technological Forecasting and Social Change* 11 (1977): 49-74.

Economic Commission for Latin America. *Perspectivas y Modiludades de Integración Regional de la Industria Automatriz en America Latina.* Santiago, 1974.

Goulet, Denis. "Dynamics of International Technology Flows." *Technology Review* (May 1978): 32-39.

Hetman, François. "Social Assessment of Technology and Some of Its International Aspects." *Technological Forecasting and Social Change* 11 (1978): 303-313.

Kindra, Guprit S. "Technology Transfer and Export Marketing Strategies: The LDC Perspective." In Alan M. Rugman, *Multinationals and Technology Transfer.* New York: Praeger, 1983.

Riesman, David. *The Lonely Crowd.* Garden City, N.Y.: Anchor, 1953.

Roman, Daniel D., and Joseph F. Puett, Jr. *International Business and Technological Innovation.* New York: North Holland, 1983.

Rugman, Alan M. *Multinationals and Technology Transfer.* New York: Praeger, 1983.

Teitel, Simon. "On the Concept of Appropriate Technology for Less Industrialized Countries." *Technological Forecasting and Social Change* 11 (1978): 349-369.

2

Technology Transfer to Third World Countries and Economic Development

A. C. SAMLI

For many decades, many poor countries have failed to develop economically. Even if the poor are not getting poorer, the rich are definitely getting richer. Table 2.1 illustrates the point. The five poorest countries in 1970 had .048 percent of the world's total income, whereas their total population accounted for 1.585 percent of total world population. In 1981 their income was up to .167 percent of the world's total income, and their population amounted to 1.692 percent of total population. If the figures for the five richest countries are analyzed, a different situation can be observed. In 1970 they had 9.741 percent of total income. In 1981 their income went up to a spectacular 26.248 percent of the world's total income. During the same period, their share of the world's population went down from 6.179 percent in 1970 to 5.644 percent in 1981. It is quite obvious that the poor countries are not making sufficient progress to get out of their centuries-long dilemma. In this chapter we first illustrate why the less developed countries (LDCs) are experiencing such a vicious circle, and then we discuss some solutions for breaking that circle. Finally, it is posited that technology transfer is the best possible solution.

THE CHARACTERISTICS OF LDCs

The LDCs share certain common characteristics, analyses of which would provide a better understanding of these countries in general. These characteristics must be analyzed without making a reference to causation. Although they may sometimes be the cause of poverty, most of them are simultaneously the effects of poverty. Thus, many of them cannot be dealt with directly since the exact causality is not readily distinguishable. Three major characteristics are overpopulation, undersupply of resources, and lack of motivation.

Overpopulation

Most of the LDCs are overpopulated. In fact, it appears that overpopulation is the most common denominator among the world's poor countries. Few of these nations, however, make a distinction between "absolute" and "relative" overpopulation.

Absolute overpopulation is considered to be a fact for countries such as India and China. In these countries, population is so large and its absolute size is still growing so fast that basic resources, even if used efficiently, are less than adequate to pull them over the poverty threshold. Some years back Gunnar Myrdal (1968) emphasized this particular point in his monumental work, *Asian Drama*. Although this observation is still quite valid, its strength has been deemphasized in recent years. We owe much of this deemphasis to China. This country has shown that if there is an absolute overpopulation concept, it is not necessarily imperative that a country reaches it automatically. The limits where an absolute overpopulation situation emerges can be put off or pushed back. However, India, Pakistan, and Bangladesh have not been so lucky so far. The key point in the condition of absolute overpopulation is the overcrowded conditions of the national land space; with the given technological state-of-the-art, the natural resources of the country are not sufficient for further economic development.

Relative overpopulation, on the other hand, implies that population, although not large in absolute terms, is growing so fast that it is outstripping

Table 2.1
Income and Population of Five Country Groups at the Lowest, Middle, and Highest Economic Levels

	Income (Pct. of world)			Population (Pct. of world)		
	1960	*1970*	*1981*	*1960*	*1970*	*1981*
Poorest[a]	—	.048	.167	1.54	1.59	1.69
Middle[b]	2.39	2.01	6.70	3.45	3.06	2.70
Richest[c]	11.79	9.74	26.25	6.64	6.18	5.64

SOURCE: Figures are computed from the 1981 world population data sheet (April 1981) and *World Population 1977* (U.S. Department of Commerce and Bureau of the Census). Figures are sums of five countries in each category.

[a]Bhutan, Bangladesh, Nepal, Chad, and Ethiopia.

[b]Bahrain, New Zealand, French Polynesia, Italy, and Czechoslovakia.

[c]Switzerland, Luxembourg, West Germany, Denmark, and Sweden.

economic gains of any kind. This situation has been true for many Latin American countries for decades. Relative overpopulation is perhaps the most common occurrence among the Third World countries.

Undersupply of Resources

The counterpart of overpopulation is, almost by definition, undersupply of resources. Just as in the case of overpopulation, undersupply of resources can be classified as either absolute or relative. Absolute undersupply of resources refers to overused soil which is not very arable anymore, which is the case in many parts of India; it also refers to depleted metal and chemical supplies that have been mined for nearly centuries. In many Third World countries some, if not all, resources have been depleted to the point where it is difficult to reverse the situation.

Countries like Haiti and El Salvador do not suffer from resource depletion in absolute terms, but they cannot produce or utilize the resources in such a way that they will be ahead of population increase and their economy will develop at a desirable pace. Inability to utilize the resources is closely related to both lack of technological development and an unnecessarily high rate of population increase. Thus, although these countries may have, in absolute terms, abundant resources, at any given time these resources are less than adequate because they are not being used effectively.

In addition, there are certain special cases where undersupply of resources is prevalent. Brazil, for instance, had the slogan "Brazilian oil for Brazilians." However, for decades the country did not have the know-how to get the oil and process it. Without the contribution of this special resource, the country's developmental process was delayed.

Lack of Motivation

The motivation issue has been discussed by scholars for many years. The basic presumption is that most LDCs cannot develop primarily because they lack motivation. The controversy relating to the cause of the motivation lack has been rather involved. Different theories have been suggested in this context. At least five separate factors have been attributed to the motivation issue and considered to be the cause. While not totally mutually exclusive, they will be discussed separately in the following pages. They are: (1) the Protestant ethic; (2) lack of know-how; (3) lack of education; (4) underemployment; and (5) wasted resources.

(1) The Protestant ethic: The Protestant ethic argument was posited rather rigorously by Max Weber (1930). Since this argument has an individualized economic message, it by and large contributes to the overall economic development from an individual's perspective. According to the

Protestant ethic, an individual must be frugal, work hard, save, and invest. Such godliness leads to very appropriate economic behavior, which results in high growth and development rates. Other religions, by definition, lack the Protestant ethic, and therefore many parts of the world have not had the benefit of this economic stimulation.

(2) Lack of know-how: Without know-how people cannot be productive. Awareness of the inability to obtain good results often is a deterrent. People cannot be motivated to work hard if they know they do not have the knowledge of how to work effectively. A very critical interrelationship appears to prevail between the motivation to work hard and technical know-how of how to produce scientifically, effectively, and efficiently.

(3) Lack of education: Most Third World countries suffer from widespread illiteracy. This lack of education is closely related to the lack of know-how mentioned above. With a prevailing low level of education, a high level of technological know-how is not possible. First, technological know-how does require a certain educational level; second, and even more importantly, without proper educational background there will be no appreciation or incentive to acquire the necessary technological know-how. Thus, lack of motivation is doubly reinforced by lack of know-how and lack of education.

(4) Underemployment: Most LDCs do not offer employment for large proportions of the labor force. Unemployment is usually very high. In addition to unemployment there is underemployment, that is, those who work do not work hard and fully. Farmers, for example, work only during the season and do not have much to do the rest of the time. Large proportions of populations have jobs that do not keep them totally occupied. The end result is less utilization of human resources. Lack of opportunity for jobs and lack of engagement in the job seriously dampen motivation. Both situations are quite widespread in many parts of the world.

(5) Wasted resources: The two broad groups of resources particularly wasted in the Third World are human resources and nonhuman resources. In addition to unemployment and underemployment issues discussed earlier, women, who comprise the largest portion of human resources (since they outnumber males), are by and large wasted in many Third World countries. They are kept out of educational, social, political, and business institutions, and they are not given the opportunity to grow and contribute to economic growth and development. As discussed earlier, lack of know-how and education leads to wasted resources despite the fact that they are scarce. In production, for example, more than necessary raw materials are used in storage, and finished products as well as raw materials are wasted in transit.

The wasted resources and the populace's awareness of this waste provide less than adequate motivation in putting forth the best effort in the development process. People, in general, are discouraged and at times enraged;

hence, they are relatively less enthusiastic to work and to become highly productive.

The lack of motivation at least partially accounts for the prevailing lack of productivity and resultant low levels of output in many LDCs. It is realistic to say that Nurkse's vicious cycle of economic underdevelopment prevails in a big way in LDCs. This concept implies a causal relationship.

THE VICIOUS CYCLE OF UNDERDEVELOPMENT

The essense of the vicious cycle is that economically underdeveloped or less developed countries cannot overcome this particular status, and they end up at the same point after having tried to develop in many different ways. The concept is illustrated in Figure 2.1.

The figure starts with the status quo, being economically underdeveloped. Because these countries are economically underdeveloped they experience low incomes. Both per capita and GNP (gross national product) are very low. Low level of income by definition implies a higher propensity to consume and a lower propensity to save. These propensities yield low levels of savings. It is well known in economic principles that savings are equal to investments.

In order to understand this concept, it is necessary to look at what might

Figure 2.1
The Vicious Cycle of Economic Underdevelopment

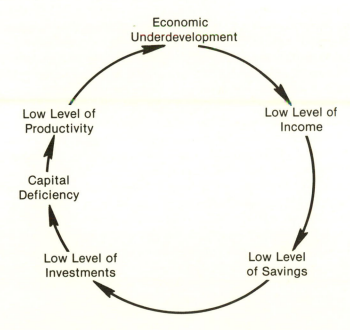

be called the Robinson Crusoe economics. Assume that Robinson Crusoe sustains himself by catching six fish a day with his bare hands. He eats five and saves one every day. At the end of the fifth day, he has enough fish that he takes the day off and develops a fishing tackle which is his capital. Once the fishing tackle is developed (savings are equal to investments), his productivity goes up (in terms of catching fish) many times more. This increase in his food supply would enable Robinson to start a vegetable garden, to tame wild goats (if any), to build a home, or to build a boat to get away some time in the near future. Thus, his increased real income (expressed in terms of increased food supply) has led to increased savings and increased investments.

As seen in the above episode, low levels of savings do not lend themselves to high levels of investments. Low level of investments, by definition, is the cause of capital deficiency. (No fishing tackles or a fishing boat, fishing nets, and so on for Mr. Crusoe.) Capital deficiency can easily be equated with low level of productivity. Even though labor is plentiful in LDCs, a minimum ratio of capital to labor is necessary to achieve a satisfactory level of productivity. Since capital is very scarce and since this situation is not likely to change, unless something special happens, low level of productivity prevails. Thus in Figure 2.1 LDCs are still at the point where they started out.

Achieving a certain degree of economic development implies breaking the vicious cycle. Unless it can be successfully broken, an LDC will not be able to improve its economic status and develop its economy.

BREAKING THE VICIOUS CYCLE

Among the numerous strategic alternatives to break the vicious cycle are (1) increased savings; (2) international trade; (3) foreign aid; and (4) technology transfer (Cassen, et al., 1982). The following section presents some of the major aspects and problems of these strategic alternatives of economic development. It must once again be emphasized that these are not mutually exclusive; however, if used together, they present an enormous problem of incompatibility. Unless extreme caution is exercised, the gains from any one of these strategies can offset the gains from others. For instance, on numerous occasions the advantages of foreign aid dissipated because the recipients were involved in wrong types of international trade. A poor country, for example, utilized the aid money to buy weapons or expensive luxury automobiles.

Increased Savings

One of the oldest strategic alternatives for breaking the vicious cycle is to increase savings. This strategy has become particularly popular in U.S. economic circles and is known as *supply-side economics.*

Savings can be increased through either of two general techniques: forced savings and voluntary savings. Forced savings in its extreme form implies slavery. If workers work hard for a mere existence-level of pay and are involved primarily in capital formation, in the long run the countries cannot help but benefit economically. On the other end of the spectrum, forced savings can be achieved by heavy taxation. Taxes can be levied to force people not to spend or consume. Total tax revenues can be utilized in capital formation.

Through voluntary savings, on the other hand, people willingly exercise special options. On one end of the spectrum is Israel's kibbutz, which for all practical purposes plays the same economic role as slavery or Siberia. Since people work very hard and are satisfied with a subsistence level of living, the fruits of their toil can be utilized for capital formation. On the other end of the spectrum are selling savings bonds or other types of government borrowing only from those who are willing to lend and using the revenues in various capital-formation activities. In this category belong innovations in the American scene such as Individual Retirement Accounts (IRAs), which are totally private and voluntary activities and can play the same role in the total economic picture.

International Trade

Assuming that trade is not one-sided and that it benefits both parties, and that the benefits of trade can be utilized in capital-formation or capital-importing activities, we may consider trading to be an important development strategy. In their trading activities, LDCs have taken two major directions: *emphasizing cash crops* and *specializing in a single commodity export.*

Many LDCs emphasize cash crops in international markets as opposed to some key products for domestic consumption. A country may for instance, use large portions of usable land for cotton to export rather than for wheat for domestic consumption.

Typically, the LDCs with an important international export commodity have relied heavily on such commodities. Oil-rich LDCs, for example, have geared almost all of their economic activities to export this important product.

Foreign Aid

One of the most logical strategies to develop LDCs is foreign aid. Many developed countries have been giving aid to LDCs for decades. Under carefully planned circumstances, these aids can be used in capital formation or can be used directly in the form of capital and hence break the vicious cycle.

Technology Transfer

Regardless of whether it is hard or soft technology, almost by definition, the successful transfer of appropriate technology can break the vicious cycle and help the LDC to develop. In transferring technology for this purpose, three specific approaches can be identified: export promotion, import substitution, and the neutral approach.

Export promotion implies bringing in the technology that would help the country break the vicious cycle by increasing its exports. This is the approach which Korea, Singapore, and Taiwan have used rather successfully. They have imported export trade-oriented technologies and have become competitive in many world markets. Their national economies developed remarkably during the 1970s.

Import substitution, on the other hand, is the choice of many LDCs that have large domestic markets and are very dependent on imports. By bringing in the technology to produce goods and services to replace imports, these countries can experience substantial economic gains which will break the vicious cycle. Developing domestic energy sources, for instance, as opposed to importing fuel from other countries is an example of this strategy.

The neutral approach covers all other areas that may not necessarily be included in export promotion or import substitution. Quite often the imported or adopted technology is utilized for new industries that previously did not exist. Or, these technologies may be used to provide balanced growth within the country by providing opportunities to increase overall efficiency. Thus, the recipient LDC can start utilizing its scarce natural resources more efficiently and hence increase its economic output.

All four of these development strategies have some serious drawbacks —or at least past experience with them has not been very encouraging.

PROBLEMS OF THE STRATEGIC ALTERNATIVES

The populace in LDCs quite often does not care for increased savings. This is due to the prevailing high propensity to consume which is typical of people who do not have too much of anything and would like to survive at least within a reasonable subsistence level. Most of the forced savings methods have not been totally welcomed by the people of LDCs, again, for the same reason. They would rather consume today than be forced to save for, say, the well-being of the next generation.

In many cases international trade forced the LDCs to produce for world markets at the expense of the people of the country. Furthermore, many countries with a single commodity export have not done well in using their newly acquired riches. Similarly, many countries that have had such an approach have experienced some drastic changes in their world markets. Sugar cane, banana, and coffee-exporting countries have experienced sudden shocks because of major changes in their world markets. The results of these sudden changes have been detrimental to the stability and growth of these domestic economies.

Foreign aid has been extremely controversial from its inception during the early post-World War II years. The principle of sound foreign aid has concentrated on two main areas, both of which are not in the mainstream of economic development, namely "military aid" and "emergency relief." Unfortunately, foreign aid and military aid have been lumped together for many years. Quite often when foreign aid is mentioned, it refers to military aid which is not really designed to help LDCs develop economically.

Emergency relief or stress relief deals with immediate economic problems that do not necessarily have any bearing for future economic development. Because of a special crop failure, if India receives emergency relief it is hardly going to help in the country's efforts to generate capital so that productivity can be increased. Aside from these two areas, that is, military aid and emergency relief, there have been other problems that have made foreign aid ineffective. Among these the most significant is that quite often the aid does not reach the right people so that it can be used in the capital-formation efforts. Corrupt organizations or governments have intercepted the aid and used it for their own personal gains.

By using this elimination process, it becomes clear that technology transfer is the best alternative in the attempt to break the vicious cycle of economic underdevelopment. Technology transfer is not free of problems. The choice of appropriate technology (Teitel, 1978), its successful transfer, and its effective implementation are all very involved topics. However, once it is established that technology may be the best way of fighting economic underdevelopment, then the road is paved to explore the intricacies of this economic development strategy.

SUMMARY AND CONCLUSIONS

All LDCs share certain common characteristics, including overpopulation, limited supply of resources, and a general lack of motivation on the part of the populace.

LDCs commonly suffer from the vicious cycle of economic underdevelopment. This vicious cycle is so prominent that economic development is equated with the breakage of the cycle. The presence of the vicious cycle is reflected by low-level productivity, which in turn stems from an acute lack of capital.

Four key strategies may help break the vicious cycle: (1) increased savings; (2) increased international trade; (3) foreign aid; and (4) technology transfer. The first three create such significant problems that the fourth, by a process of elimination, becomes most desirable. Technology transfer can break the vicious cycle by stimulating exports, by enabling the country to substitute imports, or just by improving the country's overall economic efficiency. Thus, *effective* transfer of appropriate technology is an absolute necessity in the economic devopment of LDCs.

REFERENCES

Cassen, Robert, et al. *Rich Country Interests and Third World Development.* London: Croon Helm, 1982.

Myrdal, Gunnar. *Asian Drama: An Inquiry into the Poverty of Nations.* 3 vols. New York: Pantheon, 1968.

Nurkse, R. *Capital Formation in Under-developed Countries.* London: Oxford, 1953.

Schumacher, E. F. *Small Is Beautiful.* New York: Perennial Library, 1973.

Teitel, Simon. "On the Concept of Appropriate Technology for Less Industrialized Countries." *Technological Forecasting and Social Change* 11 (1978): 349-369.

Weber, Max. *The Protestant Ethic and the Spirit of Capitalism.* New York: Scribner's, 1930.

3

Transfer of Food Retail Technology into Less Developed Countries

SANDY B. CONNERS, A. C. SAMLI,
AND ERDENER KAYNAK

Food marketing systems in less developed countries (LDCs) have been extensively studied, primarily by agricultural economists and cultural anthropologists. Both of these groups have repeatedly noted that marketing can potentially make a large contribution in LDCs, both to consumer welfare and to a nation's economic development, through improvements in food distribution. This chapter describes the traditional food distribution systems of LDCs and discusses the effects of modernization of these systems. Speculations are made about barriers to and conditions for the successful transfer of one modern food retailing institution, the supermarket, into LDCs.

ROLE OF FOOD DISTRIBUTION SYSTEMS IN LDCs

Food distribution systems can play a vital role in reducing malnutrition and poverty. Because most people who go hungry do so because the food they need costs more than they can afford, high marketing costs are an important reason why people have insufficient food. (Marketing costs are defined [47a] as the difference between the price paid by the consumer and the price received by the producer together with the utility lost due to the misallocation of the marketing system.) By designing efficient, and low-cost channels, marketing may be able to effect a decrese in food prices and an increase in real disposable income (1). This effect on consumers' income might be quite large given the high proportion of incomes spent on food among low-income consumers in LDCs (ranging from 50 percent [22, 30] to 90 percent [15]).

Efficient food distribution can influence food production and processing in LDCs. Because of the interdependence of the food distribution and production systems, improvements in food distribution can increase the amount, quality, and variety of food available and raise farm income. If the food distribution system does not serve the needs of the producer as well as the consumer, there will be a disincentive to higher production. In any case, higher production will have no effect if it does not bring food to the consumer at affordable prices (49). A focus on production alone in development programs is, therefore, insufficient. There are at least three different conditions for the provision of production incentives. (1) reasonably stable prices for agricultural products, (2) adequate marketing facilities, and (3) a satisfactory system of land tenure. Marketing can facilitate the provision of the first two of these. An effective marketing sector, then, "has a dynamic role in stimulating both production and consumption. On one hand, it activates new demands by improving and transforming farm products and by seeking out and stimulating new customers. On the other hand, it guides farmers to new production opportunities and encourages greater production in response to demand" (62: 279).

By increasing food supply through efficient distribution, marketing can ease immediate hardship on the populace caused by inadequate food supply and provide some of the necessary conditions for increased productivity in the economy as a whole (64).

Through these improvements in consumption and production, food distribution efficiency might be able to accelerate the rate of general economic development. It has been postulated that the modernization of food systems will increase labor productivity and decrease the underemployment of economic resources, particularly labor (62). In addition, marketing efficiency might promote development through its effect on the investment climate as the increased family buying power tends to reduce the market limitation barrier to investment (13). In its ability to rapidly train entrepreneurs and managers, marketing has been called the "most effective engine for economic development" (26). Such attempts will broaden the experience and knowledge base from which the LDCs can borrow to improve their present marketing systems. In addition, this type of information base can be used very effectively by the Western consultant who is trying to help LDCs to develop new and better distribution systems. Since food expenditures account for a very large percentage of the total spending budget of an average family in LDCs, such improvements in the present food marketing systems will automatically enhance the purchasing power as well as the quality of life for most of the people. Food marketing systems in LDCs may also be used as case studies for the diffusion of innovation process and comparative marketing analysis (62).

Whether the role of marketing in economic development is passive, merely accommodating itself to prevalent economic conditions, or active, influencing and directing economic growth, remains to be determined.

TRADITIONAL FOOD MARKETING SYSTEMS

Although the traditional food distribution systems in LDCs (also called "peasant markets") differ in volume and specific commodities handled, they possess many similarities. These resemblances are striking, whether one is describing markets in Latin America, Africa, or Asia. The outstanding characteristic of most retailers and wholesalers is their great number and small size (10, 14, 27, 28, 41, 68). More specifically, the existing food distribution system, particularly in urban areas, is composed of a mixture of many small neighborhood food stores, some specialized food outlets, and a few traditional plaza markets, where small-scale, highly specialized stall operators are grouped together. In this system, general food stores carry primarily staples, such as grains, sugar, flour, and oils, while bakery goods, milk, produce, fish, and meats are sold through specialized outlets. There is also a very large number of itinerant traders.

These food outlets, whatever their type, are typically family operations, each one carrying a very limited assortment of products (32). Wholesaling operations are also relatively small (62), and the same traders often perform both wholesaling and retailing functions. Traditional food retailers are usually characterized by low sales volume, small physical space and inventories, and inadequate storage facilities. In general, they possess a low technical efficiency, quite limited capital resources, and little, if any, standardization (57). The ratio of labor to sales is high, and the number of suppliers servicing these outlets is large (30).

Many believe that the seeming intensity and atomistic type of competition limits capital accumulation and firm growth and, therefore, impedes economic development (39). This fragmented retail-wholesale system is said to poorly transmit price signals and related market information to farmers, leading to faulty coordination of farm production and consumer demands. Consequently producers are often faced with uncertain product prices, oligopolistic assembly markets, and a lack of reliable market information on current market conditions.

The modernization of food distribution systems together with a reduction in the number of food merchants is often seen, therefore, as a major "entry point" to economic development (35). This strategy calls for the introduction of larger scale, more effectively coordinated wholesaling and retailing units offering higher quality and a larger variety of products at prices lower than could be achieved through the traditional, small-scale, poorly coordinated food system (62). Lower food prices would be achieved by increasing the scale of markets from individuals selling a single line of goods to a supermarket selling high-volume necessities at lower margins. Market coordination could facilitate retail purchases of large quantities at lower prices, while reductions in risk and increases in the scale of assembly, transport, and wholesale functions would contribute to efficiency and, therefore, to lower costs of operation. The reduction in food prices could, in turn, cause a significant increase in real family income and, therefore, a flow of income particularly toward low-income families. The result would be an increase in the effective demand for both food and nonfood products and services and greater investment among firms whose profits increase (33). Producers would expand production by adopting changes in technology in response to more certain market conditions, and retailer cooperative buying among small traders would be enhanced, leading to further food price reductions (66).

In some Third World countries, modernization of food distribution systems goes further than improving family income; it means adequate food intake for many citizens which can be translated in terms of increased productivity. In many of these countries large portions of the total population receive less than subsistence-level food and will be able to increase their food intake. If the people in these sectors can find work opportunities, their productivity will, by definition, increase which, in turn, will benefit the whole economy.

If, for instance, the people are surviving on 600 calories/day before the modernization process and if after modernization the food supply provides 1,200 calories/day, the people who have jobs will improve their productivity almost by definition. Thus, not only will these people be brought up to above the subsistence level, but also their increased output will benefit the whole society.

SUPERMARKETS IN LDCs

Modern supermarkets are the lead element in the modernization of the food distribution system and one of the keys to the economic development process in LDCs. The introduction of supermarkets into LDCs has been attractive to American firms as well because of the declining opportunities for growth in domestic markets (11). Because the transfer of supermarket retailing technology into LDCs may require more managerial techniques than capital (45), it has been viewed favorably by U.S. firms. Although this retailing technology varies widely in application, it is usually characterized by (1) self-service, (2) mass merchandising, including prepackaging, standardization, and grading, (3) a full-line assortment, and (4) a low margin/ high turnover operating policy34).

Although there were practically no self-service food stores outside the United States prior to 1947 (4), since then supermarkets have been introduced into numerous countries possessing a traditional food distribution system. Supermarkets have been widely accepted when introduced into rapidly developing economies such as Hong Kong and Mexico (29, 72, 73,

77, 78) and are becoming common in the Soviet Union (5, 24, 52), although they are smaller than their Western counterparts, have a limited selection, less branding, no price competition, and less attractive packaging. Supermarkets in Spain and Italy remain small and few in number (18, 19, 36). The Aurrera supermarket chain in Mexico is growing rapidly in urban areas, although small grocers remain more popular (17, 25, 69). Supermarkets throughout Asia are increasing in number and are carrying more locally produced goods (67). Migros, a Swiss food distribution cooperative, worked with the Turkish government in the establishing of modern food stores in Turkey and was successful at the beginning only in middle-class neighborhoods.

After operating in Turkey for nearly twenty years, Migros became unsuccessful in its routine retail operations because it did not pay enough attention to ongoing environmental changes in Turkey. The company tried to operate its self-service stores, supermarkets, and mobile selling trucks without considering the different needs and characteristics of the Turkish food consumers and the prevailing environmental conditions. The company's relationship with its suppliers was not good, and it could not form desired ties and relationships with the Turkish government, the local authorities, and the financial institutions. All of these inherent difficulties, of course, weakened its position and put its operations in jeopardy. Under these adverse circumstances, the company could no longer maintain its existence and decided to pull out of Turkey by selling all of its chain stores and other intermediary facilities to a Turkish holding company (47e).

The International Business Economy Corporation (IBEC), an American investment and development firm created by the Rockefeller family to operate firms in developing countries, has established several supermarket chains. A highly successful operation was established in Venezuela, and an Italian chain was sold to local investors at a substantial profit. A Peruvian venture has achieved some degree of profitability, an Argentinian subsidiary was struggling to survive, and a Puerto Rican operation was sold after experiencing considerable difficulties (43). Supermarkets in Puerto Rico are becoming more successful (16, 62) than had been previously observed (30). In every instance, however, supermarkets have been successful only among high-income consumers in LDCs (13)—precisely the opposite income segment that they were designed to benefit.

The failure to successfully transfer this supermarket technology to low-income consumers in LDCs has been attributed to a multitude of supply and demand factors. Demand-side factors include a consumer purchasing pattern that is incompatible with modern supermarkets and more suited to traditional food distribution systems. Low-income consumers in LDCs make frequent purchases of small quantities of food because of their (1) limited and often seasonal income and low cash reserves, so that they are unable to plan consumption, (2) limited storage space and little refrigeration, and (3) immobility, because of limited automobile ownership, congested streets, and inadequate public transportation (3, 10). Even when public transportation is available, consumers' low income precludes its use, leading to what Goldman (33) calls "low outreach" and a preference for nearby stores. Low literacy rates inhibit the use of self-service outlets. A large proportion of everyday transactions are conducted on a credit basis (12). Because the creditor has little capital, the number of clients per trader is restricted so that a large number of traders is required to serve the urban population. In addition, these credit arrangements are based not on legal contracts but on personal trust among acquaintances. As a result, any one trader is limited in the number of customers he or she can know well enough to trust (63, 70), again leading to a multiplicity of traders. Variety is unimportant to low-income consumers, and they do not perceive improvements in quality (35). Finally, consumers are widely dispersed, most of them living in the countryside or in small villages (57). All of these demand factors act to limit supermarket success in the low-income sectors of LDCs.

Supply-side barriers to the development of low-income neighborhood supermarkets have also been observed. Among these barriers are (1) lack of credit in LDCs to build stores; (2) lack of prepackaging, product standardization, and grading, (3) limited self-service; (4) expensive semiskilled labor and equipment; (5) political pressures that traditional stores exert, leading to laws restricting supermarket development; (6) scarce store space in urban areas; (7) rudimentary branding and mass communication; (8) lack of large and reliable suppliers; and (9) a general prejudice against trading as an occupation (4, 13, 35, 36). Without mechanization, standardization, and centralization, in terms of both administration and locating in population centers, supermarkets have been unable to attain the economies of scale that are possible for large-scale operations, thus enabling them to lower prices and compete with local traders (23).

Not only do supermarkets possess several disadvantages when introduced into LDCs, but also traditional distribution systems may possess distinct competitive advantages, thereby ensuring their survival. A fragmented market system is better suited to the needs of scattered, small-scale farmers and a scattered, relatively immobile population buying on a small scale. In addition, difficulties in transportation, storage, and communication encourage the growth of small, localized activities (19, 56). Belshaw (12) believes that the proliferation of the roles and numbers of traders is in part related to the absence of a safe, reliable system for the impersonal consignment of goods, so that goods may not be sold through correspondence. All of these conditions dictate a small-scale distribution system, gathering in many small units of supply and distribution given smaller amounts in the market.

Figure 3.1 illustrates both groups of barriers. It should be noted that only

Figure 3.1
Factors Affecting Successful Transfer of
Supermarket Technology to Less Developed Countries

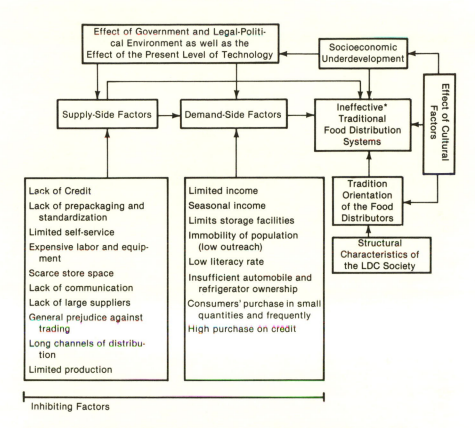

*Ineffectiveness in this figure denotes situations where the consumers' relatively scarce food monies are wasted because of improper choice of inadequate purchasing knowledge and low outreach of shoppers outside of their immediate neighborhood.

supply-side factors or demand-side factors alone would be sufficiently detrimental to the development of an efficient food distribution system. The figure also points out that, even if the supply-side or the demand-side barriers did not exist, the level of economic development or prevailing tradition orientation could provide very strong barriers. If the economy is not at a certain level, it may not be able to support efficient supermarket-type food distribution systems. (The authors are assuming that supermarkets are efficient and that the input-output relationships they display are much more favorable than their small counterparts.) Similarly, since a significant deviation from traditional food distribution systems may be perceived as foreign to the accepted order and life-styles, it may not be adopted. Hence, culture and economy are two very strong dimensions blocking improvement in food distribution. These are examined in detail in other sections of this book and so are not discussed in this chapter.

MARKETING EFFICIENCY

The failure to transfer supermarket retailing technology into LDCs has led to a reexamination of the assumption of the relative efficiency of super-markets compared to the traditional distribution system. Efficiency, however, is a term that is seldom well defined. Kohls (48) has pointed out that efficiency and welfare are often distinct in that a society may accept certain inefficiencies in order to promote the general welfare, such as a high employment rate. Similarly, a distinction is often made between input-output operating efficiency and pricing efficiency, the latter often being interpreted as a movement toward perfect competition (that is, a reduction in monopoly profits by changing the intensity of competition). Operating efficiency has also been called "technological efficiency," and pricing efficiency may also be described as "economic efficiency." Further ambiguity arises from the confusion of the level of aggregation, whether it be the economy as a whole, an industry, a particular firm, or a segment within a firm. An action that increases efficiency on one level could well decrease it on another. Here it is assumed that there is a multiple-level activity. Thus, at one level an action that will increase efficiency cannot be assumed to filter down to other levels. If similar and noncontradictory activities are not introduced at all levels, the gains that occur at one level can easily be offset in another. In addition, efficiency may be simultaneously evaluated by several measures, including the relative price of goods, costs of operation, return on sales or return on investment, sales per employee and per unit area of store space, inventory turnover, the stability of demand, and the average dollar value of purchases (31).

While supermarkets have been shown (12, 62) to be more efficient in that sales per employee and sales per unit of store area are higher than in tradi-tional stores, price has been the most widely used measure of efficiency. The evidence in this area is, however, ambiguous. Westfall and Boyd (74) report retail margins in India to be as low as 10 percent and wholesale margins falling below 5 percent. Narrow margins were also observed in Thailand (75), Africa (40, 47, 76), and the Philippines (53). Uma Lele (50) reviews many African studies of low-margin peasant marketing systems. The diffi-culty of competing with low-margin private traders has been cited as a factor inhibiting the growth of consumer cooperatives and large-scale retailing. A Puerto Rican study, however, found that food retail margins were 11 percent higher than they would be if excess capacity were eliminated and that supermarkets had lower prices for dietary staples (30). Mehren (54) notes that traditional system margins are high and rigid, as does Abbott (1). These high margins are said to be the result of (1) the weak position of many producers when bargaining with wholesale buyers, (2) high costs due to inadequate transport, storage, and handling facilities, which cause heavy losses of produce, a deterioration in quality, and increased market risk, and (3) the absence of effective competition at the retail level (1).

Whether it is efficient in regards to price, the traditional distribution system may be efficient in that it substitutes cheap and plentiful resources like labor for scarce and expensive ones like capital. Peasant marketing systems cannot be labeled inefficient insofar as they do not absorb larger quantities of scarce resources but instead substitute semiskilled and unskilled labor, providing employment and redistributing income to kinsmen less well off (8, 56). Therefore, the multiplicity of traders may be the result of the mass use of unskilled labor in the performance of the task of distribution. There is an extensive demand for the services of intermediaries, and a large sector of the population is available to perform these services at a low supply price in terms of daily earnings (6). (One might argue, however, that this surplus manpower forces the establishment of many marginal enterprises.)

Even though the traditional distribution system may be found to be the lowest cost distribution system, Collins and Holton (20) question whether cost minimization is a desirable goal. Cost minimization may be valid only when little change in production and consumption patterns is anticipated and the marketing system is performing the proper mix of services. That is, margins may be low either because marketing is being performed at a low cost or because the system is providing few services (47). A more appropriate goal, then, might be the development of a set of institutions and practices to minimize cost given anticipated changes in the methods, organization, and level of production or in the mix of goods produced. A third goal might be the establishment of channels to maximize the rate of growth of the primary and secondary economic sectors. If one of the latter two goals were to be accepted, more, not fewer, resources would be devoted to distribution.

Given the *present* state of the economies of LDCs, the small traders may be more efficient than any of their would-be competitors (56). The assumption that large-scale production, transport, and selling are more efficient may be valid in developed countries but not in less developed countries. That is, small-scale traders may be inefficient only by standards for developed countries. A set of arrangements that are economically efficient in one society may not be in another in which the availability of resources is different. The small trader may not only be "economically redundant, but actually essential to the distribution process as it is presently constituted" (56: 23). Any reduction in the number of traders would "only serve . . . to aggravate the low level of capital and the lack of employment opportunities [while] the volume of production would not be increased since the resources set free [are] already economically redundant [and] absorb resources [notably capital] in distribution which would otherwise be available for use in agriculture and industry" (8: 27).

THE NATURE OF COMPETITION

The high degree of competition among traders is said to prevent the exploitation of producers and consumers and to reward efficient traders, leading to overall economic efficiency (7). The system is usually characterized as an ideal example of monopolistic competition (44, 58). That is, despite the large number of traders, monopolistic elements or differentiation persist, partly because of the pervasiveness of credit buying (consumers resist shifting grocers once credit has been established) and because of the relative immobility of buyers and sellers (leading to the desire for locational convenience). Differentiation is also promoted by the segmentation of the population into economic and social caste systems and inadequate market information (58). This less than perfect competition is sometimes said to shield inefficient outlets from failure (30).

There is commonly little price competition in the traditional food distribution system since retailers seldom attempt to increase their sales volume or to attract customers through extensive price cutting. They often have no interest in expanding profits beyond that to provide a satisfactory level of living (10, 44). Dewey (23) observed that prices were remarkably stable and that traders were unable to raise prices significantly because of competition from other traders. As a result, there is a strong tendency toward price equalization even among firms that obtain a commodity at widely differing wholesale prices (46). At the same time, however, Mehren (54) notes that there is often no known or ongoing price in peasant marketing systems. In any case, the multiplicity of traders may not be economically redundant since they are internally stratified in terms of goods, modes of business operation, and clienteles (46), so that they do not compete with each other as much as might be assumed. It may be that none of the middlemen is making excess profits but that marketing margins are larger than they would be were there to be less differentiation (58). Mueller (58) believes that the introduction of marketing reforms such as grading, a system of weights and measures, and effective contract laws will be necessary for the elimination of many of the monopolistically competitive features of peasant markets.

DISCUSSION

Because of the failure to transfer the supermarket retailing technology into LDCs, some writers have instead argued for an *adaptation* of retailing technologies to conditions prevalent in the LDCs (12, 30). Goldman (34,

35), for instance, recommends that LDCs adopt one of the antecedent forms of the supermarket rather than its fully developed form. The aim of development, he states, should be more grocery stores of higher stages of development rather than the transformation of each store into a supermarket (32). Michaelis (55: 75) has recommended that retailing technology be adapted—not transplanted.

A modern factory can be transplanted from the United States to Asia, Africa or Latin America. The machines will function the same and the products will be identical. . . . Our distribution methods—developed to a high degree of sophistication in our intensely competitive marketplace—cannot be directly transplanted. . . . I would be the last to suggest that American marketing techniques will, or necessarily should, ever fit India's particular requirements. Rather, I would plead that—together with India and other developing nations—we explore what portions of our experience and knowhow in marketing that can be adapted to their needs.

The Organization for Economic Cooperation and Development (60) has developed criteria for assessing the appropriateness of any such proposed technology transfer into an LDC. These criteria include benefit-cost ratios, the relative cost of capital and labor, the level of local skills, local consumer preferences, and the appropriateness of local technology.

Increasing the scale of operations alone "cannot transform either the supply or market conditions. Suppliers, distributors and consumers must transform themselves *in tandem*" 57: 20). That is, simultaneous improvements in other areas are required for the successful transfer of supermarket technology because

It is characteristic of food marketing problems in countries undergoing accelerated economic development that they arise simultaneously along the line from planning of production to market demand, through transport, wholesaling, to retail distribution. These phases are so closely interrelated and the difficulty of breaking through the interdependence often so great, that success in establishing improvements in any one of the various marketing phases frequently depends on corresponding improvements taking place in others (2: 359).

Two conditions are necessary, then, for the modernization of the traditional food distribution system: (1) general improvements in other parts of the economy, making trading less attractive and, thereby, reducing the number of traders, and (2) widening transportation networks (12). These two preconditions support Cundiff's (21) hypothesis that the ability of a system to successfully adopt innovations is directly related to the level of economic development. Certain minimal levels of development are necessary to support anything beyond the simplest retailing methods. Even when the economic environment is favorable to change, the process of adaptation may be either hindered or helped by local demographic factors, social mores, government action, and competitive pressures. As Rotblat points out (63), sociocultural patterns, which are very resistant to change, must change if market development is to occur. It is not enough to change the economy alone.

Even if the economy and sociocultural patterns were to be changed together to permit the development of supermarkets, the question of how the economy would absorb the displaced workers (as capital is substituted for labor) remains. Governments in LDCs are sometimes reluctant to alter food retailing systems as trading is often used as an alternative to comprehensive employment programs (20, 45). While few traders prefer trade as employment (37), few other profitable channels of employment exist because of the relative scarcity of suitable land, technical skill, and capital. This is especially true for women and children in urban areas as there are few household duties and few schools (8). Because there are few alternative ways in which traders can be profitably employed, their opportunity costs are low and low profit margins are acceptable (23). Trading becomes relatively attractive because of the low amount of capital required for entry ($.50 to $15.00 for trade in foodstuffs in Liberia [37]). The low amount of technical and administrative skills required for trading (6, 22, 58) and the ease of the work compared to farming (9) also reduced barriers to entry. That the barriers to entry for trading are low has, however, been challenged by Handwerker (37), who states that the work is laborious, and by Sinclair (65), who observed that it took an average period of over five years for an individual coming into the city to acquire sufficient experience and capital to become a trader. Any displacement of traders by supermarkets would be especially acute in areas where women make up the majority of traders, as in Liberia (38), for alternatives would be quite low for them. Certainly, a retailing modernization program would need to be coupled with a training program, both to provide the skilled and semiskilled labor required for supermarket operation and to provide alternative employment for displaced workers.

More systematic studies are required before any policy recommendations can be made. For instance, comparative marketing studies might be able to rank LDCs along some continuum of income distribution and economic development rather than lumping them into one homogeneous class. Within any one country, careful attention needs to be paid to the various classes of traders (such as urban, rural town, and isolated rural traders, full and part-time traders, native and nonnative traders, itinerant and fixed-locality traders). Otherwise too much information may be obscured.

Furthermore, other alternatives to the traditional food marketing system, such as the employee-owned food delivery *dispensa* system (31) and cooperatives (51), require further examination. The receptivity of particular population segments to modern retailing methods might also receive further study as younger families have been observed (13) to be less concerned with personal and family relations with food merchants.

Consideration of the extension of the limitations and problems for the modernization of food retailing to nonfood retailing is also needed. Certainly, there is some degree of overlap between the two in that food retailers also sell many nonfood household items, such as kerosene, matches, and utensils. The distinction then is somewhat artificial. Modernization in one sector might then be expected to affect that in the other. The effect is likely to be less pronounced for nonfood items due to the primacy of food purchases in most consumers' budgets. In fact, the effect may be delayed. That is, modernization of the food system may stimulate the development of the nonfood system. Holton (45), however, proposes that the efficient distribution of food may appear *after* integrated distribution for other basic consumer goods (clothing and simple home furnishings). Other basic consumer goods present fewer distribution problems, being less perishable and having fewer and larger producers and less frequent consumption. The ways food and nonfood retailers differ must be considered before observations can be extended to nonfood retailing. Higher barriers to entry may exist. Handwerker (37), for example, observed that the capital required for entry into the households and cloth trade was $15 to $50 in Liberia, compared to $.50 to $15.00 for the foodstuffs trade. The trade is often dominated by nonnative traders (Chinese in Southeast Asia and Lebanese in West and Central Africa). Any generalizations made for food retailing are, therefore, not likely to be directly transferable to nonfood retailing.

Although most writers have concentrated on the transfer of retailing technology, particularly food retailing technology, from developed to less developed countries, retailing technology has also been transferred between developed countries. The most notable case is that of the hypermarket, the superstore that originated in Western Europe and has slowly been adopted in North America (59, 61). Interesting studies might be made of the conditions for the successful transfer of this retailing technology as well.

SUMMARY AND CONCLUSIONS

Because of the multiplicity of barriers and the likely dysfunctional consequences of the transfer of the supermarket retailing technology into LDCs, it is neither possible nor desirable to simply transplant this marketing form. Rather, further study is required to clarify the conditions under which the transfer may be appropriate. The possible benefits are large, but they will not be attained without careful attention to economic and social preconditions for success.

It is posited in this chapter that better and more efficient forms of food distribution technologies are very desirable for LDCs. The multiplicity of barriers to this type of technology transfer does not imply that all LDCs experience these barriers in equal terms and in equal intensity. Thus, in undertaking further studies it is extremely important to determine how food distribution technologies can be transferred to these countries. The presence or lack of these barriers and their relative intensity must be carefully explored before success and progress can take place in this important activity.

REFERENCES

1. Abbott, J. C. *Marketing—Its Role in Increasing Productivity*. Freedom from Hunger Campaign (FFHC), Basic Study No. 4. Rome: Food and Agriculture Organization of the United Nations, 1962a.

2. Abbott, J. C., 1962b. The role of marketing in the development of backyard agricultural economies. *J. Farm Economics* 44(2): 349-362 (May).

3. Anderson, Dole A. *Marketing and Development: The Thailand Experience*. East Lansing, Mich.: Institute for International Business and International Development Studies, Division of Research, Graduate School of Business Administration, Michigan State University, 1970.

4. Applebaum, William, 1956. Developments in self-service food distribution abroad. *J. Farm Economics* 38(2): 348-355 (May).

5. Barnes, Howard W., 1975. AMAer finds Soviets have long lines, little service, 19¢ bread, 700 bottles of Champagne on shelf. *Marketing News*, September 12, pp. 1, 6.

6. Bauer, P. T., and B. S. Yamey, 1951. Economic progress and occupational distribution. *Economics J.* 41 (244): 741-755 (Dec.).

7. Bauer, P. T., and B. S. Yamey, 1954. The economics of marketing reform. *J. Political Economy* 62(3): 210-235 (June).

8. Bauer, P. T. *West Africa Trade: A Study of Competition, Oligopoly, and Monopoly in a Changing Economy*. New York: Augustus M. Kelley, 1967.

9. Beals, Ralph L. *Cheran: A Sierra Tarascan Village*. Smithsonian Institution, Institute of Social Anthropology, Publication No. 2. Washington, D.C.: U.S. Government Printing Office, 1946.

10. Beals, Ralph L. *The Peasant Marketing System of Oaxaca, Mexico*. Berkeley, Calif.: University of California Press, 1975.

11. Bellenger, Danny N., Thomas J. Stanley, and John W. Allen, 1978. Trends in food retailing. *Atlanta Economics R.* 28(3): 11-14 (May/June).

12. Belshaw, Cyril S. *Traditional Exchange and Modern Markets*. Englewood Cliffs, N.J.: Prentice-Hall, 1965.

13. Bennett, Peter D. *Government's Role in Retail Marketing of Food Products in Chile*. Studies in Latin American Business No. 6. Austin, Tex.: University of Texas, 1968.

14. Bohannan, Paul, and George Dalton. *Markets in Africa: Eight Subsistence Economies in Transition*. Garden City, N.Y.: Natural History Library, Anchor Books, 1965.

15. Boyd, Harper W., Jr., Abdel Aziz et Sherbini, and Ahmed Fouad Sherif, 1961. Channels of distribution for consumer goods in Egypt. *J. Marketing* 25(6): 26-33 (Oct.).

16. *Business Week*, 1964. Food chain with a Latin flair. No. 1811, pp. 93-95, 98 (May 16).

17. *Business Week*, 1979. Jewel Cos: scoring in Mexico with U.S. supermarket techniques. No. 2608, pp. 120, 122 (Oct. 22).

18. Carnahan, Ann, and William Carnahan, 1971. Legal tangles complicate Italian food marketing. *Adv. Age* 42(52): 21 (Dec. 27).

19. Carson, David, 1966. Marketing in Italy today. *J. Marketing* 30(1): 10-16 (Jan.).

20. Collins, N. R., and R. H. Holton, 1963. Programming changes in marketing in planned economic development. *Kyklos* 16: 123-137.

21. Cundiff, Edward W., 1965. Concepts in comparative retailing. *J. Marketing* 29(1): 59-63.

22. Dannhaeuser, Norbert, 1977. Distribution and the structure of retail trade in a Philippine commercial town. *Econ. Dev. and Cult. Change* 25(3): 471-503 (April).

23. Dewey, Alice. *Peasant Marketing in Java*. New York: Free Press of Glencoe, Crowell-Collier Publishing Co., 1962.

24. Dietrich, Robert F., 1975. No red ink at this red super. *Progressive Grocer* 54(8) (Part 1): 60, 62 (Aug.).

25. Downer, Steve, 1978. Marca libre—Mexican-style generics? *Adv. Age* 49(44): 58 (Oct. 30).

26. Drucker, Peter F., 1958. Marketing and economic development. *J. Marketing* 22(3): 252-259 (Jan.).

27. Firth, Raymond. *Malay Fishermen: Their Peasant Economy*. Hamden, Conn.: Archon Books, Shoestring Press, 1968.

28. Fox, Richard G., 1967. Family, caste, and commerce in a North Indian market town. *Econ. Dev. and Cult. Change* 15(3): 297-314 (Apr.).

29. Fujii, John, 1979. Supermarkets are changing with consumers' needs. *Far Eastern Economic R*. 106(50): 83-85 (Dec. 14).

30. Galbraith, John Kenneth, and Richard H. Holton. *Marketing Efficiency in Puerto Rico*. Cambridge, Mass.: Harvard University Press, 1955.

31. Gamble, S. H. *The Dispensa System of Food Distribution: A Case Study of Monterrey, Mexico*. New York: Praeger, 1971.

32. Goldman, Arieh, 1974a. Growth of large food stores in developing countries. *J. Retailing* 50(2): 50-60 (Summer).

33. Goldman, Arieh, 1974b. Out reach of consumers and the modernization of urban food retailing in developing countries. *J. Marketing* 38:8-16 (Oct.).

34. Goldman, Arieh, 1975-76. Stages in the development of the supermarket. *J. Retailing* 51(4): 49-64 (Winter).

35. Goldman, Arieh, 1981. Transfer of a retailing technology into the less developed countries: the supermarket case. *J. Retailing* 57(2): 5-29 (Summer).

36. Guerin, Joseph R., 1964. Limitations of supermarkets in Spain. *J. Marketing* 28: 22-26 (Oct.).

37. Handwerker, W. Penn, 1972-74. Entrepreneurship in Liberia. *Liberian Studies J*. 5(2): 113-147.

38. Handwerker, W. Penn, 1974. Changing household organization in the origins of marketplaces in Liberia. *Econ. Dev. and Cult. Change* 22(2): 229-248 (Jan.).

39. Handwerker, W. Penn, 1979. Daily markets and urban economic development. *Human Organization* 38(4): 366-376 (Winter).

40. Hawkins, H.C.G. *Wholesale and Retail Trade in Tanganyika*. New York: F. Praeger, 1965. (Cited by Hollander, 1970.)

41. Hodder, B. W., and U. I. Ukwu. *Markets in West Africa: Markets and Trade Among the Yoruba and Ibo*. Ibadan, Nigeria: Ibadan University Press, 1969.

42. Hollander, Stanley C., 1969. The international shopkeepers. *MSU Business Topics* 17(2): 13-23 (Spring).

43. Hollander, Stanley. *Multinational Retailing*. East Lansing, Mich.: Institute for International Business and Economic Development Studies, Graduate School of Business Administration, Michigan State University, 1970.

44. Holton, Richard H., 1953. Marketing structure and economic development. *Quar. J. Economics* 47(3): 344-354 (Aug.).

45. Holton, Richard H., 1956. Food retailing and economic growth. *J. Farm Economics* 38(2): 356-360 (May).

46. Isaac, Barry L., 1981. Price, competition, and profits among hawkers and shopkeepers in Pendebu, Sierra Leone: an inventory approach. *Econ. Dev. and Cult. Change* 29(2): 353-373 (Jan.).

47. Jones, William O., 1970. Measuring the effectiveness of agricultural marketing in contributing to economic development: some African examples. *Food Research Institute Studies in Agricultural Economics, Trade, and Development* 9(3): 175-196.

47a. Kaynak, E., 1975. *Food Retailing Systems in a Developing Economy*. Bedfordshire: Cranfield Institute Press, 28.

47b. Kaynak, E., 1981. Food distribution systems: Evolution in Latin America and the Middle East. *Food Policy* 6(2): 78-90 (May).

47c. Kaynak, E., 1979. A refined approach to the wheel of retailing. *European Journal of Marketing* 13(7): 237-245.

47d. Kaynak, E., 1980. Government and food distribution in LDCs—the Turkish Experience. *Food Policy*, 5(2): 132-245 (May).

47e. Kaynak, E., 1980. Transfer of supermarketing technology from developed to less-developed countries: the case of Migros-Turk. *Finnish Journal of Business Economics* 21(1): 39 49.

48. Kohls, R. L., 1956. Toward a more meaningful concept of marketing efficiency. *J. Farm Economics* 38(1): 68-73 (Feb.).

49. Kriesberg, Martin, 1968. Marketing food in developing countries: second phase of the war on hunger. *J. Marketing* 32: 55-60 (Oct.).

50. Lele, Uma. *The Design of Rural Development: Lessons from Africa*. Baltimore and London: Johns Hopkins University Press, 1975.

51. Lele, Uma, 1981. Cooperative and the poor: a comparative perspective. *World Development* 9(1): 55-72.

52. Luck, David J., and Daniel B. Bosse, 1975. AMAers tour showplace Soviet supermarket. *Marketing News*, September 12, p. 7, 9.

53. Lugrin, Jean P. *Chain Store Management in the Philippines (Price Stabilization Corporation—Prisco)*. United Nations Technical Assistance Program Document ST/TAA/K Philippines/5. New York: United Nations, 1954. (Cited by Hollander, 1970.)

54. Mehren, George L., 1959. Market organization and economic development. *J. Farm Economics* 41(5): 1307-1315 (Dec.).

55. Michaelis, Michael. Distribution in developing economies. *Boston Conference on Distribution*, 1961. (Cited by Wadinambiaratchi, 1965).

56. Mintz, Sidney W., 1956. The role of the middleman in the internal distribution system of a Caribbean peasant economy. *Human Organization* 15(2): 18-23 (Summer).

57. Moyer, Reed. *Marketing in Economic Development.* Occasional Paper in International Business, No. 1. East Lansing, Mich.: Institute for International Business Management Studies, Graduate School of Business Administration, Michigan State University, 1965.

58. Mueller, Willard F., 1959. Some market considerations in economic development. *J. Farm Economics* 41(2): 414-425 (May).

59. O'Neill, Robert E., 1974. Inside the hypermarket. *Progressive Grocer* 53(5): 43-48, 50, 148 (May).

60. Organization for Economic Cooperation and Development (OECD) and the Food and Agriculture Organization (FAO) of the United Nations. *Critical Issues on Food Marketing Systems in Developing Countries.* Report of Joint Seminar, Paris, October 18-22, 1976. Paris: OECD, 1977.

61. Parker, A. J., 1975. Hypermarkets: the changing pattern of retailing. *Geography* 60 (Part 2) (267): 120-124 (Apr.).

62. Riley, Harold, Charles Slater, Kelly Harrison, John Wish, John Griggs, Vincent Forace, José Santiago, and Idalia Rodriguez. *Food Marketing in the Economic Development of Puerto Rico.* Research Report No. 4, Latin American Studies Center, Michigan State University, 1970.

63. Rotblat, Howard J., 1975. Social organization and development in an Iranian provincial bazaar. *Con. Dev. and Cult. Change* 23(2): 292-305 (Jan.).

64. Samli, A. Coskun, 1965. Exportability of American marketing knowledge. *MSU Business Topics* 13: 41 (Autumn).

65. Sinclair, Stuart W., 1976. Informal economic activity in African cities: proposals for research. *J. Modern African Studies* 14(4): 696-699 (Dec.).

66. Slater, Charles C. Market channel coordination and economic development. In *Vertical Marketing Systems,* ed. by Louis P. Buckin. Glenview, Ill.: Scott Foresman, and Co., 1970, pp. 135-157.

67. Stockwin, Harvey, 1976. Letter from Manila. *Far Eastern Economic R.* 91(4): 62 (Jan. 23).

68. Tax, Sol. *Penny Capitalism: A Guatemalan Indian Economy.* Smithsonian Institution, Institute of Social Anthropology Publication No. 16. Washington, D.C.: U.S. Government Printing Office, 1953.

69. Trevino, Ruben, 1980. Growth in Mexican supers stimulates promo use. *Adv. Age* 51(21): S10 (May 12).

70. Wadinambiaratchi, George, 1965. Channels of distribution in developing economies. *Business Quar.* 30(4): 74-82 (Winter).

71. Ward, Barbara E., 1959-60. Cash or credit crops? An examination of some implications of peasant commercial production with special reference to the multiplicity of traders and middlemen. *Econ. Dev. and Cult. Change* 8: 148-163.

72. Ward, Mary, 1978a. Superstores: giants of Japan retail scene. *Industrial Marketing* 63(1): 80-81 (Jan.).

73. Ward, Mary, 1978b. 7-Eleven units fill demand for convenience shopping. *Industrial Marketing* 63(1): 82 (Jan.).

74. Westfall, Ralph, and Harper W. Boyd, Jr., 1960. Marketing in India. *J. Marketing* 25(2): 11-17 (Oct.).

75. Wiggleworth, E. F., and Jiri Botan, 1966. Retailing trends in Thailand. *J. Retailing* 42: 41-51 (Summer).

76. Winder, R. Bayly. The Lebanese in West Africa. *Comparative Studies in*

Society and History, April 1962, pp. 292-333. (Cited by Hollander, 1970.)

77. Yavas, U., E. Kaynak, and E. Borak, 1981. Retailing institutions in developing countries: determinants of supermarket patronage in Istanbul, Turkey. *Journal of Business Research* 9(4): 367-379 (Dec.).

78. Yavas U., E. Kaynak, and E. Borak, 1982. Food shopping orientations in Turkey: some lessons for policy makers. *Food Policy*, 7(2): 133-140 (May).

4

A Technology Transfer Model to Third World Women Toward Improving the Quality and Quantity of the Food Supply

A. C. SAMLI AND JANE H. WALTER

Although much attention has been given to food deficiency in Third World countries, this problem remains as acute now as it was in the past (Wortmann and Cummings, 1978). Perhaps the least understood factor behind this problem is food management. Indeed, one's management of existing food supplies, qualitatively and quantitively, accounts for much of the food deficiency (Ritchie, 1976). A model is presented in this chapter illustrating how food management—physical handling and distribution of food—and its nutritional utilization are woefully neglected areas in the Third World countries (Cain and Dauber, 1981). Hence, developing such a technology and transferring it successfully will provide a breakthrough not only by enhancing women's role in development in these countries but more importantly by accelerating the basic economic development of these countries.

This chapter has three major components. The first component deals with an exploration of food supply in a society; the second explores food management at the household level; and the third examines problems of technology transfer in issues of food utilization in Third World countries.

A MODEL OF FOOD SUPPLY

In the final analysis, the food supply in a society is not only how much food that society can produce, but also how the society handles the food supply in terms of physical distribution and how that society uses the food supply (Figure 4.1). Although much has been written on food production, very little if any attention has been devoted to the physical handling of the food products (Newland, 1977). Even more neglected is the proper food-use issues at the household levels in Third World countries.

Figure 4.1
A Model of Food Supply

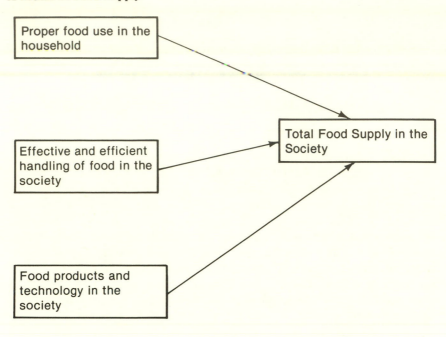

Food Production and Technology

Most colleges of agriculture and nutrition, particularly in U.S. land-grant universities, have developed a multitude of advanced techniques in agricultural and food production. These efforts have led to the so-called and highly controversial "green revolution" and other facets of highly increased agricultural productivity. Obviously, proper transfer of appropriate techniques to Third World countries is important in coping with the problems of underdevelopment. However, many of the techniques are either too complicated or too costly to be truly useful. The work in this area has begun and is likely to continue for an indefinite period of time.

Physical Distribution and Handling of Food

One of the reasons why food production efforts have failed in many Third World countries is not that production techniques and their application have been inadequate but that there has been a failure to develop efficient distribution systems. Indeed, most agriculturalists are so involved in food production issues that they usually overlook the fact that undistributed agricultural output is the same as lack of basic food. Numerous cases in economic development and marketing texts deal with the failure to distribute the food that was successfully produced. Inadequate distribution systems, that is, warehousing, transportation, communication, grading, and packaging, have all too often offset the strides that have been made in food production and food technology.

The Use of the Food Supply

Notwithstanding production and distribution, the way a society uses its food has a direct impact on its total food supply available. It has been stated, for example, that the best part of grains in the United States are being fed to livestocks and pets rather than being utilized for human consumption. While the United States may be in a position to afford such a luxury, most Third World countries cannot. One of the most important aspects of food usage in a society takes place in the household. This particular aspect of food supply in a society is perhaps the greatest challenge for the women in Third World countries. The rest of this chapter deals particularly with this aspect. It should be understood that this issue is not more important than or mutually exclusive of the other two issues, that is, production and distribution. However, food preparation at home is perhaps the greatest challenge for those concerned with women in development issues.

FOOD MANAGEMENT AT THE HOUSEHOLD LEVEL

In many parts of the world, particularly in those countries where the food suppy is limited, food management at the household level is often inefficient (Cain and Dauber, 1981). Food management at the household level is considered in three parts: processing, storing, and consuming (Figure 4.2).

Processing

Because most homes in Third World countries are not well equipped, food processing at the household level is less than efficient. Without sharp knives or running water in the kitchen, fresh vegetables may be cut improperly, that is, too deeply, therefore, wasting substantial amounts of food, or may unnecessarily peel because of inadequate water, causing a substantial food loss.

In addition to deficiencies in the kitchen, lack of food preparation information may increase the problem. For example, excessive cooking may cause much of the nutritional value to be wasted and the actual amount of the food to be reduced, if not totally diminished. For instance, in many parts of Turkey corn is cooked a very long time in order to make it more "digestible."

Figure 4.2
Food Management at the Household Level in Third World Countries

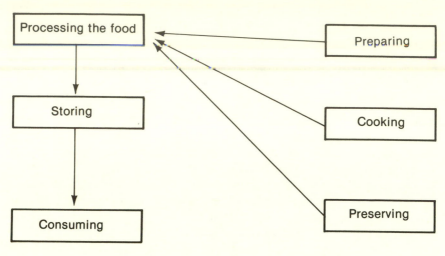

Lack of proper cooking facilities may also aggravate the problem: Burning or not being able to cook the food, therefore wasting it, are commonplace occurrences. Many kitchens in the Third World are so underequipped that even if the knowledge were to be present, it would be almost impossible to prepare the food to give optimum food value.

Even if the food is properly prepared and cooked, preservation poses a serious problem which, therefore, indirectly affects the food supply. Climatic conditions coupled with the lack of some basic preservatives also negatively affect the food supply.

Storing

Third World households more than most other households in the world lack storage space; therefore, risk of spoilage coupled with insufficient amounts of food leads to inadequate use of food supply. Thus, many parts of the world could do better with improved storage facilities at home rather than a new and elaborate food industry.

New, simple technologies are being developed to reduce post-harvest food loss. For instance, weevils and rodents destroy nearly half of the food stored in rural Cameroon homes. Small technological advances can reduce that loss by at least half (Henn, 1976).

Consuming

Lack of knowledge of proper nutrition combined with cultural imperatives leads to less than optimal use of the food supply. For instance, certain ethnic groups have a diet based on an abundance of starchy foods. As a result, while lacking some necessary foods, these ethnic groups are also wasting some foods by consuming too much of them.

Thus, three factors—poor processing, inadequate storage, and narrow consumption patterns—affect the existing food supply at the household level in societies where food is acutely limited. This type of mismanagement at the household level intensifies the overall problem disproportionately.

TRANSFERRING FOOD UTILIZATION TECHNOLOGY

Clearly, the food supply in Third World countries can be enhanced by improving the food use process at the household level. Based on this premise, part of the economic development process and Agency for International Development activities must be related to technology transfer of food preparation and utilization. Such a model is presented in Figure 4.3. Such a model has four components: (1) the country, (2) the sender, (3) barriers to transfer, and (4) receiving countries' housewives.

The Country

As Figure 4.3 illustrates, a technology specifically tailored for a particular Third World country must be developed regarding food utilization and processing. Such a technology will have at least two specific and sequential steps. First, a careful analysis of food preparation processes and available unused food sources must be undertaken in order to establish the direction and parameters of the technology. Second, once the food preparation processes and unused food sources are identified, the prioritization process must take place. This prioritization process will determine which unused food sources should be tapped first and which aspects of ongoing food preparation practices should be altered. Thus, every country may have to have a different formula for developing a food preparation process designed to increase the overall food supply. In addition to developing the food preparation process which is tailored to the special needs of each country, cooking and preserving must also be incorporated into the technology that is going to be transferred to these countries. The next step is to determine the nature and specifics of the technology transferred.

The Sender

The country that is preparing the technology to be transferred must have particular awareness of the needs and capabilities of the recipient country. Preparing the technology is not sufficient unless it is structured in the proper format for transfer. This is evidenced by the efforts to introduce soybeans as a protein supplement into the existing diet. It was necessary to present combinations of soybeans with commonly accepted foods.

Figure 4.3
A Technology Transfer Model of Expanding Food Utilization in Third World Countries

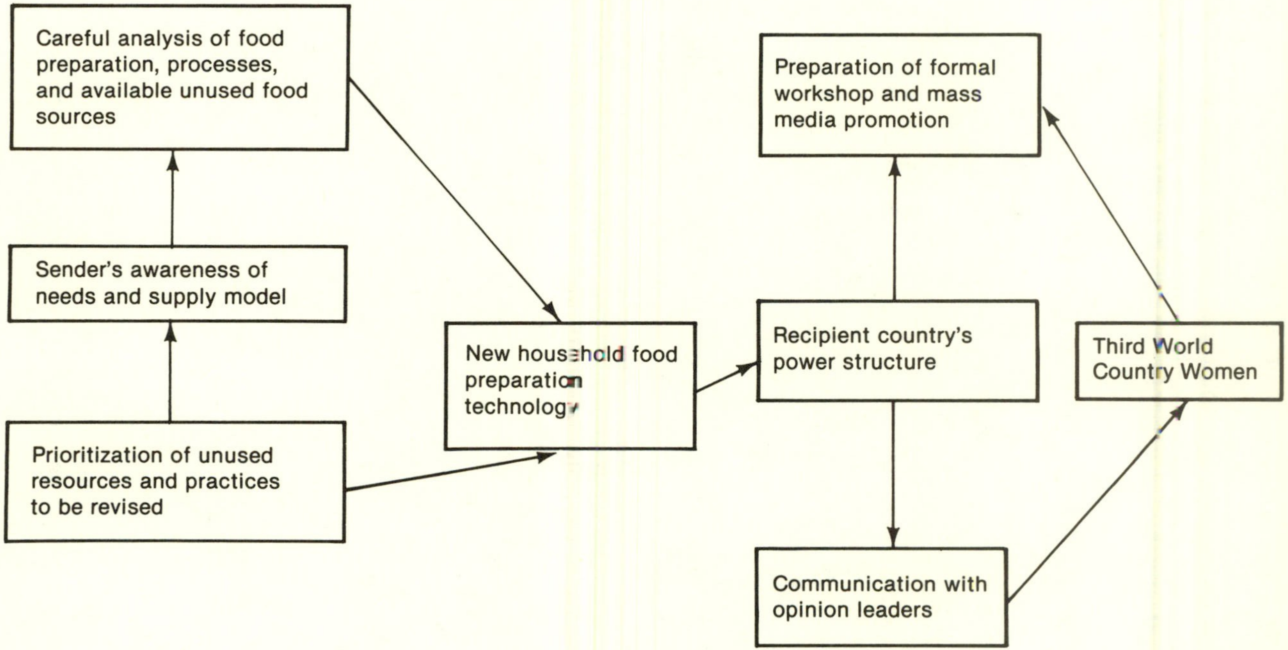

Barriers to Transfer

In addition to the traditional cross-cultural communications barriers (Moran and Harris, 1979), there are two distinct layers of additional communication barriers to transferring the technology related to food processing and consumption: (1) the existing power structure, and (2) communication of the message to the individual. While the first can be described as the power structure barrier, the second may be termed the tradition barrier.

The power structure barrier implies that the Third World is a man's world. Indeed, the the existing power structure is practically all male. Thus, in order to be transferred, the proposed technology must go through the male barrier. In order to go through this barrier successfully, one must work with the prevailing power structure rather than try to change or destroy it. Working with the power structure barrier implies not threatening or upsetting the balance but rather gaining acceptance. Thus, enhancing the awareness of the male power structure as to the possibility of increasing the food supply is necessary to go through the first barrier. In essence, therefore, it may be said that woman's development in the Third World countries is a function of increased education and enhanced awareness or sensitization of men.

Most of the Third World countries are strongly tied to traditions and hence are not readily open to new ideas such as modifying ways of preparing staple dishes. This traditional orientation cannot be readily overcome. Joint efforts must be made to transfer technology. Examining the cultural barriers implies preparing the technology properly and promoting it effectively. The two most important aspects of this promotion are the mass media and the opinion leadership. The mass media have to communicate, within the constraints of the country's values and culture, that there are more effective ways of achieving traditional goals or performing traditional tasks of preparing the food and feeding people at the household level. Research indicates that different mass media and different promotional techniques are prevalent and effective in different countries. Therefore, proper use of the mass media in this technology transfer is of the essence. Opinion leadership and communication networks also function differently in different countries. Determining the identity of the opinion leaders who influence household practices is very important, for they can be used as liaison persons for the technology transfer process.

In many tradition-oriented countries, the mothers or other female elders are opinion leaders in the areas of cooking and household management. Thus, in each country as well as in each community informal communication networks penetrate the populace. In an effort to transfer the proposed technology successfully, it is necessary to determine the nature of this informal communication network.

In addition to preparing the appropriate technology, the sender must undertake preliminary research to determine the communication process prevalent in each community. Research (Zaltman, 1965; Young and Young, 1961; Rogers and Cartano, 1962) has shown that in order to determine the opinion leaders in the existing informal communications networks, three separate techniques are employed: (1) sociometric; (2) key informant; (3) self-designating techniques (Zaltman, 1965). All of these techniques were developed in the early 1960s and are still quite appropriate for Third World consumer research.

(1) Sociometric technique: This technique involves asking the members of a group or a community to whom they go for advice and information about food processing and household management (Katz and Lazarsfeld, 1955). Once the information flow prevalent in that community is established, it is possible to detect the opinion leaders.

(2) Key informant technique: Here the researcher questions those people in the group or the community who can identify the opinion leaders in that group or the community. In such cases without developing the general pattern of the prevailing communication systems, it becomes possible to directly identify the opinion leaders (Young and Young, 1961).

(3) Self-designating technique: Individuals are asked to determine the degree to which they perceive themselves as opinion leaders (Rogers and Cartano, 1962). This technique may not determine the prevailing comunication network completely or immediately identify opinion leders as the second method does. However, it is effective in identifying some of the true opinion leaders who in turn can influence the behavior of local women. Any one of these techniques, or a combination of them, can be used in order to penetrate the tradition barrier and carry the technology message to the individual.

Receiving Countries' Housewives

The relative role of the sexes varies dramatically from culture to culture. In many Third World countries, the type of technology transfer discussed in this chapter needs to be accepted by the males of that society and of the households so that it can be adopted by the women. In fact, this is why Virginia Tech's International Programs have used not only Mothercraft centers but also Fathercraft centers in Haiti to improve diet practices. These centers raise the fathers' sensitivity and awareness of the importance of diet in order to improve the overall health of the family. In other cultures, networking among women can be very effective in reaching the grass roots level in terms of technology transfer.

One last means of communication is the cooperative system. In India, for instance, a number of very successful women's cooperatives provide possible models for technological improvement. In the process, they provide the means for technology transfer in many aspects of life, including household management (Tinker, 1981).

SUMMARY AND CONCLUSIONS

This chapter makes three premises: the food supply can be partially improved by proper food utilization at the household level; expanded technologies can be developed to improve the food utilization process in different countries; and transferring these technologies to the appropriate grass roots recipients is a very complicated task.

In addition to very expensive and time-consuming efforts in improving food production and distribution techniques, if food consumption technologies were to be nominally emphasized, a substantial proportion of the food shortage problem in Third World countries would be reduced. At least part of the food research related to development should be considered within the scope of women in development considerations.

Prevailing insensitivities to the receiving country's needs and prevailing conditions within that country can cause expensive errors on the part of the sending country. Thus, a technology transfer model to improve the food supply in Third World countries must be made *country specific.*

REFERENCES

Belden, G. C., et al. *The Protein Paradox: Malnutrition, Protein-Rich Foods and the Role of Business.* Cambridge, Mass.: Harvard University Press, 1964.

Cain, M., and R. Dauber. *Women and Technological Change in Developing Countries.* Boulder, Colo.: Westview Press, 1981.

Cavasgil, T. S., Lyn S. Amine, and Edward Vitale. "Marketing Supplementary Food Products in LDCs: A Case Study in Morocco." *Food Policy* (May 1983): 111-120.

Henn, Jeanne K. "Report on Women Farmers and Their Relationship to ZAPI de L'Est." Washington, D.C.: World Bank, Rural Development Division, March 1976, Mimeo.

Katz, Elihu, and Lazarsfeld, Paul F. *Personal Influence.* New York: Free Press of Glencoe, 1955.

Miner, M., ed. *Protein Enriched Cereal Food for World Needs.* St. Paul, Minn.: The American Association of Cereal Chemists, 1969.

Moran, Robert T., and P. R. Harris. *Managing Cultural Differences.* Houston: Gulf Publishing Co., 1979.

Newland, Kathleen. *The Sisterhood of Man.* New York: W. W. Norton, 1977.

Ritchie, Jean A.S. "Impacts of Changing Food Production, Processing and Marketing Systems on the Role of Women." *Impacts of the World Situation.* Proceedings of the World Food Conference. Ames: Iowa State University Press, 1976.

Rogers, Everett M., and David G. Cartano. "Methods of Measuring Opinion Leadership." *Public Opinion Quarterly* (Fall 1962): 439-440.

Tinker, Irene. "New Technologies for Food-Related Activities: An Equity Strategy." In Cain and Dauber, *Women and Technological Change.*

Wortmann, S., and R. Cummings. *To Feed This World.* Baltimore: Johns Hopkins University Press, 1978.

Young, Frank W., and Ruth C. Young. "Key Informant Reliability in Rural Mexican Villages." *Human Organization* (Fall 1961): 141-148.

Zaltman, Gerald. *Marketing: Contributions from the Behavioral Sciences.* New York: Harcourt, Brace & World, 1965.

5
Technology Transfer to Eastern Europe

STANLEY J. PALIWODA AND
MARILYN L. LIEBRENZ

Technology may be said to have four main components:

- The technology embodied in products whose manufacture requires extensive research (high-technology products): a small volume of exports can, for example, transfer a major technology if—as in the field of computers—the product can be easily copied.
- Sales of patents, licenses, and know-how, whereby various inventions, production processes, and operating devices are distributed between countries.
- The direct investment that allows the purchaser of a factory to obtain his or her productive and technical capital.
- The official and private technical assistance which is intended to improve the level of the recipient country, mainly through training (teaching, courses, vocational training).[1]

C. Wolcott Parker, in a paper to the Licensing Executives Society, stated that "technology was created by the human mind responding to the necessities of survival."[2] There is a congruency between technology transfer and communication. Without communication there is no demand for goods and services; thus, no technology is needed or used, and none is transferred. However, since technology is being transferred in greater and greater amounts, it follows that there needs to be more and more communication. Within the context of East-West trade, this matter is allied to politics. John R. Pegan has described the special nature of technology transfer:

in some respects, technology transfer is a very special business, unlike any other. The most fundamental, distinguishing attribute of this basic business is that it is utterly dependent on the availability of proprietary technology for transfer to others in need of it. Without the protective property rights in the technical product of intellectual effort, as afforded by patent or trade-secret laws, there is no proprietary technology and no business of technology transfer. This fundamental and unique nature of technology transfer as a business is no respecter of ideology.[3]

While communication is essential for people to know of a specific technology, it is also a limiting factor of technology transfer. The need for technology per se is boundless but lack of communication is likely to limit this need from being satisfied.

TECHNOLOGY TRANSFERS TO EASTERN EUROPE

Technology sales to Eastern Europe are predicted to rise as the global economy continues to improve. Despite warnings that the region's economic prospects may not be as favorable as broadcast, as a result both of inflation and its internal high pricing policies with the Soviet Union in regard to petroleum purchases,[4] the basic forecast appears quite positive.

Thus, the attention on technology transfers to this region is warranted, particularly in view of the uncertain future of East-West relations and détente. The East European countries are a particularly valuable region for study inasmuch as the citizens of this region are not under great restrictions in regard to the industrialized West—primarily the United States but also Western Europe. Representatives from Eastern Europe are permitted to visit key defense areas in the United States—territories that are off limits to the Soviet people. East European trading companies do not have to be registered with the U.S. government, and their personnel need not file as foreign agents. The discovery that some of these East Europeans function as industrial intelligence agents for the Soviet Union[5] may or may not be a realistic picture for the group as a whole.

The whole question of whether transfer technology should be extended to the Eastern Bloc has come down to a controversy between business-related interests, which support increased technology sales from the industrial West, and defense sectors (primarily in the United States), which discourage technology sales. The apparent rationale of business is that "if we do not offer such sales, our competitors will."[6] The alternative position, held primarily by government and state representatives, is concerned not only with "protection" and weapons systems, but also with an overall trade perspective which foresees increased competition growing from technology sales. The idea is that a one-time sale carries the potential for ongoing competition.

In addition, some officials have described a potentially vicious circle of "energy and high-technology trade: the more energy the Soviets sell to Europe, the more incentive the Europeans will have to sell high technology to the Soviets, and this, in turn could help to increase Soviet energy exports to Europe."[7] France's recent sales of nuclear products to the USSR provides just one illustration of this situation. One type of product, the small personal computer, appears to carry additional problems. Even curtailing the technology behind the manufacture of the smaller computers would appear inadequate inasmuch as the computers themselves are now small enough to carry in suitcases and are found worldwide.[8]

The position of the United States on technology transfer has become increasingly restrictive in the 1980s, although the 1979 Export Administration Act, which expired in September 1980, was temporarily extended by President Ronald Reagan until the U.S. Congress could reach a consensus on the amendments. At issue is not only national security, but also the use of export sanctions to achieve foreign policy goals, which are sometimes achieved to the detriment of individual corporate loss of both image and finances. One example is the cost to Caterpillar Tractor whose sales of pipe-laying machinery to the USSR were suspended in 1978 by then President Jimmy Carter. By the time the sanctions were lifted in August 1983, estimates of damages to Caterpillar ranged in the neighborhood of $400 million. Use of these sanctions for foreign policy pressure is becoming increasingly ineffective with the growing availability of alternative suppliers, as evidenced in prior grain sales by Latin America, especially Argentina, and, in the pipe-laying instance, by the Japanese corporation, Komatsu.[9]

The security rationale, however, is the major incentive for the stricter controls which Central Intelligence Agency officials are openly urging for scientific exchanges between the United States and the Eastern Bloc. This area carries major policy implications in the technology transfer area, particularly in the research fields.[10]

COCOM

Traditionally, the Coordinating Committee for East-West Trade Policy (CoCom), based in Paris, has placed a watching brief on so-called strategic exports to the East European Bloc. However, not all Western or Organization for Economic Cooperation and Development (OECD) member states with highly developed techniques are members of CoCom. Indeed, several nations place a high value on their independence and freedom from any form of political alignment. In this respect, Switzerland has long achieved a role of arbiter in international disputes, but Sweden, in another connection, has been seen to be a source of ''leakage'' of so-called strategic exports to Eastern Europe. Since Sweden is not a member of CoCom, no law or agreement is being broken. The substitution effects of Western exports to the Eastern Bloc should be applied to all of East-West trade, but timing is also important. As Nye has pointed out:

technology is not like a precious metal to be hoarded. It is more like a fine Rhine wine. He who hoards it too long is left with bottles of worthless vinegar. With time, any technology will spread—as Britain found out with the textile technology in the 19th Century and the U.S. discovered with nuclear technology in the 1940s.[11]

Analysis of exports to Communist countries processed under validated license reveals that very small shares (1 to 3 percent) of U.S. exports were judged to have enough potential application to military industrial production in Communist countries to merit evaluation under the validated license procedure.[12] More as a result of disagreement between its members than as a direct consequence of this, CoCom now has only a short list of items that form the basis of a common group of published exports to Eastern Europe. In recent years, the United States has effectively strengthened this list by prohibiting any American company or subsidiary abroad from supplying listed goods. The United States still has key positions in aeronautics, data processing, engines and turbines, scientific apparatus, organic chemistry, and electronics in particular. These six sectors are responsible for half of the nine East European countries' deficit with the United States.[13] Even though four-fifths of U.S. trade with the Eastern Bloc is accounted for by agricultural products, yet it is the United States and Britain that have technology balances that are structurally in surplus. This is in contrast with the rest of the industrialized countries (Europe and Japan), which are traditionally in deficit. In 1981, 81 percent of U.S. and 40 percent of British technology earnings derived from foreign subsidiaries.[14]

It appears that the United States' political position is that the list of CoCom-controlled items should be as wide as possible, to avoid the application of even nonweapon-related products toward weapons usage. However, many members of CoCom and some members of NATO plus Japan would prefer to see the CoCom-controlled items narrowly defined—so that increased trade is possible.[15]

The incentives for the Eastern Bloc to acquire Western technology are ever increasing, particularly as the computer and telecommunications revolution continues to take over. The Eastern Bloc faces updating competition, not only from the United States and Japan, but also, increasingly, from China. Thus, while the sales of technology from the United States to the Eastern Bloc may be down via conventional channels, the incentives for obtaining high-technology equipment are becoming greater. One example of this "purchase or purloin" strategy came to light in November 1983, when customs officials in West Germany and Sweden seized a Digital Equipment Corporation VAX 11/782 computer bound for the USSR. The equipment had been routed via South Africa prior to Euorpe. It was seized because of its most questionable future usage: the operation of missile guidance systems.[16]

In addition to the immediate concern accompanying the seizure of the illegal VAX computer export, the situation prompted demands for increased regulations on the part of the U.S. Department of Commerce to limit the multiple licenses of high-technology products to the members of CoCom, and to Australia and New Zealand.[17]

One of the major problem areas, even through CoCom, is that the number of alternative suppliers is readily increasing, while the interconnectiveness of the global economies indicates that a control policy hurts not just that immediate company or even country, but some of that country's allies as well—as the above example readily indicates. William A. Roct, former director of the U.S. State Department's Office of East-West Trade (who resigned in protest over the tightening of controls to the Soviet Union), maintains that limitations on technology exports should take the form of "negotiations (with CoCom members or other U.S. allies) on strengthening controls on items which have direct, rather than indirect relationship to the national security of the U.S."[18]

It was in one of the key U.S. categories listed above—turbines—that a confrontation arose recently between the United States and its West European allies who had been contracted as suppliers to the Soviet oil pipeline. John Brown Engineering Limited, a British company supplying gas turbines which incorporated a General Electric license, was being cut off from supplies by the American government but was simultaneously ordered to supply the Soviet Union by the British government. If it obeyed British orders, it would face reprisals from the U.S. government affecting its American subsidiaries. If it chose not to do so, it would face heavy unemployment among its British workforce, together with lost orders worth millions of pounds, and possible British government reprisals. It is important to note that it is no longer possible to insure against such political risks with the ECGD.[19]

Industrial espionage and theft is one of the most "productive areas" for Soviet and East European intelligence sources, that is, the "procurement of production equipment technology, as opposed to actual weapons systems," as noted by Lawrence J. Brady, former assistant secretary for trade administration within the U.S. Department of Commerce.[20]

The United States has taken a number of measures to attempt to control unwarranted technology flows to the Eastern Bloc. These measures include:

- Classification of the bulletin of the Defense Department's Defense Technical Information Center as "confidential."
- Restricted availability of the National Technical Information Service listing of nearly 80,000 annual technical reports.
- FBI briefings to all defense contractors on Soviet espionage tactics as of 1982.
- Establishment of an interagency Technology Transfer Intelligence Committee as of 1982.
- A 1982 confidential agreement between the U.S. and its Western allies to tighten up on technology transfers to the Eastern Bloc.

- A 200-percent increase in the number of individuals monitoring exports for the Department of Commerce since 1982, particularly concentrating on the activities of California's Silicon Valley firms (Operation Exodus).[21]

Additional controls on visas for travelers from the Eastern Bloc were applied as of May 1983, not only in the United States, but also throughout the CoCom community nations."

TWO-WAY TECHNOLOGY FLOWS

Technology transfer rarely constitutes an equal two-way flow, even over time, between transferor and transferee. An estimate of the East-West license trade reckons that, since 1965, 1,500 licenses have been sold by the Eastern Bloc to the West (USSR—400; Czechoslovakia—400; Hungary—300; German Democratic Republic (GDR)—300; and Poland, Bulgaria, and Romania—100).[23] For the same period, a West German source estimates East European countries to have purchased 2,400 licenses from the West, including 500 by Yugoslavia.[24] It is important to point out, however, that the sources are different and that the figure for Eastern Bloc sales of licenses in the West, although not contradicted, would appear to be at least generous. One fairly extensive research study cites ninety licenses which have been sold by Poland alone, the majority of which were sold during 1971-80.[25]

It may be in this area of "reverse" technology transfer that the greatest strides may be made, particularly in light of the current détente between the Eastern Bloc and the West. By the end of 1983, Hungary had announced a series of measures designed to increase its export of goods and, presumably, technology, to the West, including the less traditional non-European markets. While the inclination to seek export markets is not new among East European nations, the easing of restrictions and the magnitude of reforms in Hungary to encourage additional business appear to make it the Soviet Bloc's most "easy-going" economy at present.[26]

Increasing consumer acceptance of goods from the Eastern Bloc, especially Eastern Europe, also appears to be helpful in aiding possible future reverse flows of exports, including technology.[27] However, foreign policy matters play a major role here; hence, should conflicts between the West and the East escalate, consumer acceptance of the goods, regardless of the desirability of the items or the information, would possibly decrease.

Indeed, technology transfer to Eastern Europe is frequently seen as being a one-way street, transferring eastwards the sophisticated items of machinery, process controls, and know-how which will in the end "bury us."[28] Since communism views history as being on its side and its truth as invincible over time, it becomes difficult to separate the questions of politics from those of trade. Particularly as technology relates to a transferral of current state-of-the-art techniques, elevating the capability of the transferee to that of the transferor, there are inevitably political considerations and involvement in this area. With world demand contracting, it is true now more than ever that possession of technology has become the supreme arm for gaining, consolidating, or extending trading positions.

Trade and politics in the East European sphere are inseparable. Trade is seasonal and fluctuates greatly with the warmth of the political climate. Many of these technology transfer deals which are being developed today were planned several years ago during the period of East-West détente. The early 1970s witnessed relaxed controls over East-West trade, making possible the realization of several very large projects. On the Western side, CoCom controls were lifted and on the Eastern side, attempts were made to encourage joint East-West ventures by means of facilitating legislation. Table 5.1 is an operational variable analysis of the ICA and the joint equity venture on East European soil. Table 5.2 examines the conditions relating to joint equity ventures in Eastern Europe. Figure 5.1 provides a concise overview of the advantages and problems facing technology transfer, incorporating both nonequity agreements and joint equity ventures.[29]

EASTERN EUROPE

Although Eastern Europe is a rather homogeneous area, it might be informative to consider some of the unique characteristics of each individual country in the region, especially in relation to technology transfers.

Romania, for instance, was the only East European country in 1981 to belong to the International Monetary Fund (IMF) and the World Bank. It also held most-favored-nation trading status with the United States, but this status was jeopardized in March 1983 because Romania was found to be imposing a tax on emigrants. According to one expert, the suspension "could halve Romania's exports to the United States."[30] Romania's trading needs in regard to imports include equipment and technology, especially in the areas of energy, computers, and other electronic products, metallurgical and chemical industries, and agriculture. U.S. trade with Romania was also negatively affected by the easing of trading restrictions between Romania and the European Economic Community (EEC), resulting in greater trade between Romania and the EEC. The greatest problem facing Romania is the lack of hard currency, requiring projects and sales to incorporate countertrades and joint ventures whenever possible.

Poland, haunted by internal strife and labor unrest, appears to be seeking more basic goods than high-technology products. This is the result more of necessity than of choice. The development of natural resources, as well as housing construction and agricultural improvements, reflects the country's immediate needs but not its high level of industrialization. Poland was the third largest Council for Mutual Economic Assistance (CMEA) exporter to the West in 1981, behind the USSR and the GDR.[31]

Hungary literally broke away from the "cumbrous foreign trade systems

Table 5.1
An Operational Variable Analysis of the ICA and the Joint Equity Venture

Operation Variables	Industrial Cooperation Agreement		Joint Equity Venture	
	Possible Advantages	*Possible Disadvantages*	*Possible Advantages*	*Possible Disadvantages*
Ownership	None, no company finance involved	Lack of control	49% equity stake	Weakening of company equity base
Venture control	Contractual limitations, plant Eastern responsibility	Limited control	*De facto* control greater than equity share	Inability to reconcile objectives
Venture capital	No capital investment by company	ICA entails acceptance of goods m.u.l.[a]	Capital and managerial investment	Commitment of company resources
Return on investment (ROI)	Fast	Speed of project rests with Eastern partner	Gradual ROI shows willingness to stay in market	Venture has to achieve profitability first
Risk sharing	Contractual liability only	Diminished risks diminish opportunity for spectacular profits	Half-share only	Eastern partner may refuse to kill-off an unprofitable joint venture
Venture duration	Fixed duration	Renewal or extension requires separate contract	Unlimited	Termination a possible problem
Western company repayment	Hard cash and goods	Adjustment to Western business cycles	Goods m.u.l.[a] and hard cash	Subject to Eastern taxes
Manufacturing	Extra facility at cost	May flood market eventually	Extra plant at cost	Exposure at risk

Operation Variables	Industrial Cooperation Agreement		Joint Equity Venture	
	Possible Advantages	*Possible Disadvantages*	*Possible Advantages*	*Possible Disadvantages*
Management skills	Limited, contractual obligations	Costs of this transfer may be greater than anticipated	Full access	Too great a dependence on the Western partner
Marketing	Lower cost goods m.u.l.[a]	Coordination with Western business cycles	Lower cost good m.u.l.[a]	Investment in capital, machinery and management
Market expansion	Western access to CMEA and limited Eastern access to West via partner	Ability to vary deliveries according to demand	Western access to CMEA and limited Eastern access to West via partner	Sales priced only in 'hard' currency
Pricing	Lower costs	Western inability to forecast Eastern expectation	Lower costs	All costs priced in 'hard' currency only
Quality control	Goods to Western quality standards	Free access but geographical distance and costs of quality control	Goods to Western quality standards	Free access but geographical distance and costs of quality control
Research and development	May be included or may lead from an ICA	Dependent upon mutual capabilities	Ability to capitalize on Eastern strengths	Difficulties of coordination
Updating of technology transferred	Contractual	Ambiguity of contract act definition	Closer integration	Sharing of current company specific technology

SOURCE: S. J. Paliwoda, *Joint East-West Marketing and Production Ventures* (Gower, 1981).
[a]Made under licence (m.u.l.).

Table 5.2
Conditions Relating to Joint Equity Ventures on East European Soil

	Pct. of Total East-West Cooperation in 1978	ICA Share of Cooperation	No. of Joint Equity Ventures in Country	Maximum Permissible Share of Equity	Position in Local Economy: Separate/Integrated	Management Control	Accounting System	Legal Parameters
BULGARIA	3.5%	Major	3 active	No Limit	Separate	Director, Joint Management Board	Only one rate of exchange for commercial transactions, the offered rate. 25% of the Western partner's share of profits may be repatriated after payment of taxes	Decree 535 of March 1980
HUNGARY	24.2%	Major	5 active	49%	Separate	Director, Joint Management Board	Settlement in forints, but Hungary close to being a market economy: fair value of forint. Hungarian National Bank guarantees to contribute share besides repatriation of profit, amortisation, and share in event of liquidation	Decree 19 of 1970. Decree 28 of 1972. Decree 7 of 1974. Decree 7 of 1977
POLAND	17.2%	Total	0	49%	Integrated	0 joint-ventures in force at present	Tourist rate of exchange for joint equity ventures. All accounting performed in mutually agreed hard currency. State guarantee on the transfer of profits and capital, subject to conditions. New legislation is pending however.	Law of 20 December 1928. Law of 20 March 1928. Decree of 14 May 1976. Decree of 7 February 1979

	Pct. of Total East-West Cooperation in 1978	ICA Share of Cooperation	No. of Joint Equity Ventures in Country	Maximum Permissible Share of Equity	Position in Local Economy: Separate/ Integrated	Management Control	Accounting System	Legal Parameters
ROMANIA	8.9%	Major	3 active	49%	Separate	Director, Joint Management Board	Tourist rate of exchange for joint equity ventures. All accounting performed in mutually agreed hard currency. State guarantee on transfer of profits, amortisation, and share of property in event of liquidation, subject to conditions	Foreign Trade Law No. 1 of 1971. Decrees 424, 425 of 1972
YUGOSLAVIA	29.3%	0	200+ but many dormant	49%	Integrated	Director, Joint Management Board, responsible for matters relating to contract (technology), marketing, profits, etc.) Workers' Council	Settlement in exchange dinars. State guarantee of transfer of profits and capital, subject to conditions	Decree of 9 February 1978. Law of 30 March 1978. Law of 1 March 1978

SOURCE: Revised and updated from S. J. Paliwoda, *Joint East-West Marketing and Production Ventures* (Gower, 1981). See also "Business International S.A.," *Business Eastern Europe*, January 28. 1983.

Figure 5.1
The Technology Transfer

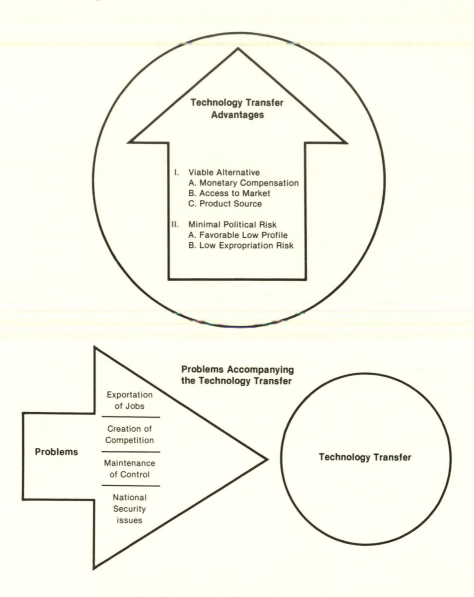

SOURCE: Marilyn L. Liebrenz, *Transfer of Technology: U.S. Multinationals and Eastern Europe* (New York: Praeger Publishers, 1982), pp. 15, 18.

of Eastern Europe" through its late 1983 attempt to improve its trading balance, even if this improvement may be detrimental to its socialistic orientation. "More than 150 Hungarian companies now have the right to trade independently without going through specialized Foreign Trade Organizations," notes *The Economist*. The country is even encouraging competition among those same organizations.[32]

Hungary joined the IMF in 1982 and appears increasingly oriented toward exports. This would indicate an even greater need for current technology, but the problems facing the country in this area include a slowness to adapt products to the world market, maintenance of product quality, and adequate supplies of spare parts.

Czechoslovakia conducts less trade with the West than do the above-cited countries, but the country does possess a high level of industrial development as well as abundant grain harvests which supplement other local agricultural supplies. Despite the country's desire for more manufactured goods, its licensing procedures for obtaining much of the technology, from the United States at least, have proved difficult. A hard currency shortage has also been highly detrimental.[33]

Bulgaria's trade, too, has concentrated more on Western Europe than on the United States. The country did permit joint equity projects with the West as of March 1980, generally as a means of attracting hard currency, but also as a means of improving its industrialization base. Typewriters and leather footwear were the two leading U.S. imports from Bulgaria in 1980.[34]

The German Democratic Republic continues to increase its trade with the Federal Republic of Germany as well as with neighboring Czechoslovakia. Both merchandise and human traffic between the borders of the two Germanies continue to increase. In fact, East Germany's dependence on the West and the West's economic benefits are so great that East Germany "can scarcely afford to shrink back into isolation, [as] the country owes western banks nearly $10 billion and about 80 percent of all hard currency earnings are said to service those debts."[35]

These distinctions among the major East European nations appear to have more influence on the specific forms of technology desired or on the particular ability of one country to establish payment for its needs than on totally affecting technology transfers from one East European country to the next.

EAST-WEST TRADE

The following profile of East-West trade emerges:

- Foreign trade in Eastern Europe and the Soviet Union is a state monopoly. First, this gives rise to the charge of "whipsawing,"[36] that is, the ability of a large buyer to play off potential sellers against one another to obtain maximum price breaks or other contractual concessions. This charge arises since it is possible to enter the market only through the Foreign Trade Enterprise (FTE) specializing in that particular product. Thus, the FTE is a monopoly buyer on behalf of an entire nation for that product. Second, as national purchasing agencies, FTEs often buy in volume, and it is alleged that the bigger the order at stake, the more tempted the Western firm is to make concessions to win the contract.

- In 1983 the East-West détente became an historical concept; its future is uncertain.

- East-West trade is dominated by the multinational corporations, particularly in certain key industrial sectors. In many respects the reason may be the barriers to entry created by the structure of the East European markets themselves.

- Today's large industrial ventures owe their existence to the "heady" days of détente.

- Transferral of technology across two quite different socio-politico-economic blocs has produced organizational difficulties quite different from those we may have come to expect at the Western interfirm level.

- Communist countries, taken together, purchase a relatively small share of the West's total high-technology exports (approximately 5 to 7 percent total).[37]

- The share of high-technology products in total Western exports to Communist countries (12.6 percent in 1976) is similar to the high-technology products share in Western exports to the world (10.9 percent in 1976).[38]

- In spite of the rapid growth of Western exports to Communist countries, the proportion of high-technology products within these exports has remained relatively constant.[39]

- The United States is the West's fourth leading exporter of high-technology products to Communist countries. In 1976 the United States accounted for 13.7 percent of all such exports, compared to its approximately 10 percent share of such exports to the world.[40]

- U.S. exports of high-technology products accounted for 9.5 percent of total U.S. exports to Communist countries in 1976, in comparison with a 17.2 percent share in U.S. exports to the world.[41] (Again it is not only the statistic that is revealing, but also the fact that this was at the peak of détente.)

- The lack of availability of hard currency reserves therefore leads to attempts to find local substitutes for Western machinery specifications in project plans and inevitably to countertrade deals;

- East European joint equity ventures are secondary to Industrial Cooperation Agreements (ICAs) which are purely contractual in nature and stipulate the duration and extent of the respective parties' responsibilities and obligations.

- The reverse flow of technology from the East to the West is not taking place to any appreciable extent. A few important licenses have been acquired from Eastern Europe and the Soviet Union, but it is small compared to West to East traffic. Soft contact lenses introduced by Bausch and Lomb were of Czechoslovakian origin, and the Soviet Union has provided important licenses relating to smelting and foundry technology in particular. Continuous casting, evaporative stove cooling, dry coke quenching, and electroslag remelting are only a few of the technologies which have been picked up by Japanese steel companies such as Nippon Steel or

Kobe and Ulvac. Others, such as 3M, Kaiser Aluminum and Chemical, Babcock and Wilcox, Deering Milliken, Bristol-Myers, and JR McDermott, have purchased patents and know-how from the Soviet Union and Eastern Europe.[42] On the other hand, Western companies that announce an exchange of licenses or framework agreements to cooperate may be engaged mainly in industrial reconnaissance—assessing the actual state of the art in the said industry and little more. See Table 5.3 for Eastern European licenses purchased by Western companies.

- There appears to be a growing debate in the United States as to the treatment of subsidized exports, including technology, from state-controlled economies, under the issue of unfair competition. While currently concentrated in the area of lower-priced manufactured goods from socialist countries such as China, the implications here could also affect relations with the Eastern Bloc.[43]

- Inability to accept the project management concept, other than to a limited degree in the Soviet Union where it is possible to cross-over FTEs, remains a major problem. It means that each individual sector of industry with its own FTE contributes only its specific share to large national projects. There is no organization to oversee, phase, or integrate the contributions from the separate FTEs. Since each FTE has a target for export and a budget for imports, essential purchasers of equipment are often delayed until a supplier is found who may be willing to accept a certain amount of payment in goods, that is, countertrade. This may add years to the length of delay in commissioning a new industrial plant. The Kamaz truck plant in the Soviet Union[44] and the MF plant at Ursus outside Warsaw, Poland,[45] are cases in point.

- Labor turnover in Eastern Europe is high. Theoretically, there is no unemployment, but even with high levels of overmanning, there is still unemployment with low productivity. Moreover, there is little in the way of worker incentive and satisfaction. The system that exists is capable of punishing but not of rewarding. Mismanagement, which is itself a loss term, is an indictable offense. The entrepreneur in Eastern Europe who does succeed in a speculative gamble will earn a bonus this year but higher production targets next year, which will cause further disenchantment among an already greatly disenchanted labor force. This situation recalls a Soviet workers' saying of the 1970s: "As long as the bosses pretend they are paying us a decent wage, we will pretend that we are working."[46]

- Training of the local workforce by Western companies engaged in ICAs or joint equity ventures has often been seen to be an open-ended commitment, first, because of worker mobility, but, second, because of promotion. Workers who have been trained in Western methods are sought after in their own country and may earn more secure promotions if they work outside of their enterprise thereafter.

- Large payments are planned as part of the five-year planning cycle, and often essential inputs are scheduled to arrive from plants yet to be developed but which have not yet done so at the time of plan preparation. The problem is great, particularly as many of these projects are "greenfield sites" requiring that housing, roads, canteens, and shops be erected first.

- Modifications within an ICA to the contracted-for-product specification may be made or suggested while tooling up is proceeding elsewhere. Contractually, there may be a requirement to supply product modifications, although there may well be a clause—as we will see later in the case of MF—that seeks to define exactly what constitutes a product modification and what instead constitutes a "new" technology. The ability to absorb product modifications varies with the transferee's actual technological capability.

Table 5.3
Licenses Recently Sold to U.S. Companies by COMECON Countries

	Technology	Buyer	Seller
Medical-biochemical	Surgical stapling guns	U.S. Surgical 3M	USSR
	Soft contact lens	National Patent Development	Czechoslovakia
	Anticancer drugs	Bristol-Myers	USSR
	Cardiovascular drug	Squibb	German Democratic Republic
	Psychotropic drug	American Home Products	USSR
	Method for producing calcium pantothenate	Diamond Shamrock	German Democratic Republic
	Cardiovascular drug	Dupont	German Democratic Republic
	"Vitride" chemical reducing agent	National Patent Development	Czechoslovakia
Energy	*In situ* coal gasification	Texas Utilities Services	USSR
	Heller-Forgo dry cooling process	Babcock & Wilcox	Hungary
	Method for making armored drilling hoses	Gates Rubber	Hungary
	OSO dewatering screen for coal	National Standard	Poland
Metallurgy	Electromagnetic casting of aluminum	Kaiser Aluminum & Chemical Reynolds Aluminum Alcoa	USSR

SOURCE: John W. Kiser III, "Tapping Eastern Bloc Technology," *Harvard Business Review* (March-April, 1982), p. 88.

Table 5.3 *(continued)*

	Technology	Buyer	Seller
	Roller dies	Harrisburg Steel	Hungary
	Electromagnetic casting of copper	Olin	USSR
	Method for titanium nitriding of tool steels	Multiarc Vacuum Systems	USSR
	Magnetic impact bonding	Maxwell Laboratories	USSR
	Flash butt welding	J. R. McDermott	USSR
	Evaporative stave cooling of blast furnaces	Andco	USSR
Miscellaneous	Rock hammer "Hefti"	Joy Manufacturing	USSR
	Pneumatic trenching tool "Hole Hog"	Allied Steel & Tractor	USSR
	Hydrocyclone "Triclean"	Bird Manufacturing	Czechoslovakia
	Spray printing of carpets	Deering Milliken	German Democratic Republic
	Inertial core crusher for extra hard rocks	Rexnord	USSR

TECHNOLOGY TRANSFERENCE

Having thus outlined briefly a few salient points relating to East-West transfer of technology, let us now consider the actual mechanics of such operations.

While this discussion concentrates on the specifics of technology transfer between the industrialized West and Eastern Europe, it is also valuable to examine a summary of technology transfer means, legal and illegal, between the West (especially the United States) and the Soviet Union as published in 1982.[47]

Legal: Complete turnkey sales (buy one factory and copy it); direct investment in Eastern Europe (siphoned off by the USSR); patents and licenses with extensive teaching effort; joint ventures and joint production development with Western firms; technical data and engineering documents; proposals, presale negotiations, and sales presentations; commercial visits; governmental and industrial equipment sales; sales of products; scientific, technical, and student exchanges; and open literature.

Illegal: Hostile intelligence service acquisitions (spies); recruited agents and industrial espionage (recruited agents, either for greed or ideological reasons); illegal arms trade; illegal trade in other commodities; third country diversions (channeled through middleman countries); captured in war; and end-user diversions (uses other than overt purposes for which product/ technology was obtained).

The other side of this analysis of technology transfer, however, is to question how the Eastern Bloc is able to purchase technology, particularly relatively high-level technology given this area's hard currency constraints and lower standard of living. One example comes from Rank Xerox, the office equipment firm that sold some $40 million worth of copiers to CMEA and Yugoslavia in 1983. Some of the techniques followed by Rank Xerox are as follows:

- Patience is needed, for negotiations may take years, and up to eighteen signatures may be needed for approval.

- Domestic production of relatively high-technology products is in its infancy; products are often desired and needed.

- Copiers are particularly difficult to sell because of the political/cultural aversion to anything that "copies" information; yet, sales were accomplished.

- The idea is to be seen and heard as much as possible, specifically, outfit an exhibition train and travel through Eastern Europe; similarly outfit mobile vans and continue traveling—a portable exhibition show; establish permanent show-rooms and service centers as feasible—often with joint venture partners; sponsor sporting events and arts contests for publicity; show at trade fairs, hold seminars, put on exhibitions; and use direct mail and advertising whenever possible.

- Manufacturing centers should be set up (the competition, including the Japanese, will do so if you do not).

- Training on site and in other countries should be provided (again, if you do not, other competitors will).

- Expertise should be acquired in "creative financing," including countertrade and other ways in which the payment for the products becomes possible.[48]

The benefits that Western firms may obtain through ICAs with Eastern European foreign trade organizations and state enterprises have been summarized by Martin Schnitzer as follows: "access to markets, political and social stability, stable labor conditions, comprehensive education, lower operating costs, and new technology."[49] However, Schnitzer notes that the two most important benefits are access to markets and lower operating costs, although technology flows are also important. These flows apply not only to the United States and Eastern Europe but also to other countries. For example, patent rights for manufacturing the Hungarian-designed compact refuse burner spread to France, Italy, and West Germany.[50]

TRANSFER SMOOTHNESS

Given the two different social, political, and economic systems of East and West, success of transfer will depend on how much the respective parties interact, and not just on the degree to which the contract allows them to. In many instances, some form of organizational change may be forced on the Western partner in order to allow a more effective integration between partners. Because of the East's organizational structure and bureaucratic rigidity, many special departments or units have been created specifically for the purpose of troubleshooting trading problems with Eastern Europe. Control Data, ICL, Massey-Ferguson (MF), and ICI all have special sections that deal with specific problems such as countertrade, that is, part payment of contract value via repurchase of goods. GKN,[51] in fact, found itself in the middle of a row after winning a £40m contract to supervise the expansion and modernization of a drop forging plant for the East German motor industry, Ludwigsfelde. The problem was that GKN had agreed to take and market East German trucks in part payment for its work, much to the chagrin of British Leyland.

One organizational problem peculiar to East-West business is that it requires the addition of a specialist unit or department. There have also been problems at several other levels which until now have only been hinted at.[52] One such problem is the state of the technology being transferred and the present level of the recipient's competence. This constitutes the essential difference between a general technology that is industry-wide and one that is system- or company-specific. When we assess Eastern Europe on these technological criteria, East Germany and Czechoslovakia are clearly the most industrialized, and Bulgaria has a special importance in the production of forklift trucks. Poland, which has invested more heavily than any other East European country, cannot be included in the East German and Czechoslovakian level. Poland, an agricultural country, has been undergoing rapid industrialization. The problem involved in technology transfer to Poland is one of insufficient infrastructure in terms of skilled employment, factory availability, and even electrical power generation to keep pace with an expanding industry.

CENTRALIZED PLANNING

When a project is earmarked for national priority status, inputs essential to its operation are more readily received. However, the problem of factory availability is endemic to the East European system, as is the lack of hard currency reserves to make purchases, either windfall or planned, from the West. In times of trouble, there is the lack of project management which may stagger the project. Furthermore, this lack may cause distortion in the priorities and individual contributions along the lines of critical path analysis to ensure the timely completion of essential parts of an important project. Although there is some coordination in the Soviet Union where it is possible to integrate purchases and countertrade obligations among several foreign trade enterprises, this is not the usual pattern and does not in any event cover project management. The evidence points to the larger Western companies having to deal with five or more East European FTEs[53] in an uncoordinated manner. As both the FTE sales target and import budget must be considered, the FTEs attempt to sell to those who are in turn supplying goods to them. The narrow specialties of the foreign trade centralized structure create an irony whereby the Western machine-tool supplier receives purchase orders for his Eastern machine-tool client and manufacturer. Inevitably, this is a major source of discontent, delay, and sheer waste of resources. Business international S.A. reported the chronological sequence of an order for shoemaking equipment which involved the countertrade acceptance of shoes made on existing East European production lines as part payment for the new machinery.[54] The following stages were involved:

1. The importing FTE applied to its industrial ministry for approval to import the shoemaking equipment. Since the machinery under contract met the established technical standards, the application was forwarded to the Ministry of Foreign Trade.

2. The Ministry of Foreign Trade checked the financing, and verified the availability of shoes for export and the willingness of the shoe-exporting FTE to link its sale with the import of shoe manufacturing equipment through another FTE. The Ministry of Light Industry obtained a pledge from the shoe manufacturer that the needed shoes would be supplied under a countertrade contract.

3. The Ministry of Foreign Trade asked the Foreign Trade Bank to tie the import and export transactions.

4. With the Foreign Trade Bank's hard currency license in hand, the Ministry of Foreign Trade advised the Ministry of Light Industry that the shoe export would be accounted to the leather industry investment quota.

5. The Ministry of Light Industry passed its approval to the exporting FTE, which in time confirmed the countertrade delivery.

6. The MFT issued the import license for the shoemaking equipment and the export license for the shoes.

As Business International points out, what may have been expected to take perhaps one or two weeks for each stage of the procedure—and thus a total of nine to ten weeks—took in excess of six months. Thus, even when permission is forthcoming, one must still allow for delays. According to Dr. Stanley J. Paliwoda, the two items that must therefore be engineered into any price quotation are the countertrade element and the procrastination factor. First, it is important to beware of increasing countertrade demands in excess of the conventional maximum of 30 percent of contract value. In some cases, the punitive penalties for nonacceptance of countertrade are now being implemented. This does not allow for absorption into the contract price. Second, the procrastination factor is inherent in any large project but more so in the East European Bloc where permission to export must first be granted from one's national government. Since the imposition of martial law in Poland, the United States has become more involved in East-West trade with blanket laws on technology sales. The whole area of East-West trade remains sensitive.

Credit is not a problem, however, as money will be found for essential projects. Repayment has not been a major problem to date, although Poland and Hungary's financial position remains precarious. A moratorium may often be imposed for a few months, which further increases the operating costs of companies that do business in Eastern Europe, thereby imposing yet another barrier to entry for small to medium-sized Western firms. Yet, even when a project has not been successful because of delays in its implementation in Eastern Europe, the chances are that it may continue to remain profitable for the Western partner, as long as it continues to be paid for the period in excess of its contractual commitment. The danger is that Western markets and trends could be seriously affected by the mass production and sale of inferior articles made by semiskilled or badly trained operatives using technologically inferior machines, which were bought in Eastern Europe to conserve hard currency plant expenditure. In fact, this danger remains theoretical, but the possibility has aroused enough fear to ensure the institution of control procedures to prevent such a situation from ever arising.

APPROPRIATENESS OF TECHNOLOGY

The key element here is that the size and the planning horizon for many of these very large projects are determined by the East Europeans themselves. They work out their own national priorities in a five-year plan that is integrated within a five-year plan for the CMEA region which allocates productive specialization to its member states. Likewise, the appropriateness of the technology is not always open to discussion. Many of the problems that surround the delays over the Massey-Ferguson (MF) tractor plant in Warsaw (hailed to be the largest in the world upon completion) stem from the fact that its size, timing, and transferral of manufacture of model prototypes were determined by the Poles themselves, not by MF. In such a situation, the company is forced to provide what is asked or else allow a competitor to do so. If the competitor does so, there may be subsequent ramifications for certain regional markets closer to that area of production. Longer-term effects may be important enough to influence rather hasty short-term decisions. With regard to MF[55] again, the initial agreement called for thirty-eight versions of the tractor in 3-, 4-, and 6-cylinder engine sizes. However, as separate FTEs were involved and purchasing for this massive project was not coordinated, many licenses were bought that may never be used. One such purchase was that from the MF subsidiary, Perkins Engines Limited, of a license for 6-cylinder engine production in the south of Poland. Waste and delays, both of which cost money, are endemic to the central planning system.

The question of leverage,[56] that is, control which the transferor of technology possesses over the recipient, has been shown to vary enormously. In the case of General Tire in Romania, leverage was found to be close to zero as there was little actual interest in trading. In Poland where there has been interest in utilizing Western licenses and producing Western-branded equipment, this "leverage" does not have to be used; it is usually accepted and implicit in the running of these operations. This is because they are seeking to engage in export-intensive industries that have relatively higher value added, and thus require quality control and inspection procedures. Yet at the same time, the concept of value added is also built into the licensing and the ICAs which ensure a return for the Western transferor. International Harvester, for example, continues to supply engines to Poland. As the volume of production increases and the license fees are paid, this continued trade assures an increasingly important source of extra sales.

In areas like Poland where agriculture remains in peasant hands and farming is undertaken chiefly by horses, it is difficult to understand why a tractor plant would be commissioned to produce a range of the very latest models. Some people argue that horses are particularly important in the south of Poland where flooding takes place regularly and where four-wheel-drive tractors would not perform as efficiently.[57] The integration and degree of fit of the manufactured product into the domestic East European economy poses yet another research question which is outside the scope of this work.

In the case of Poland, the leading purchaser of technology in the 1970s, the decision as to the appropriateness of the areas of technology and their level of sophistication was made by the then premier, Edward Gierek. As a former miner in France, Gierek had identified wealth with heavy engineering, and so under his regime in Poland many investments were channeled into steel, coal, shipbuilding, crane-building, tractors, and the like, all of which are mature industries that have suffered during the present recession.

Since the level of appropriateness was being decided elsewhere, all the

Western companies could do in the competitive supply situation that ensued was to facilitate the transferral of technology. For the MF tractor plant in 1974, this meant creating a special project team that had a massive support staff of over 140 people but that was designed to integrate the Polish operation into MF's structure, so that all future documentation for the tractor models to be transferred would automatically be sent to the Polish partner. In 1983 MF had perhaps only six staff members who handled problems arising from the Polish project; all other information needs were met routinely by other parts of the organization.

HOW TECHNOLOGY TRANSFER HAS BEEN RECEIVED

Ideologically, the East Europeans make heavy use of words such as cooperation and partnership, even when only simple exporting transactions are involved. However, there may be a desire to be allied to established Western manufacturers and to share in their production, particularly as the production function in Eastern Europe is physically separate from research. In that region, it is therefore harder to innovate and to persuade local production that new models should be engineered and produced. Certainly, the Ursus Tractor Factory had produced its own new range of tractor prototypes but was overruled in favor of MF models as cooperation with MF would confer access to new tractor designs and technology: branding and trademarks of products bought back by MF. International marketing is an area in which the East Europeans are particularly weak. Here, MF was handling the export distribution for Western markets so that Ursus could export to the West only via MF. Ursus remained free to handle its own distribution for other markets, although its products were not to include the MF logo, livery, or other trademarks. Eastern Europe's weakness in marketing relates back to Marx and the labor theory of value whereby any expenditure on services is construed as constituting an overhead. Yet, as international society progresses from manufacturing to services, it becomes harder to justify an economic law that relates only to the value of labor without redefining it for modern conditions. Keynes himself warned of the dangers of being "a slave to a defunct economist."[58]

In the case of the cooperation between Fiat and Pol-Mot of Poland, we have an example of an ICA that enabled the transferee not only to digest the technology sent across but also to make a "quantum leap." Armed with the technology acquired from Fiat, Pol-Mot's production enterprise, FSO (which has replaced the previous trademark Polski-Fiat, which is believed to have been embarrassing to Fiat), has produced a car with its own resources, named the Polonez. This marks a departure from the manufacturing under license syndrome. It is believed that Fiat did not wish to involve itself in this new model, and so the Poles undertook this work on their own. What has emerged is a car which, although quite stylish in appearance, is mechanically geriatric by Western standards.[59] While an interesting departure, it is not likely to be repeated.

Coles Cranes Limited is another British manufacturer with long-established industrial cooperation with Bumar of Poland. Yet its expectation of being able to formally ratify an agreement for the joint research and development of a new hydraulic crane came to nought, despite intense activity and negotiations over a period of years. Coles subsequently developed a model of its own. What this case shows is the professional competence Bumar gained as a result of working closely over the years with a Western firm.

BARRIERS TO TECHNOLOGY ABSORPTION

There are two categories of barriers: real and imagined. Both sides must be willing to make the cooperation work. The real and imagined barriers include:

- Possible embargo on CoCom approval.
- Lack of hard currency for all purchasers, except those purchasers with national priority status.
- Poor infrastructure.
- Poor management in the Eastern Bloc.
- High costs of technology transfer as a result of the factors above. David J. Teece states that substantial resources must be utilized, not only to transmit technical information, but also to ensure its successful absorption.[60] Their costs will vary considerably according to the number of previous applications of the innovations and how well the parties understand the parties involved. Accordingly, Teece believes that it is entirely inappropriate to regard technology as something that once acquired by one firm can be made available to others at zero social cost. Substantial fees may have to be charged to reflect the resource cost of transmitting technical information. Furthermore, since substantial investment is required to effectively utilize an innovation, the governments involved might want to protect the transferee's investment in technology transfer as well as the transferor's investment in R&D. In order that imitation may proceed at a socially desirable rate, a degree of patent protection to licensors and licensees might be called for under some circumstances, assuming that the transferor is not a perfect price discriminator and that the technology fees reflect the cost of transmitting the technology.
- Irregular supplies of components and part-assemblies from within the local East European economy.
- Transportation difficulties occasioning delays.
- Lack of an overall license strategy. Kiser cites a Soviet official as stating that ministries have no systematic approach to patent protection for Soviet products

and inventions.[61] Of seventy research and design institutes in the Ministry of Instrument Making, only nine even recommended taking out foreign patents; in the Ministry of Automobile Production, only 7 of 200 research and design organizations recommended such action.

- Producing for export without having a current domestic supply, therefore not having product and/or process experience.
- The state monopoly of foreign trade, its monopsonistic FTE buyers, and the fragmentation of responsibility among FTEs with no coordination taking place for large projects.

CONDITIONS NECESSARY FOR A SMOOTH TRANSFER

As noted earlier, the incidence of joint equity ventures in relation to ICAs is small. ICAs owe their strength to the fact that the contract determines the duration and respective duties of either party, just as it determines the price net of all local taxes. Local taxation or compulsory disbursement taxes[62] create a particular headache for the efficient and profitable operation of joint equity ventures, for new taxes are often created to deal with the establishment of a new joint equity venture. Without prior notification, such taxes can materially affect the profitability of such ventures as can productivity both through high labor turnover rate or low motivation.

For ICAs the key to success lies in the contract. The greater the project size, the more the important points have to be clearly defined. An examination of the Massey-Ferguson ICA bears this out. MF concluded its agreement with the Polish FTE for agricultural machinery, Agromet-Motoimports, in 1974 after four years of negotiations. The original agreement, which was for a fifteen-year period, in effect comprised four agreements:

1. A general agreement outlining the objectives of the two partners and the method of arbitration.
2. A license agreement stipulating the rights of both parties, the specific manufacturing rights, and the extent of production line improvements to be conveyed. The licensing rights which MF confirmed are for use in Poland only. There is also a clause which broaches the thorny problem of when a new tractor also constitutes a new technology. It has been agreed that the modifications that have been made will be passed on to the Polish side, but when a new technology is involved, not subject to the present agreement, then it can be transferred under a separate agreement. The clause defines a new technology as a new technological concept such as a hydraulic motor.
3. An ICA covering economic and commercial relations, the method of paying expenses on both sides, the level of buyback, and the pricing structure for goods bought by either side. The price basis is MF world prices, and either side offers discounts, but the Polish discount is larger than the British discount to Poland

because of the marketing and distribution costs MF will incur with the Polish products.

4. A project implementation contract covering planning and schedule timetabling. MF is responsible for designing the new plant and supplying the technology: the Poles are completely responsible for implementing the contract. The contract involves the manufacture in Poland of eight basic MF tractor models.[63]

The Poles wanted a "complete" tractor, a license that was "without holes," that is, all the inputs which MF used in their manufacture had to be included in this transfer of technology. However, since MF bought out more than half the components used in its manufacturing plant at Banner Lane, Coventry, this request was received coolly and almost led to a break between the two parties. Finally, a compromise was reached on the two greatest points of contention:

1. The two parties agreed on a list of goods which Massey-Ferguson could not be expected to provide, for example, rubber tires. It was understood that if the Poles lacked any item on this list, then they would have to acquire that technology on their own, as it was not part of the contract. However, in separate negotiations with potential suppliers, the Poles, eager to minimize the hard currency cost of these purchases, sought countertrade deals from its suppliers, which proved to be a contributory factor in the three-year delay[64] in the Poles' production schedule.

2. A further list of exclusions consisted of all items presently made in Poland and, therefore, Poland probably already had the necessary manufacturing capability for them. The Poles themselves would have to meet the problems of adapting these products to production requirements.

Access to facilities and information transfer are crucial components in any technology sale. In terms of Eastern Bloc license sales to the West, Kiser reports that Energy Sciences experienced no restrictions of its ability to inspect the particle-beam accelerator used at the Institute for Nuclear Physics in Novosibirsk.[65] Not only did executives from Southwire Company visit the facility in the Caucasus (which makes aluminum from nonbauxitic aluminate), but also the Soviets reportedly told them of an improved second-generation process technology that had not yet been introduced.

POSTSCRIPT: EAST-WEST COOPERATION IN THIRD COUNTRIES

There are no estimates of how many companies are actually engaged in third market activities, perhaps because of company confidentiality or because few bilateral ICAs that allow third market activity have been effective. Third market cooperatives describe the joint or complementary activities of Eastern and Western enterprises in countries other than those in which the parties are domiciled. The United Nations Economic Commission for Europe (UNECE) views the third market cooperative as being a logical development and defines it as encompassing the following characteristics:

- Joint selling and after-sales services of products in third markets which may or may not have been manufactured by the parties under coproduction, licensing, or subcontractual arrangements.
- Joint tendering and/or project implementation in the turnkey plant and civil engineering factors in third countries.
- Joint ventures for manufacturing, marketing, or services, which may be domiciled in a partner's country but which serve third markets as well.
- The marketing of a cooperation partner's products or services in a third country without the direct participation of the partner's enterprises that supply the products. This type of marketing may encompass the provision of after-sales service and spare parts in addition to sales promotion and physical distribution.[66]

Tripartite cooperation is yet another special form whereby a partner from a developing country is actively involved in the design and implementation of the project.

Third country cooperation has not necessarily evolved from bilateral ICAs, for many partners have been drawn specifically to this form of relationship without prior cooperation experience. The particular advantages are seen from the fact that world markets are shrinking; hence, one must even reconsider not only markets that have been overlooked in the past but also new forms of trading relationship. First, there is the question of market access afforded by the Eastern partner perhaps also with the furnishing of soft credits. Second, the product offering is Western, usually bearing an identifiable Western brand name, but Eastern in terms of labor and content.

Single entity trading such as that of the Manchester-based Polibur Limited, a subsidiary of Burmah Oil and of Polimex-Cekop of Poland, enables the trading organization responsible for the sale of turnkey plants in the petrochemicals sector to wear two quite different hats, changing nationality almost upon the appearance of a prospective client. Third market cooperation allows for profit-sharing and for disposing of countertrade obligations. Another British company, Cementation Limited, which is responsible for the construction of hotels in Gdynia, Poland, accepted a countertrade that consisted of Polish labor to a given value. This value base would be used on foreign construction sites, but for the Poles there was the advantage not only of getting their hotels cheaper but also of ensuring that their workforce was being trained in construction methods by a Western company.[67]

While third market activity can be found in nearly all industrial sectors, UNECE has named the three sectors that are showing the fastest growth: vehicles, including passenger cars and commercial vehicles; plant engineering and contracting; and services for industrial capital equipment producers and operations.

SUMMARY AND CONCLUSIONS

East-West trade is a very small part of total foreign trade, with Hungary being a possible exception. This is only one part of the picture, however. Trade statistics do not reflect the fact that Western-imported machinery may have higher productivity than that of its Comecon counterparts. D. W. Green and H. S. Levine, therefore, undertook a study, calculating the stock of imported and domestic machinery separately and the contribution of these separate components to the growth of Soviet industry.[68]

In their initial study, the authors concluded that Western machinery is approximately fifteen times more productive at the margin than indigenous machinery. Moreover the growth of industrial production from 1968 to 1973 would have been only 28.4 percent without those additional imports of Western machinery (instead of the actual 33.4 percent). In other words, approximately 15 percent of the growth rate would have been foregone. These calculations were subsequently revised, but still showed that Western machinery installed in Soviet industry was about eight times more productive at the margin, which implies that about 2.5 percent of the 1968-73 industrial output growth rate would have to be subtracted.[69] Admittedly, these studies rest on a number of debatable assumptions, but they do establish beyond doubt that the transfer of technology is much more important to the Soviet economy than a superficial examination of trade statistics would suggest.

The diverging paths of economic conveyance and political divergence have been traditional features of East-West trade. Sobeslavsky and Beazley offer a more optimistic view: "The agreement to disagree has been one of the fundamental principles of political and commercial practices in the West and it seems that it has not been applied in the area of East-West relations, thus enabling both sides to engage in what has aptly been described as 'transideological cooperation.' "[70]

Nevertheless, Sobeslavsky and Beazley also express certain doubts:

The perpetuated state of ideological and political divergence cannot but militate against the current Western policy of letting the companies involved in East-West transfer of technology supply the socialist countries with the high technology they themselves are not able to develop. Undoubtedly powerful arguments against this technology transfer may be considered on economic, political and moral grounds Indeed it seems incongruous of the western countries that they would help support political and economic systems which in virtually all conceivable respects are alien and inimical to their own, and it is irrational that such a policy is accompanied by enormous defense expenditures whose main purpose is to shield the West from the military threat of Warsaw Pact countries.[71]

Even so, the arguments for trade will continue to weigh more heavily since trade offers mutual benefit and, even at the lowest level, provides a channel of communication.

NOTES

1. *Conjoncture* 9 (October 1982): 130.

2. C. Wolcott Parker, "View of Things to Come in Technology," *Les Nouvelles* 17, No. 1 (March 1982): 27.

3. John R. Pegan, "Basic Business in a Changing World," *Les Nouvelles* 17, No. 1 (March 1982): 51.

4. "East European Economies: Looking Up," *The Economist*, December 17, 1983, p. 41.

5. Jim Drinkhall, "Security Loophole, East Bloc Businessmen Freely Come and Go in U.S. Defense Areas," *Wall Street Journal*, January 23, 1984, p. 1.

6. Stuart Auerbach, "Control on High-Tech Export Criticized," *Washington Post*, January 22, 1984, p. G4.

7. "Why Paris Is Peddling Its Nuclear Wares in Moscow," *Business Week*, December 26, 1983, p. 39.

8. Gerald F. Seib and Eduardo Lachica, "U.S. Argues for Curb on Western Exports of Personal Computers to the Soviet Bloc," *Wall Street Journal*, January 31, 1982, p. 38.

9. Christine Tierney, "Senate to Begin Grappling with Thorney Issue of Export Controls," *Barron's*, February 6, 1984, p. 30.

10. Peggy Mevs, "Export Controls," in Gary Clyde Hufbauer, ed., *U.S. International Economic Policy 1981* (Washington, D.C.: International Law Institute, 1982), pp. 8-11.

11. Joseph S. Nye, Jr., "Technology Transfer Policies," *Issues in East-West Commercial Relations*, A compendium of papers submitted to the Joint Economic Committee, U.S. Congress, January 12, 1979, p. 16.

12. Hedija Kravalis, Allen J. Lenz, Helen Raffel, and John Young, "Quantification of Western Exports of High Technology Products to Communist Countries," in *Issues in East-West Commercial Relations*, ibid., p. 35. See also *Technology and East-West Trade*, Office of Technology Assessment, U.S. Congress (Allenheld, Osmun/Gower, 1981).

13. *Conjoncture*, p. 133.

14. Ibid., p. 137.

15. "Wedded to Politics," *The Economist*, January 7, 1984, p. 65.

16. Lisa Miller Mesdag, "Soviet-Bound Computer," *Fortune*, December 26, 1983, p. 165.

17. Stuart Auerbach, "Tougher Rules on High-Tech Exports Asked," *Washington Post*, January 19, 1984, p. B1.

18. William A. Root, "Trade Policy: The U.S. Needs to Listen to Its Allies," *Business Week*, November 21, 1983, p. 22.

19. "UK Exporters Lose Cover on Sanctions," *Financial Times*, April 21, 1983, p. 7.

20. Catherine Jacobson, "The Technology Transfer Issue," *Business America*, May 31, 1982, pp. 2-4.

21. Caryle Murphy and Alison Muscatine, "U.S. Fights Escalating Battle to Control Technology Brain," *Washington Post*, June 19, 1983, p. A12.

22. Dan Morgan, "U.S. Outlines New Visa Policy to Safeguard Industrial Data," *Washington Post*, May 6, 1983, p. A9.

23. John W. Kiser III, "Tapping Eastern Bloc Technology," *Harvard Business Review* (March-April 1982): 85.

24. Ibid., p. 88.

25. Jerzy Cieslik, *Transnational Corporations in East-West Trade: The Case of Poland* (Warsaw: Central School of Planning and Statistics, Research Group on Transnational Corporations, 1982), p. 16.

26. Amity Shlaes, "Hungary Moves to Liberalize Economy," *Wall Street Journal*, December 28, 1983, p. 16.

27. Robert D. Hisrich, Michael P. Peters, and Arnold K. Weinstein, "East-West Trade: The View from the United States," *Journal of International Business Studies* (Winter 1981): 119.

28. This is a paraphrase of the often quoted remark made by the late premier, Nikita Khrushchev: "We will bury you."

29. Linda S. Droker, "U.S.-Romanian Trade Trends, January-December 1980," *East-West Trade Policy Staff Papers*, U.S. Department of Commerce, International Trade Administration, April 1981, p. 16.

30. "Business Bulletin," *Wall Street Journal*, March 3, 1983, p. 1.

31. Gary Teske, "U.S.-Polish Trade Trends, January-December 1980," *Ditto re Romania*, May 1981.

32. "Business Brief—East-West Traders Raise the Curtain," *The Economist*, January 7, 1984, pp. 64-65.

33. Lawrence R. Kessler, "U.S.-Czechoslovak Trade Trends, January-December 1980," *Ditto re Romania*, April 1981.

34. Deborah A. Lamb and Thomas Moore, "U.S.-Bulgarian Trade Trends, January-December 1980," *Ditto re Romania*, April 1981.

35. William Drozdiak, "Germans on Both Sides Mend East-West Fences," *Washington Post*, January 8, 1984, p. A15.

36. *U.S.-U.S.S.R. Trade and the Whipsaw Controversy*, Excerpts from meeting March 30, 1977, Advisory Committee on East-West Trade, U.S. Department of Commerce, Bureau of East-West Trade, August 1977.

37. Kravalis, et al., "Quantification," p. 43.

38. Ibid.

39. Ibid.

40. Ibid.

41. Ibid.

42. Kiser, "Tapping Eastern Bloc Technology." p. 85.

43. Art Pine, "Debate Begins on How U.S. Should Treat Export Subsidies of Non-Market States," *Wall Street Journal*, November 3, 1983. p. 34.

44. George D. Holliday, "The Role of Western Technology in the Soviet Economy," *Issues in East-West Commercial Relations*, p. 82.

45. S. J. Paliwoda, *Joint East-West Marketing and Production Ventures* (Hampshire, England: Gower, 1981).

46. Hedrick Smith, *The Russians* (London: Sphere Books, reprinted 1981), p. 265.

47. Jack Anderson, "How to Acquire U.S. Technology by 19 Methods," *Washington Post*, September 20, 1982, p. C15.

48. "Communist Paper-Chase," *The Economist*, December 17, 1983, p. 68.

49. Martin Schnitzer, *U.S. Business Involvement in Eastern Europe: Case Studies of Hungary, Poland, and Romania* (New York: Praeger, 1980), p. 29.

50. Ibid., p. 32.

51. Simon Jones, "How to Win Countertrading," *Marketing*, July 9, 1980. See also S. J. Paliwoda, "East-West Countertrade Arrangements. Barter, Compensation, Buyback and Counterpurchase or 'Parallel' Trade," University of Manchester Institute of Science and Technology (UMIST) Discussion Paper 8105, March 1981.

52. A more detailed analysis of the general and company-specific factors leading to success or failure are reviewed in Stanley J. Paliwoda and Marilyn L. Liebrenz, "Expectations and Results of Contractual Joint Ventures by U.S. and U.K. MNC's in Eastern Europe," *European Journal of Marketing* 18, No. 1 (1984): 25-33.

53. Jerzy Cieslik and Boguslaw Sosnowski, "Transnational Corporations in East-West Trade, The Case of Poland," Central School of Planning and Statistics, Warsaw, Research Group on Transnational Corporations, Working Paper No. 1, 1982. See also Jerzy Cieslik, "Western Firms Participating in the East-West Industrial Cooperation: The Case of Poland," *Management International Review* 23, No. 1 (1982): 69-75.

54. Business International SA., *Business Eastern Europe*, March 11, 1983.

55. Paliwoda, *Joint East-West Marketing* (Hampshire, England: Gower, 1981).

56. Marilyn L. Liebrenz, *Transfer of Technology: U.S. Multinationals and Eastern Europe* (New York: Praeger, 1982), p. 318.

57. Discussions with Dr. Maria Konieczna, Academy of Agriculture, Wroclaw, Poland.

58. John Maynard Keynes who ironically was born the year Karl Marx died.

59. *Financial Times*, April 23, 1983.

60. David J. Teece, *The Multinational Corporation and the Research Cost of International Technology Transfer* (Cambridge, Mass.: Ballinger, 1976), p. 100.

61. Kiser, "Tapping Eastern Bloc Techology," p. 89.

62. A term coined by Iancu Spigler, *Direct Western Investment in East Europe* (Oxford: Holden Books, 1975). See also Paul Jones, *Taxation of Multinationals in Communist Countries* (New York: Praeger, 1978).

63. Paliwoda, *Joint East-West Marketing*, p. 161.

64. This delay has been extended considerably, as in 1983 (agreement signed in 1974 for production to commence June 1978) there were no complete production lines anywhere in the new plant. It is now scheduled for 1986-87, but this is dependent on GKN being allowed to complete a large new foundry at Lublin to supply castings for the new plant.

65. Kiser, "Tapping Eastern Bloc Technology," p. 90.

66. "Recent Developments in Industrial Cooperation—Cooperation in Third Markets," *Economic Bulletin for Europe* 33, No. 1 (March 1981): 135-155.

67. Paliwoda, *Joint East-West Marketing*, p. 88.

68. D. W. Green and H. S. Levine, "Implications of Technology for the USSR," in *East-West Technological Cooperation*, NATO Colloquium, 1976, Brussels, p. 43, reported in V. Sobeslavsky and P. Beazley, *The Transfer of Technology to Socialist Countries* (Hampshire, England: Gower, 1980), p. 106.

69. Ibid., p. 108.

70. Ibid., p. 115.

71. Ibid.

6
Technology Transfer Within Eastern Europe

STANLEY J. PALIWODA AND
MARILYN L. LIEBRENZ

The Soviet Union and its satellites in Eastern Europe still adhere to the cult of Lenin. The significance of this fact is that since they went neither the way of the Americans in their revolution nor the way of the Chinese with a "Cultural Revolution," the Soviet bloc still owes its legitimacy to the thoughts and writings of its leaders at the turn of the century. Although qualifications are possible and attempts are made to show how modern technological adaptation coincided with the ideas of Lenin,[1] quantum leaps have to pass the ideology test and prove that they are within the mainstream of communism.

RELATIVE INDUSTRIAL STRENGTHS WITHIN EASTERN EUROPE

Czechoslovakia and the German Democratic Republic (GDR) are the most highly industrialized countries in Eastern Europe and the most dependent on energy imports from the USSR. Bulgaria has a particular strength in both hoists and forklift trucks. Both Hungary and Bulgaria have demonstrated a proficiency to be agriculturally self-sufficient. Hungary's "economically adventurous" moves in 1983 and 1984 represent one approach to improving its own economic position—stressing both its industrial expertise and its agricultural abilities. However, apart from the technology and techniques that other countries in the Eastern Bloc desire to make their own industrial enterprises more productive, the Hungarian reforms appear to be focused on trade with other portions of the world, not its Comecon allies. Others such as Poland are still industrializing. Eastern Europe is more dependent on the Soviet Union than vice versa. Philip Hanson reports that exports to the USSR are of the order of 6 percent of total West European output, and imports from the USSR account for 7 percent of total domestic expenditure in Eastern Europe.[2] Fuel and raw materials constitute about half of Soviet exports to Eastern Europe, while machinery accounts for half of the Eastern European trade with the Soviet Union. There is evidence, however, that the Soviet Union has not fully profited from trade with Eastern Europe and that it has achieved more in the way of political integration than financial success by not raising its oil prices, for example, directly in line with prevailing world market "spot" prices.

TECHNOLOGY TRANSFER: OFFICIAL PLAN COORDINATION TECHNIQUE

The Council for Mutual Economic Assistance (CMEA or Comecon) is the vehicle for economic progress and cooperation within the Eastern bloc. The Warsaw Pact is the term used for military defense of the bloc.

The CMEA was established in 1949 to expand trade and credit relations among member states of the block and to try to specialize in production and circumvent the strategic embargoes imposed by the NATO alliance.[3] In July 1971 the Comprehensive Program for Socialist Economic Integration was adopted to try to resolve macroeconomic problems in several areas such as agriculture, transport, foreign trade, and currency relations. The program covered fifteen to twenty years and built on previous cooperation.

The CMEA program proposals were built into the individual plans for each member state with the hope of achieving economic convergence within the bloc and a sizable increase in economic and industrial developments within the member states.

The First Coordinated Plan for Multilateral Integration Measures, 1976-80, was designed to take this goal further. It spelled out concrete obligations for each member country with regard to the joint construction of several large economic projects in fuel, energy, and raw materials to the value of some 9 billion rubles,[4] together with proposals for production, scientific, and technical collaboration. The Soyuz gas pipeline came under this plan, with other plants for the production of pulp, ferriferous raw materials, and others. There are proposals for five long-term programs within the next ten to fifteen years to meet the growing needs for energy, fuel, basic raw materials, food and consumer goods, to raise the standard of mechanical engineering, and to develop transport. A number of bilateral agreements on specialization and cooperation in production have been signed to 1990.

The Second Coordinated Plan covers the period 1981-85. It has five sections and deals with the joint construction or projects in building, by joint efforts of industrial installations at the expense of the interested countries (5 measures); specialized and joint production on a multilateral basis (13 measures); scientific and technical cooperation projects (13);

multilateral integration measures (10) intended to accelerate the economic progress of Vietnam, Cuba, and Mongolia; and uniform standards and specifications (24 measures).[5]

Commitments under the first section exceed 2,500m rubles and include. continued construction of the 4m KW Khmelnitskaya atomic power station in which Hungary, Poland, and Czechoslovakia share half the expenses for half the output; continued construction of the 750 KV power line as a second link between European USSR and Eastern Europe; research, design, and development on 1,000 MW power units with water-moderated reactors; mutual deliveries of equipment for atomic power stations; and an agreement with the GDR, Cuba, Poland, and Czechoslovakia to invest 43 percent in the USSR's Mozyr factory for production of nutrient yeast from highly purified petroleum paraffins. In compensation beginning in 1984-85 these countries will be getting a protein product of high food value essential for livestock breeding.

The second section of the Second Coordinated Plan provides for the exchange of 20,000 million rubles' worth of specialized products within this five-year period. Energy development is dependent on the agreement on multilateral international specialization and cooperation in manufacturing atomic power plants for 1981-90. Cooperation is provided for the production of components for Lada cars. Four hundred million rubles' worth of cars will be supplied. The USSR supplies its partners with ammonia, methanol, high and low pressure polyethylene, nitrogen and potash fertilizers. The CMEA supplies the USSR chemical pesticides, varnishes and paints, bleaches, and chemically pure substances. The CMEA countries also divide their efforts among the manufacture and mutual deliveries of equipment for open-cast mining and for enrichment of solid fuels, ferrous and nonferrous metal ores, chemical raw materials, and the making of mining machinery. Poland, the USSR, and the GDR are the biggest exporters of mining equipment.

The East European countries and Cuba have agreed on specialization in the manufacture of 150 hp (and more powerful) tractors, a set of farm machines for these, and livestock breeding equipment. The volume of their mutual deliveries will top 5 million rubles in five years. Hungary, the GDR, the USSR, and Czechoslovakia are the biggest exporters of these items.[6]

The CMEA countries are carrying on their cooperation in developing and building integrated container transport system facilities. The system improves cargo transportation, especially foreign trade cargoes.

The third section of the Second Coordinated Plan covers problems connected with power, fuel, raw materials, livestock breeding, mechanical engineering, and electronics. The interested CMEA countries will continue their cooperation in developing a 500 MW MHD generator, which is to be built and put into commercial operation in the USSR. Yet another joint effort, but a more peripheral one, deals with new methods of converting solar, wind, and geothermal energy into electricity and heat. The partners are said to be building silicon-based solar cells, a 10 KW generating unit of a photoelectric solar station, and sixteen 30 KW wind-operated power plants.

The development of the economy of each of the member states is reflected in each state's Five-year plan which incorporates the spirit at least of CMEA specialization. The Soviet Union for the period to 1985 plans a large increase in agricultural output and in freight carried by rail, but a decrease in capital investments and state and cooperative retail trade. Productivity has escaped the system. As N. A. Tikhonov explains:

One of the key tasks of the Eleventh Five Year Plan is the fuller and more effective use of fixed production assets. They are growing rapidly but the proper returns on them in many cases elude us. The plant in use often operates at less than full capacity. . . . The fixed assets on many collective and state farms are not being used rationally enough. Owing to poor maintenance and storage, machinery at times quickly becomes unusable and is written off before its rated service life has expired. . . . The rate of return on investment and other economic indicators are adversely affected by delays in putting new production plants into operation. . . . We have to make an appreciable headway in increasing capital investment productivity.[7]

INHIBITORS TO TRADE WITH THE EASTERN BLOC

The near proximity of the East European countries to each other, combined with the lack of many trading barriers, would indicate a strong propensity for trade among the countries of the Eastern Bloc. However, the combined lack of hard currency has, instead, prompted these countries to seek other markets. They especially concentrated on those of the industrialized West or developing countries with surplus cash flows. Such trading or even manufacturing collaboration might be highly beneficial to all parties concerned in terms of the products developed or produced.[8] This search for trading media has been detrimental to the interregional trade flows among the East European countries more than between these countries and the Soviet Union.

While the USSR may rank second in the world in total output and first in the manufacture of tractors, harvesters, diesel and electric locomotives, and metal-cutting lathes, its productivity is desperately low. Specialization of production may enable concentration to take place in specific areas, but lethargy and stupor are endemic to the Soviet system. Initiative is not recognized as an ideologically healthy concept; therefore, it is safer to satisfice than to maximize, especially when the rewards for doing so will only be a small bonus and higher output targets the next year. But the pain of failure is accompanied by the criminal charge of mismanagement. Inertia is the status quo

Until 1983, four alternative economic models were available to the Andropov regime: conservative, reactionary, radical, and liberal.[9] Conservatism means virtual retention of the status quo with minor modifications. Reactionary involves political modernization, restoring order and discipline via the secret police, perhaps ending the virtual lifetime tenure of the party and management elite, and freeing the "hidden reserves" characterized by a large degree of underemployment. The radical model must entail the decentralization of planning and management, retaining central planning without assignment of directive targets to enterprises. The Soviet leadership would have very little interest in supporting self-management or other forms of worker control. If the radical model succeeded in generating vigorous entrepreneurship, large incomes would be earned in eliminating disequilibria in the centrally planned economy. A liberal model would conserve the traditional planning methods for most of the economy while liberating present restrictions on private enterprise—the withdrawal of the socialized central planning sector to the "commanding heights" of the economy. There would be a private-public sector interchange; decisions would be made on pricing, but the private sector could fill a gap in retailing. Over time, however, inertia creates its own strategy, its own vested interests for retaining the system as it is, and thus resistance to change. The evidence that emerges is that Soviet premier Andropov spent a great deal of his energies in an inner-cabinet struggle for power with the faction that supported Chernenko. The ability to change the system and decide how it should be changed are still two key questions which are unlikely to receive immediate attention, despite the pressures of a creaking Soviet system.

In recent years Soviet exports going to Comecon have fallen and even a more dramatic fall in Comecon's exports to the Soviet Union has been experienced.[10] The Soviets are warning that they cannot guarantee unlimited supplies of fuel and raw materials to the Comecon area and that Comecon member countries should join forces to conserve precious resources and avoid duplication of effort. Soviet pressure, therefore, exists to increase investments in coal, nuclear power, and other alternatives by 150 percent in the next decade.[11]

In some instances, the Soviet Union had been providing a form of trade subsidization to its satellites. It provided oil at less than the world market price on an import basis. It also paid more than the world price for some of the products exported from those same satellites, or it provided exports to some countries, even when repayment was not always certain.[12] These subsidies to Eastern Europe were estimated to have totaled $21 billion in 1980 and were presumably increased as a result of Poland's unrest.[13] Again, apart from the political and commercial ties which the subsidies have created between the USSR and other Eastern Block countries, they have also promoted increased trading activity among themselves.

The Soviet oil-pricing measures, based on a five-year rolling average of world prices, also have less ability to adapt to unusual situations, including the recent worldwide oil price drop. As a result, in recent years the cost of

Soviet oil to its allies has become higher than it would be on the open market. It also appears that, as of late 1983-early 1984, the USSR was encouraging the CMEA nations to develop their own energy sources, including coal, nuclear power, and other alternatives, so that Soviet oil might be exported to countries outside CMEA at higher export rates.

Part of this weaning strategy appeared to include not only increasing the price of Soviet oil sold to Eastern Europe, but also of reducing oil shipments in general—hence, the directives to increase their own energy output 150 percent.[14] This policy could hurt Czechoslovakia and East Germany substantially, because of their quite timely high level of industrialization but no oil reserves.

In fact, it appeared that the promise of high-energy petroleum from the Soviet Union could greatly increase trade between its East European neighbors and the USSR. The fluctuations in the world oil prices make the prospects rather undependable. Regardless of the availability of this resource, the present Soviet pricing policy with regard to petroleum makes purchases by the Eastern Bloc higher than the world rate, which was abnormally low in late 1983 have become available. The annual statistical yearbook of the Soviet Union has been growing smaller and less detailed each year.[15]

SKILLS, CAPABILITY, AND PROSPECTS
FOR INTEGRATION WITHIN CMEA

In an analysis of the future of the CMEA, Marer has said that both centrifugal (creating separation) and centripetal (moving toward the center) forces have affected regional integration.[16]

Centrifugal forces include the existing structure of production in Eastern Europe; problems of coordination; and inefficient pricing systems. Centripetal forces include the worldwide energy crisis; Western inflation and recession; the growing importance of trade blocs; and numerous other factors contributing to the hard currency indebtedness of the East European countries. Many of these external events have increased the attractiveness for CMEA countries of intrabloc economic relations and have provided a momentum for CMEA integration. Marer also points out that Soviet economic involvement with Eastern Europe seems to have been costly for the USSR to 1976 (the point at which he was writing).[17] He concludes that "it is not obvious that the USSR will attempt to push integration much further than it now stands." This is in line, too, with 1983 pronouncements from Moscow as viewed earlier.[18] The "exchange of inefficiencies," which is how the trade exchange may be seen between the USSR and its satellites, is evidenced by the fact that they all have a specialist foreign trade enterprise charged with responsibility for selling surplus and inferior merchandise in the economy to the USSR.

CMEA has passed through the following stages:

1. The 1950s, with bilateral relations led by the USSR.
2. The 1960s, the Khrushchev era when the CMEA was created as a supranational body, and attempts were made at an international division of labor and specialization of production.
3. The 1970s, beginning with the 1971 Comprehensive Program for Integration.

A number of problems continue to inhibit progress; these are discussed in the following sections.

Centrifugal Forces Hindering CMEA Integration

1. The existing production structure in Eastern Europe, which was originally geared to postwar Soviet demands and bilateral trade with the USSR rather than multilateral trade within the Comecon bloc.
2. Problems of coordination since the negotiators and spokesmen for the foreign trade enterprises are often, if not always, divorced from production.
3. Inefficient domestic and CMEA price systems based on a moving average for four years at a time, creating an hiatus when commodities move suddenly and sharply. However, the Soviet Union was not slow to change the rules for pricing Soviet oil to its neighbors, although the price is still subsidized. This creates centrifugal pressure whenever it is cheaper to import from the West or, alternatively, sellers of low-priced goods find buyers outside the bloc.
4. Bilateralism, which is an obstacle since trade within each commodity group must be bilaterally balanced.
5. Noncompatible economic guidance mechanisms existing within Eastern Europe. Recently, the USSR has been moving toward a Hungarian model but at a cautious pace. Two of the most important all-union ministries are the Ministry for Heavy and Transport Building and the Ministry of General Machine Building which are experiencing "experimental" changes in management. The decree appears to reflect the growing conviction among Soviet economists that detailed planning from the center in such a huge, diversified, and geographically spread-out economy is counterproductive.[19]
6. Inability to compare investment costs and contributions. The economic rationality of investment decisions, especially those involving joint investment projects, is difficult to establish to everyone's satisfaction.
7. Excessive gestation periods. The average investment project takes too long to complete.[20]

Centripetal Forces for Integration

Overall, trade with the West averages about one-third of the value of Eastern Europe's total trade turnover. Traditionally, the East Europeans have paid for their Western purchases with a net export surplus in food, raw materials, and semimanufactures. The Western recession has ensured that these markets either no longer exist or are stagnant. CMEA members therefore fall back on themselves for a solution because of the following factors:

1. Energy crisis. Suddenly oil prices had gone beyond the scope of many of the East European nations' ability to pay. Thus, the Soviet Union, with a fixed period price, was relied upon more heavily as a supplier.

2. Western inflation. Oil had much to do with inflation in the West. As low value-added exports from the Eastern Bloc did not fare as well as higher value-added Western imports, the terms of trade worsened, particularly for Poland, Hungary, and Romania. Hungary has since joined the International Monetary Fund (IMF) following the example of Romania, which was the first East European member in IMF. Poland submitted a membership application but as of 1984 was still awaiting an official response.

3. Western recession. The market for Eastern goods crumbled, particularly Eastern exports of beef and agricultural products.

4. Enlargement of the European Economic Community (EEC). Reduced Western market access and increased protectionism within a larger EEC. It was now more difficult than ever for foodstuffs and basic materials to find a market.

5. Impaired credit standing. Poland, for example, exceeded its ability to service foreign debt interest, never mind the capital amount itself. There was no surplus for purchases other than those that were deemed to be absolutely essential.

6. Intra-CMEA trade. Such trade becomes more attractive.

7. Greater importance of trade blocs as shown by the EEC.

8. End of further experimentation with economic reforms.

9. Abatement of pressures for supranationalism.

10. Changes in world market price of energy and raw materials.

11. Fewer obstacles to ruble convertibility.

12. Eastern European loans of hard currency through CMEA banks.

13. East-West Industrial cooperation. This may promote CMEA integration.

Certain branches of Soviet industry have made extensive use of Western technology (the VAZ project involved the transfer of 380 licenses), but many sectors of industry have not. Their development has been based overwhelmingly on indigenous technology supplemented by technology acquired within the CMEA. Julian Cooper points to these activities, characterized by high levels of socialist self-reliance, as being in the production of weapons, optical equipment and many types of consumer goods, coal mining, nuclear power, rail transport, much of the electronic, radio, and telecommunications industry, and agriculture (except for the provision of quality fertilizers).[21] This view is therefore at odds with that of A. C. Sutton.[22] Stanislaw Gomulka has pointed to a large body of evidence which indicates a high degree of resource misallocation in both conventional production and research and development (R&D), a large but rather slow and often wasteful investment activity, and a generally high resistance to innovation, especially in existing enterprises.[23] The contribution of Soviet and East European R&D activity to the world flow of new inventions is negligible. In the 1970s, in the figures cited by Gomulka,[24] Comecon countries imported about ten times more licenses in terms of dollars paid than they exported. The exports represented merely 1 percent of the estimated total of world exports.

EAST EUROPEAN CAPACITY TO INTEGRATE

Satisfying the need for energy will have a substitute effect in all of the CMEA economies and across their industries. Marer and Montias estimate that more than 100,000 people are directly involved in carrying out various CMEA functions and activities.[25] In addition to its permanent commissions, the CMEA has two regional banks; scientific institutes; interstate conferences on ad hoc problems; intergovernmental commissions dealing with specific issues; and many conferences of nongovernmental organizations that maintain loose ties with the CMEA.

The few firms in Eastern Europe that are jointly owned by enterprises in member countries include:

1. Haldie (1959: Katowice, Poland) between Hungary and Poland: extracting and processing coal waste products.
2. Agromash (1965-) between Hungary and Bulgaria: producing machinery for vegetable and fruit harvesting and processing.
3. Intromash (1965:) between Hungary and Bulgaria: producing specialty equipment for transport machinery and equipment used in factories.
4. Drubhba (1972: Zawiercie, Poland) between the GDR and Poland: producing cotton yarns.
5. Service (1975: Zielona Gora, Poland), a subsidiary of Interatom: providing instrument maintenance of nuclear-technical equipment imported by Poland.

The small number involved and the small scale of their operations indicate the problems that arise in this area for ventures other than those that have coproduction on a compensation trade basis.

The CMEA Comprehensive Program of 1971 created the International Economic Association (IEA), with a looser organizational structure than the joint enterprise. The IEA has authority to negotiate specialization agreements and conclude contracts at the governmental level. Marer and Montias have identified eight IEAs in Eastern Europe:

1. Interatominstrument (1972: Warsaw) by six East European states excluding Romania: cooperation in research, production, and sales of nuclear-technical equipment, with authorization to trade with third countries.
2. Interatomenergo (1973: Moscow) by seven East European states plus Yugoslavia: cooperation in research, planning, construction, and supply of nuclear power plants.

3. Assofoto: (1973: Moscow) between the USSR and the CDR: joint planning in the photochemical industry.

4. Intertextilmash (1973: Moscow) by seven East European states plus Yugoslavia: cooperation in research, production, and sales of textile machinery, with trade with third countries to be authorized "in the future."

5. Interkhimvolokno (1974: Bucharest) by seven East European states plus Yugoslavia: cooperation in research, production, and sales of chemical fibres.

6. Domokhim (1974: Moscow) between the USSR and the GDR: joint planning in domestic (household) chemical products with company sales outlets in the founding countries.

7. Intertlkonpr bor (1974) by seven East European states: cooperation in measuring instruments.

8. Interport (1974: Warsaw) between Poland and the GDR: apparently, cooperation involving port facilities in the two countries.[26]

To these may be added Interlighter International Shipping Corporation,[27] the joint water transportation system of Bulgaria, Czechoslovakia, Hungary, and the USSR which handled 1.5 million tons of goods during 1978-83.

Marer and Montias conclude that the importance "of the joint enterprises and the IEA's lies in the possibility that they may provide the legal and experimental basis for creating socialist multinational corporations which potentially could play an important role in CMEA integration."[28]

Theoretically, the concept of socialist multinationals has been explored before, but Stanley J. Paliwoda maintains that there is no substance to this theory.[29] The basis on which the socialist enterprises is founded—their articles of incorporation—is central planning, not growth or profitability. They do not have a role for professional management as in the West, and the instances of antonomy are also generally limited. In addition, marketing, which is so important in the West, is seen in the East as only an addition to overhead. Hence, branding and promotion do not receive the same attention relative to a Western multinational. Moreover, foreign direct investment in the West is much less in number and value than is reported by McMillan.[30] With the exception of perhaps Nafta (UK) Limited, these investments are simply sales and distribution outlets. There are no manufacturing outlets or investments of particular note with the exception of Nafta (UK), which is a wholly owned Soviet subsidiary that uses BP to refine its oil and then retails it through a network of a few hundred service stations in England and Wales. Research on the socialist multinationals is currently being investigated by an international team of investigators funded by the Institute for Research on Multinational Corporations.[31]

The development of gas fields is likely to provide some energy relief to Czechoslovakia and the GDR which are the region's most energy import-dependent. Soviet planners currently have 4,030 megawatts, with 15,910 megawatts planned. Bulgaria, Czechoslovakia, Hungary, and the GDR have twelve operating reactors, and the bloc plans to quadruple capacity.[32] In any event, it is likely that in the next five to ten years problems concerning both the cost and size of Soviet oil and gas supplies to Eastern Europe will be critical.[33]

TECHNOLOGY TRANSFERS EFFECTED

The USSR claims more than 490 Soviet-aided projects in the last five years (1978-1983). Soviet-assisted power plants generated 37 million KW. Within the USSR there are two 4 million KW power stations for generating electricity for CMEA. The integrated power grid covers a territory with 220 million people. The USSR also has a nationwide integrated gas supply system and industrial complexes in West Siberia; Angora-Yenisu; Timano-Pechora; South Yakuutian; Pavlodar-Ekibastuz; South Tajikistan; a petro-chemical center at Tobolsk, Tomsk; and the Baikul-Armur railway. The Soviet Union has also built the Urengoy gas pipeline to the West and instituted the Soviet Food Program whereby investment has increased but productivity has declined. Successive years of bad harvests, poor quality equipment, and difficulties in storing and handling crops all led to the urgency of implementing a food program. The situation in the other East European countries is described in the following sections.

BULGARIA

Bulgaria specializes in the development of electronics and electrical energy and hauling equipment, shipbuilding, instrument-making, certain machine tools, and agricultural machines.[34] This country accounts for 35 percent of output of electric trucks in CMEA countries and 90 percent of exports of CMEA electric trucks. Bulgaria cooperates in the establishment on Soviet soil of additional capacity for the production of metals, pulp, and timber-logging in order to meet its own needs in these deficit materials. Twenty years ago machinery and equipment accounted for 12 percent of its exports, but now the percentage is approximately 50 percent. The Bulgarians receive Soviet help in the following concerns: Kremikovtski iron and steel works; Bourgas oil refining; Stara Zagora nitrogen fertilizer plant; Maritsa-East steam power plant; Kozlodoni atomic power plant; methyl metacrylate plant in Stara Zagora; vinyl chloride and polyvinyl chlorate; house-building complexes in Stara Zagora, Pleven, Burgas, Tolbukhin, and Pazardzhik; chlorine-producing enterprises in Devna; acetaldehyde plant in Burgas; phthalic anhydride plant in Ruse; tire retread shop in Pazardzhik and tire factory in Vidin; 98 percent of steel and rolled metals; 100% of pig iron, copper, and zinc; 80% of electricity (452,000 KW); 100% of oil refining; iron and steel sector (which has been built up almost entirely with Soviet assistance in Ihitiman for hoisting gear and farm machinery); cement plant construction in Temalkovo; Bobov-Dol coal mines; spiral seam pipe-plant in Seplamviri for USSR-Bugaria gas main; and Vinitsa-Albertirtsa electricity transmission line built jointly by the USSR, Bulgaria, Czechoslovakia, Hungary, and Poland.

In addition, Bulgaria and the USSR cooperate on the Soyuz gas pipline; the cellulose combine in Ust-Illmal; the asbestos plant in Kiembaevsk; the Mir energy system; and railway lines and motorways from Moscow-Sofia (to be updated).

Bulgaria has helped with: cigarette factories in Stara Zagora and Haskovo; capacities for low-voltage electrolytic condensers in Kyustendil; the ferromagnite plant in Pernik; the woolen knitwear factory in Petrich; the Faience tile factory in Isperih and eleven other projects; the "record" machine-building plant in Plovdiv; the diesel engine plant in Varna; and a plant for electronic chips in Stara Zagora.

In return for its participation in big construction projects on foreign soil, Bulgaria annually receives an additional 50,000 tons of pulp, 40,000 tons of asbestos, over 1 million tons of iron ore, 9,000 tons of ferroalloys, and considerable quantitites of natural gas and electric power from the USSR as well as nickel from Cuba. Over a ten-year period Bulgaria is also to receive more than 32,000 square meters of natural gas in return for its contribution to the Soyuz pipeline. Around 35 percent of the pulp imported from the USSR will come from the UST-Ilmck combine, and more than 40 percent of the iron ore coming from the USSR will be the result of Bulgaria's participation in integration projects.

CZECHOSLOVAKIA

The USSR traditionally accounts for one-third of Czechoslovakia's foreign trade but covers its needs for basic fuels and raw materials either completely or to a crucial degree.[35] Of the total 7.275 billion convertible ruble exports to CMEA, 4.6 billion is machinery and equipment; and 1.75 billion is accounted for by cooperation and specialization, of which 1.53 billion falls into the machinery and equipment sector. Bulgaria takes the largest share—30 percent—of Czechoslovakian exports under cooperation and specialization. Overall, the USSR has the largest share—61.7 percent (62.4 percent in the case of machinery and equipment).

The commodity structure of Czechoslovakian exports/imports in relation to the socialist countries has remained virtually unchanged. In general, engineering goods accounted for more than 63 percent of total exports; raw materials, semifinished goods and materials for more than 20 percent; durable goods for 16 percent; and farm produce, food industry raw materials, and foodstuffs for about 1 percent. In imports, the largest item (accounting for nearly 53 percent) consists of raw materials, semifinished products and materials, followed by machines and equipment (36 percent), farm produce and food industry raw materials (more than 5 percent), and industrial goods (nearly 6 percent).

Czechoslovakia's needs of crude oil, natural gas, electricity, bituminous coal, brown coal, briquettes, cast iron, aluminum, calcinated soda, ammonia potash, nitrogen, and mixed fertilizers are covered almost exclusively by imports from the socialist countries. Czechoslovakia also takes from these countries decisive amounts of oil products, iron and manganese ores, bauxite, sulphur, raw phosphates, cooking salt, ferroalloys, copper, zinc, lead, nickel, sulphuric acid, tobacco, and tobacco products.

In 1982, Czechoslovakian exports made under cooperation and specialization contracts accounted for approximately 26 percent, of which machines and equipment totaled 34 percent. Czechoslovakia has participated in multilateral integration projects with machinery and consumer goods deliveries for the fodder yeast plant in Mozyr, USSR, and with the delivery of part of the technological equipment, building material, and other goods for the Khmalnitskaya nuclear power plant in the USSR.

The CMEA Framework Agreement on multilateral cooperation in the sphere of development and organization of industrial robots under specialization and cooperation arrangements runs to the end of 1995.

In keeping with the emphasis on energy production, Czechoslovakia plans to "produce 21 Soviet-designed, 440-Mw reactors by the turn of the century—10 of them for export to other Comecon members. (This program is probably too ambitious, Western observers say, given likely production delay problems in assembling an adequate labor force and the heavy financial strain on the potential export customers. Most serious of all, the required investments are reportedly starving other sectors of the Czech economy of needed capital.")[36]

Czechoslovakia has a Program of Robotization for the Seventh Five-Year Plan under which 3,000 industrial robots are to be installed by the end of 1985 and 13,000 by the end of 1990, saving 5,500 workers by 1985 and 30,000 by 1990. More than 200 robots and industrial products have been made to date. The principal makers are ZPA Presov, Kharlat Snina, Tesla Kolin, Skoda Plzen, Baz Bratislava. ZIS Detva, ZEZ Praha (Horice plant), and ZTS Kosice (Bardejor plant). Successful applications are in use at AZNP Mlada Boleslaw (automobiles); ZIS Dubnicanad Vahom (heavy engineering); CZM Strakonice (motorcycles); ZVL Kysucke Nore Mesto (engineering); and VSZ Kosice (metallurgy).

The chief coordination of research and development of industrial robots is located at the Metal Industry Research Institute at Presov. (HM 160 universal manipulation was developed jointly with the Soviets.)

Another important cooperation program is the program for multinational cooperation in the development of new types of color TVs and equipment for color TV. Other areas include data processing machinery, manufacture of equipment for nuclear power plants, antifriction bearings, tractors and farm machines, equipment for processing solid fuels, ferrous and non-ferrous metals, and raw materials for the chemical industry. The cooperating institutions include Skoda Plzen (engineering), CAZ Praha (automobiles), Tesla Praha (electronics), VUSTE (Research Institute of Engineering Technology and Economics), Inorga (organization and control), CKD Polovodice (semiconductors), TST Praha (machine tools), and Romo Fulnek (consumer goods). Other projects underway involving cooperation include radio transmission station equipment (V-1 Bolhunice power station, Dukovary power station), and Mochovce power station (all three with 1,760) megawatt capacity); Czechoslovakian-supplied rolling and other equipment for Soviet-aided plants in Turkey and India; pulp and paper companies in Vranov and Zilina; an unbleached sulphate pulp at Ruzabberok; and the Prague underground railway.

GERMAN DEMOCRATIC REPUBLIC

The presence of West Berlin in East Germany has produced revenue for the German Democratic Republic. West Germany pays more than $1 billion for transportation and similar services annually. This revenue, in turn, provides the GDR with income that encourages additional purchases within the Eastern Bloc.[37]

The GDR has initiated the following projects: High pressure ethylene installation Polymer-60, annual capacity of 60,000 tons at Leuina, doubling capacity and allowing it to export 45% of electricity and 100% of natural gas output; large-panel house-building complex in Zwickau; radio-transmitting station equipment; Janschwilde thermal power plant (3 M KW); power bloc for Boxberg, the largest brown coal-fired station in Europe (3,500 megawatts); equipment for the hot-roll crosscutting installation at Eisenrhuttenstadt; equipment for the bushed roller chain at Vortspitt; cooperation in television; and joint prospecting for oil, gas, and solid minerals.

HUNGARY

About 95 percent of Hungary's total imports originate from socialist countries; about 80 percent of all Hungarian exports of machinery and equipment are directed to socialist countries. Hungary annually receives 6.4 million tons of oil from the USSR and 4.5 billion m^3 of natural gas.

Hungary supplies 7,200 Ikarus buses, other bus components worth some 200 million rubles, and spare parts for passenger cars and lorries worth 30 million rubles to the USSR. In return, Hungary receives 26,700 automobiles (including 25,000 Lada cars), nearly 3,000 trucks and special purpose vans, and 23 million rubles' worth of cooperation products.

Hungary's automotive industry operates under four agreements with the USSR:

1. Specialization agreement relating to finished automobile industrial products. Buses are exchanged for trucks.
2. Specialization and cooperation agreement of automobile subassemblies. The RABA Works supplies rear axles for Soviet buses and trolley buses in exchange for front axles. Power-assisted steering wheels and universal joints go to the Hungarian car industry.
3. Agreement relating to speed change gears. Speedy deliveries direct components to the USSR. Lvov's automobile works provides hydromechanical change speed gears for Ikarus buses.
4. Cooperation agreement on Lada cars. In exchange for various car accessories, the Volga automobile factory, FAZ, has agreed to supply 1,500 D. Lada cars to Hungary.

The backbone of Hungary's commercial vehicle manufacture is a vertical cooperation among three large concerns: the Hungarian Railway Carriage and Machine Works (RABA); the Csepel Auto Works at Szigetszentnuklos; and Ikarus with its plants in Budapest and Szekesfehervar. These firms developed jont projects in the 1960s to make buses as they set up large-scale bus making in Hungary. Planners could count on sizable demands from CMEA member countries, especially the Soviet Union. The Hungarian vehicle industry was therefore developed to meet domestic and other CMEA demand. However, in the 1970s growing Western demand required higher specifications, which required further cooperation.

Hungary's cooperation agreements with India include supplying 400,000 auto electronic sets, that is, ignition switches, horns, and windscreen wipers. Over 60 percent of products sent to the USSR are made at the Bakony Works of Veszpren for Togliatti, for which the Soviets deliver 15,000 cars in return. The Bakony Works cooperates with the Polski-Fiat Bielsko-Biala plant and supplies 150,000 sets. Beginning in 1982, Fiat agreed to buy 100,000 Bakony distributors per year. In addition, 150,000 distributors were bought by Yugoslavia's Zastava plant, and 150,000 were to be bought by Romania's Dacia plant. The Bakony equipment is based on a British license. Interestingly, turbo-recharging equipment which operates regardless of the number of revolutions per number (featured by BMW) was developed in Budapest.

RABA (the Hungarian Railway Carriage and Machine Works) at Gyor is widening its production range by producing garden tractors under a license that was obtained from one of the factories belonging to the Czechoslovakia Agrozet Trust. The first series was turned out in 1983, and additional series were scheduled for the following years. Fitted with a Yugoslavian engine, it is able to handle about two dozen different agricultural implements.

With regard to exports of machine products, the most recent branch is the instruments industry. A new enterprise, the Micro Electronics Company, was founded to increase the manufacturing of microelectronic components. The average age of its exported products is four years; the age of the vehicles (buses, lorries, motor trains) hardly exceeds five years.[38]

Chicken factories have been sold by Babolna Agricultural Combine. Recently, four big chicken factories were delivered to the USSR in an 80 million ruble project. Approximately 1 million square meters of aluminum-coated panels, fourteen different structural units, and 150 km of feeding and drinking lines had to be transported. All of them were loaded onto 8,000 wagons, including some specially made carriages. Some specialists from Soviet poultry stations were trained at Babolna in industrial breeding technology. Several breeding plants at Babolna have achieved better results in the fattening of chickens than was anticipated. Specialists will stay one year to supervise the project. Regular charters deliver 2.1 million parent couples and 23.1 million Broyler Tetra chicks, as well as the so-called premixes and vitamins which are essential ingredients of the feeds.[39]

The unconventional reforms in Hungary's business projects are unprecedented, as noted by Paul Marer: "what's new is the openness to so many kinds of changes on so many levels."[40] The changes made in Hungary's system during 1982 and early 1983 appear to have paved the way for even greater revisions, with future changes including shareholding companies and the establishment of a competitive commercial banking system.[41] These changes would not only restructure Hungary's domestic and foreign trade, but would also increase the flow of technology and facilitate access to such information throughout the Eastern Bloc through Hungary.

At present, Hungary's technology qualifies more as know-how than as high tech. One example is its chicken-farming operations. The specialists who conduct the poultry sales provide knowledge designed to produce higher quality chickens. In actuality, the information involved here may not be sufficiently technical to warrant the specialist's ongoing presence, but the day-to-day adherence to rigid guidelines and the quality control exerted over the initial months illustrate a form of technology transfer. The Soviet Union and Czechoslovakia appear to be the Eastern Bloc's two major purchasers of chicken factory technology at this point in time.[42]

Other areas of industrial trade activity are as follows: 59% of oil refining; 30% of steel and aluminum; 35% of pig iron; 98% cold rolled plate; 100% hot rolled plate; oxygen converter shop capacity of 1 million tons of steel at Danube; steel works; Paks atomic power station (1,760 megawatt); co-operation in the manufacture of Rubin and Temp TVs; precision casting shop at Csepel; iron and steel mill in Budapest; cement plant in Belapatfalva; automated air traffic control at Ferihegy Airport (first in the CMEA); grain elevator in Gynongyos; diesel fuel hydroblasting plant, 1 million tons in Szazhdombatta; and Tiza oil refinery, 3 million tons in Leninvaros.

POLAND

Poland's large trade deficits have been as exasperating in the East as in the West and have influenced trading relations.[43] Poland's trade deficit with the USSR amounted to around 1.5 billion rubles in 1981, 1.2 billion in 1982, and an estimated 1 billion in 1983. The USSR agreed to scale down Polish exports of consumer goods without curtailing its own exports of consumer goods to Poland. The talks with the chairman of the Soviet State Committee for Planning, Nikolai Babakov, which were held in Warsaw in early 1983, also dealt with the matter of unfinished and discontinued investment projects in Poland, which the country is not capable of completing on its own. Discussed was Soviet participation in the completion of some departments at the Huta Katowice metallurgical complex and in the Pokoj and Jednosc smelting plants.

Other cooperation projects include 18% electricity generation, 61% of oil refining, 79% of pig iron, 52% of steel, 48% of rolled metals, and 31% of coke; equipment for a rubber regenerating plant in Bolechow; hydrogen peroxide at the Alwena chemical plant near Krakov; 397 km standard gauge 1,520 mm) railway line from the USSR to Katowice put into operation—for iron ore (?), plus shipping coal, sulphur, engineering and farm produce to the USSR; a large house-building complex in Dabrowa Gornica; a caustic soda plant, Giurgiu with 200,000 capacity and 62% of hot rolled plate; 50% of steel pipes; 64% of coke; a concrete discharge pipe factory in Ostrow Wielkopolski for building the Warsaw metro; equipment for the Pszczyna Wierzbica cement plant (2.2 million tons) prefabricated construction equipment for greenhouse blocks, each of 6 hectares area; 500,000 KW turbo-unit Kozienice thermal power plant; Polanec thermal power station (eight steam boilers each, capable of 650 tons of steam per hour); blueprints for the Rzarnowiec atomic plant; and air vacuum installations at the Blachownja oil refinery in Kedzierzyn.

The hardships being placed on Poland as a result of the hard currency cash flow problem have resulted in a desperate shoe shortage. The shoe factories, representing an investment of more than $6.5 million for equipment and raw materials, lack the currency to import some essential additional materials such as glue.[44]

ROMANIA

With oil reserves running low, Romania may increasingly have to turn to the CMEA for energy imports. Projects involving cooperation up through 1982 include the following: 50% of electricity; equipment for 1,400 tandem cold-rolling mill, Golati; "30-102" tube mill at Zalau; "25-114" tube welding mill at Zimnicea; large-panel house-building complex in Bucharest; caustic soda plant at Gh. Gh-Day; oxygen-producing plant in Craiova;

viscose cellulose plant in Braila; pentane, isopentane isomerization plant in Ploiesti; equipment for radio-transmitting stations; three steam boilers, each of which produces 420 tons of steam an hour; two heat and power supply turbines for Gelati thermal power station; and equipment for the extension to the Deva thermal power plant, Romania's largest.

Oil refining, established in Romania during the 1970s, has the capacity but, at present, does not have the petroleum to operate the refineries.[43]

The 1984 Winter Olympics brought Yugoslavia worldwide attention and publicity, as well as some valued revenues. It is hoped that these contests will encourage interchange among the Eastern Bloc countries, as well as with other countries, especially as the Eastern Bloc athletes did well in the Olympics.

Projects involving cooperation include: 29% of electricity, 39% of steel, 46% of pig iron, and 75% of lead and zinc extraction; Birac plant with capacity of 600,000 tons of alumina; steel shop at Skopje (850,000 tons of slab); aluminum plant (50,000 tons); in Titograd, Cmarska iron ore pit (9.3 million tons) mine and concentration factory in Stariy Trg; equipment for cast radiator plant in Zrenjan; equipment for battery factories in Probistip and Srebenica; thermal electric power stations with total capacity of 1.2m KW, including the NoviSad, Brtolan-111 and Mglderik thermal power station. (The Soviets account for 27% of electricity); equipment for Titovy Rudinisi coal mine; iron and steel in Smederevo; coke-oven at Zenica steel complex; Zletoro Sasa mining and ore-enrichment enterprise; nickel mine and factory in Prishina; oil-refining installation and bitumen-producing installation at Pancevo; co-production of cast radiators; boilers and fittings at Zrenjanin; and automobile batteries at Srebrenice and Probiship.

SUMMARY AND CONCLUSIONS

Although not fully developed there appears to be technology transfer among CMEA countries through trade and cooperation. Further developing in this cooperation depends upon availability of resources. Smith has predicted that the growth of resources available for development will be determined by three factors: First, a slowdown in the growth of, or a possible fall in, domestic energy supplies, which will make it necessary to direct investment to areas with a high incremental capital: output ratio, and this will reduce the ability to command resources from outside the bloc. Second, slowdown in the rate of growth of the industrial labor force. Finally, the pressure of increased liabilities undertaken by the bloc in the shape of the admission of Vietnam, together with the expected increase in the cost of military and development aid extended to non-Bloc members.[46]

NOTES

1. Konstantin Popov, "The Socialist Countries; Economic Integration—The Embodiment of Lenin's Ideas," *USSR Foreign Trade* No. 4 (1981): 5-9.

2. Philip Hanson, "Soviet Trade with Eastern Europe," in Karen Dawsha and Philip Hanson, *Soviet-East European Dilemmas* (London: Heinemann, 1981), p. 91.

3. The Consultative Committee (CoCom) which meets in Paris is not exactly an arm of NATO, as France, which is both host to it and a member remains outside NATO.

4. The Soviet ruble is officially worth 1.06 = .91, but the unofficial or "black market" rate is allegedly five times higher.

5. "The CMEA Integration Programme," *Soviet Europe* 6, No. 141 (n.d.): 16.

6. S. J. Paliwoda, *Joint East-West Marketing and Production Ventures* (Hampshire, England: Gower, 1981), Chapter 1.

7. N. A. Tikhonov, "Guidelines for the Economic and Socialist Development of the USSR for 1981-5 and for the Period Ending in 1990," Report to the 26th Congress of the Communist Party of the Soviet Union, February 27, 1981, Novosti Press Agency, Moscow.

8. Marilyn L. Liebrenz, *Transfer of Technology: U.S. Multinationals and Eastern Europe* (New York: Praeger, 1982), Chapter 5.

9. J. S. Berliner, "Managing the Soviet Economy: Alternative Models," *Problems of Communism* (January-February 1983): 40-56.

10. Michael Simmns, "Moscow Tells Comecon to Prepare for Hard Times," *Guardian*, May 31, 1983.

11. "Can Mother Russia's Allies Be Weaned from Her Oil?" *Business Week*, October 24, 1983, p. 85.

12. Charles Wolf, Jr., "Costs of the Soviet Empire," *Wall Street Journal*, January 30, 1984, p. 32.

13. Michael Dobbs, "Economic Stagnation at Root of East Europe's Ills," *Washington Post*, December 13, 1982, p. A22.

14. "Can Mother Russia's Allies Be Weaned," p. 192.

15. Amity Shaes, "Soviet Watchers Face Growing Secrecy on Kremlin's Economic, Crop Statistics," *Wall Street Journal*, February 10, 1984, p. 30.

16. Paul Marer, "Prospects for Integration in the Council for Mutual Economic Assistance (CMEA)," *International Organisation* 30, No. 4 (Autumn 1976): 631-648. Note that the lists reproduced here have been lengthened from the original.

17. Ibid.

18. Simmons, "Moscow Tells Comecon."

19. A. Robinson, "Moscow Seeks to Learn from Hungary's Experience," *Financial Times*, August 10, 1983.

20. I. V. Maevskii and V. I. Maevskii, *Nekotorye Voprosy Izmereniya Ekonomiches' oi Effektyiynostj* (Moscow, 1970), p. 95, quoted in V. Solomin, *Voprosy Ekonomiki*, No. 1 (1977): 62.

21. Julian Cooper, "Western Technology and Soviet Economic Power," Paper delivered at the 1983 Millennium Conference: Technology Transfer and East-West Relations in the 1980s, London School of Economics, May 1983.

22. A. C. Sutton, *Western Technology and Soviet Economic Development*, 3 vols. (Stanford, Calif.: University Press, 1969, 1971, and 1973).

23. Stanislaw Gomulka, "The Incompatibility of Socialism and Rapid Innovation," Paper delivered at the 1983 Millennium Conference: Technology Transfer and East-West Relations in the 1980s, London School of Economics, May 1983.

24. Ibid., p. 3.

25. Paul Marer and John Michael Montias, "CMEA Integration: Theory and Practice," in *East European Economic Assessment*, Part 2: Regional Committee Congress of the United States (Washington, D.C.: U.S. Government Printing Office, July 10, 1981).

26. Ibid.

27. *Hungarian Economic Information*, 1983/13.

28. Marer and Montias, "CMEA Integration," pp. 631-648.

29. S. J. Paliwoda, "Multinational Corporations: Trade and Investment Across the East-West Divide," *Journal of Management and Decision Economics* (December 1981): 247-255.

30. C. H. McMillan, *Direct Soviet and East European Companies in the West*, Working Paper No. 2, East-West Commercial Relations Series: Institute of Soviet and East European Studies, Carleton University, Ottawa, Canada, 1978.

31. The Institute for Research and Information on Multinationals, Paris, is sponsoring an integrated program of research on the investment activities of socialist foreign trade organizations in Britain, Ireland, and Sweden.

32. "Can Mother Russia's Allies Be Weaned," p. 85.

33. Alan H. Smith, "Economic Factors Affecting Soviet-East European Relations in the 1930's," in Dawsha and Hanson, *Soviet-East European Dilemmas*, p. 113.

34. *Bulgarian Foreign Trade* (March 1981): 3; (May 1962): 5.

35. *Czechoslovak Foreign Trade* (March 1983): 7; (February 1983): 6.

36. "Can Mother Russia's Allies Be Weaned," p. 197.

37. William Drozdiak, "Germans on Both Sides Mend East-West Fences," *Washington Post*, January 8, 1984, p. A15.

38. *Hungarian Economic Information*, 1983/15, p. 3; 1982/23, p. 5; 1982/22; Adam Torok, "Hungary and the International Cooperation of Auto Industries," *Marketing in Hungary* (1982), pp. 31-36.

39. *New Hungarian Exporter* 32, No. 11 (November 1982): 5.

40. Amity Shaes, "Hungary Moves to Liberalize Economy, Already Soviet Bloc's Most Easy-Going," *Wall Street Journal*, December 28, 1983, p. 16.

41. Ibid.

42. Victoria Pope, "East Bloc Tries Hungary's Methods," *Wall Street Journal*, February 10, 1983, p. 35.

43. *Polish Economic News* 3 (40A), February 15, 1983.

44. Dobbs, "Economic Stagnation," p. A22.

45. Ibid.

46. Smith, "Economic Factors," p. 113.

7
China's Four Modernizations Program and Technology Transfer

RUSTAN KOSENKO AND A. C. SAMLI

The Oriental World has manifested a remarkable genius for absorbing Western science, technology, and industrial development—to such an extent that it has become more than competitive with its erstwhile benefactors. Japan is a notable example. Equally impressive have been the performances of Hong Kong, South Korea, Singapore, and Taiwan.

The People's Republic of China is in the process of duplicating that success, but with a distinctively different approach. China's formula for becoming a super economic power by the year 2000 is simple: a massive transfer of Western technology. As a result, China's appetite for Western goods and technology is insatiable. The estimates have placed the total cost for imported know-how to be $170 billion by 1985 and $600 billion by the year 2000 (1, 2). (The original estimate was $200 billion. The $170 billion estimate reflects the inherent internal problems to technology transfer and the decreasing investment capital available to fund this project.)

Despite this immense potential, since 1979, China has scaled down, postponed, or canceled about 700 large- and medium-sized projects which were originally in the ambitious economic modernization program (27). This "readjustment" of goals is indicative of China's difficulty in absorbing massive doses of new technology. Furthermore, Beijing's leaders now question the country's ability to cope so quickly with so many technical projects.

For China, then, the lesson is clear. There is little compatibility between "know why and know how!" Thus, successful technology transfer is a two-edged sword, simultaneously determined by an importer's ability to absorb the new technology and by the exporter's ability to provide a favorable transfer.

This chapter explores these issues. It attempts to establish a procedure to be used in assessing China's ability to absorb technology and it proposes a strategy for the successful transfer of technology by American firms.

THE FOUR MODERNIZATIONS PROGRAM

The post-Mao leadership under Deng Hsiao-Ping has evoked a *volte-face* from the dogmatism of Mao. The current ideology espouses that "advanced techniques and experience are the common wealth of the working people of the world." Subsequently, "every country as it develops is bound to absorb and make use of, to a greater or lesser degree, scientific and technological achievements of other countries." The new order does not see self-reliance as "self-seclusion" or as a rejection of foreign trade and technological transfer. "Learning from other countries" and "making foreign things serve China" are considered proper to China's economic modernization. Buttressing this current mood is Deng Hsiao-Ping's statement that "to import (advanced technology and equipment) is for the purpose of learning from them and promoting our own inventions instead of using them to replace our own (technology)." Thus, new directions in economic policy are manifest in the four modernizations program (1).

The four modernizations program—the program to modernize agriculture, industry, national defense, and science technology—seeks to propel China into the front ranks of the world's industrial powers. The size of this venture is akin to the Industrial Revolution of the 1800s.

While the line of Western firms bearing their magic elixirs has been forming since 1971, momentary euphoria seems to have blinded Western businessmen as they scramble for their piece of the modernization pie. They have forgotten that the Chinese have a propensity for excess. The Great Leap Forward campaign was designed to industrialize and modernize china instantly (without any aid from the West). Instead, the country almost starved. The Cultural Revolution was to change Chinese society. It did and in time almost wrecked the government. Now they are on a massive buying spree, talking in terms of debts and loans running into hundreds of billions of dollars. All this for a country with foreign currency holdings of $2 to $4 billion, in addition to probably $2 billion in gold and an annual trade volume of $36.7 billion in 1980 (4).

Financial considerations can slow the progress of the modernization train, but the problems encountered in the importation of technology by a less developed nation can damage the tracks and bring the modernization train to a resounding halt.

PROBLEMS OF TECHNOLOGY TRANSFER

Technology transfer to less developed countries (LDCs) has been an area of wide-range interest and significant research (4, 5). These studies have pointed to the inherent problems of technology absorption by an LDC. An improper transfer could inhibit the modernization process, and could have adverse socioeconomic and political repercussions for the home nation.

Many technology proponents have argued that much of the present technology transferred to LDCs is totally inappropriate. They argue in favor of offering more technologies that recognize the labor-abundant/capital-scarce conditions of a nation and that help raise the standard of living of the predominately rural composition of the society, instead of capital-intensive transfers (6). The key area of contention is the concept of "appropriate technology." Although some pundits equate "appropriate" with small-scale or labor-intensive technologies, others contend that it should not be determined by the "level of its scale or sophistication" but rather by how effectively the transferred technology addresses the inherent problems of a particular *socioeconomic* system (7).

Internal problems are indigenous to China. Beijing's leaders have discovered the hard realities of the above. They fear that their new economic direction has "uncaged a dragon." Their citizens have earnestly taken to newly introduced free enterprise, market-oriented prices, profits, and cash bonuses. These policies are now felt to be undermining the very basis of the socialist society.

Any rapid economic development and industrialization brings with it cultural effects. Not only are there effects of industrialization on individuals, but also new relationships are developed with prevailing economic institutions and the very social structure begins to erode. It is replaced with a more Western orientation.

Nurkse demonstrates the poignancy of Western emulation:

When people come into contact with superior goods or superior patterns of consumption, with new articles or new ways of meeting old wants, they are apt to feel after a while a certain restlessness and dissatisfaction. Their knowledge is extended, their imagination stimulated, new desires are aroused, the propensity to consume is shifted upward. . . . New wants . . . can be important as an incentive, making people work harder and produce more (29).

The party's main organ, *The People's Daily,* is replete with warnings.

If planned production and [distribution] do not cover the main body of China's economy, the state-owned economy will disintegrate . . . and the socialist economy will become controlled by the unbridled, spontaneous force of the market economy. . . . In the past few years, we have initiated a number of reforms in the economic system. . . . This orientation is correct, and its gains are apparent. . . . However, cases of weakening and hampering the state's unified planning have been on the increase. Hereafter, while continuing to give play to the role of market regulation, we must on no account neglect or relax unified leadership through state planning (30).

Therefore, China faces a monumental task—finding a happy medium between two incompatible systems.

Further exacerbating this new economic direction is the havoc it plays on societal behavior. The pursuit of individual profit has replaced the egalitarian ideal. State-owned factories are hoarding materials, withholding taxes, and raising prices, and profits are dominating behavior. In addition, the disparities between rural and urban workers are widening. As a result, wage increases and further expansion of free markets have been halted. All this has been at the expense of the key motivating factor to induce people to greater production efficiency. The people have gotten used to fatter pocket money and the luxury goods they can now afford (30).

China is faced with a formidable task. It needs to institute new economic initiatives devoid of ideologically unacceptable blemishes on the nation's social and political fabric. Thus, it would be no mere tautology to say that the speed with which the leaders can deliver the goods to the people will largely determine the speed with which the people will deliver the goods to the leaders.

THE U.S. DILEMMA

Critics of development modes place the onus on the exporting nations. American firms find themselves with a perplexing task: the Chinese continue to insist on receiving the most up-to-date technological information and capital equipment. However, China as well as other LDCs might not be equipped to absorb sophisticated technology effectively or efficiently (8). The natural outcome of the dilemma is one of guarded suspicion of foreign firms and accusations of insensitivity to development needs. For the American executive this situation endorses the "Ugly American" image and entails a setback not only for the development of the modernization process, but also for beneficial lateral trade.

U.S. firms have two options: (1) not to sell the highly technical industrial capital equipment and therefore avoid future unpleasant bilateral confrontations, and (2) to sell the demanded equipment and take short-term benefits at the expense of long-term potential. At first glance neither option is optimal. China's total trade was $36.7 billion in 1980 alone, an increase of 23.8% over 1979. Imports accounted for $18.5 billion; exports recovered $17.9 billion. These were increases over 1979 of 17.9% and 30.9%, respectively. The U.S. share of this trade pie is 13%, and estimates indicate that U.S. firms will have an increasing share of expanding trade which will reach a total of $170 billion by 1985 (9, 31). As a result, the first option cannot be accepted since it does not provide any profitable prospects. However, the second option can be more palatable. Our model of technology transfer presents the core aspects of a technology transfer that U.S. firms can utilize in order to eliminate costly future business-related confrontations with China and promote long-term trading opportunities.

GOVERNMENT POLICY AND THE EXPORTER

Any transfer of technology is really governed by the exporter's government policy vis-à-vis the transferee nation. Fortunately for U.S. firms, the change from a hitherto containment to a coexistence policy has invigorated exporting optimism. Normalization of relations and extension of the more favorable tariff structure of most-favored-nation status to China have put American firms on an equal footing with competitive foreign suppliers (10).

Recently, however, the Reagan administration has made technology transfer a "cause célèbre." Under the rubric of national security, the administration controls exports of critical technology. The concern is how to plug the holes in the high-tech sieve.

Washington's concern over controlling U.S. technology transfers is matched by its confusion over how to do so. There is no clear definition of "critical technology," and businessmen question whether it can be controlled at all if the Europeans and the Japanese play the export game by different rules.

More debilitating to American business interests is the morass of conflicting bureaucratic red tape. The U.S. Department of Commerce exercises control over technology transfer using the *Commodity Control List*. It is an 800-page book of products and technologies marked for control. But the Defense Department also plays a major role. It has its own, albeit, longer list called the *Militarily Critical Technologies List*. We can clearly visualize the bureaucratic morass (32, 33) when we consider that Commerce has two additional partners: the State Department, because of the foreign policy implication of high-tech trade; and the Treasury Department, which makes its contribution through the Customs Service.

This aim of control extends beyond U.S. borders. The State Department uses economic blackmail to force a number of neutral and nonaligned countries to tighten their technology transfer policies. The most recent targets were Austria, England, and France (34).

Although initially directed at the Soviet Union, the administration policy on controlling the "forbidden fruit" has reached China. Washington is refusing export permits for high-tech goods to Hong Kong if the buyer is wholly owned by the Communist Chinese or if there is a risk that the equipment will end up in China. One such company, Hua Ko, is not deterred. Hua Ko claims it can buy much of the boycotted technology from Europe or Japan. Not only technology transfer but also training is a target for scrutiny. The U.S. government is looking more closely at the training of Communist Chinese at American firms under existing agreements with China.

Despite these bureaucratic constraints, U.S. firms intending to transfer technology to China must be concerned with at least two critical issues: (1) the technology selected for transfer; and (2) the nature and scope of the support service system that is required for a given level of technology.

Figure 7.1 depicts a general technology transfer model that should be considered as a requisite to any transfer of technology to China. Although this descriptive model was developed with primarily China in mind, it is applicable to other Third World countries as well.

Figure 7.1
Technology Transfer Model

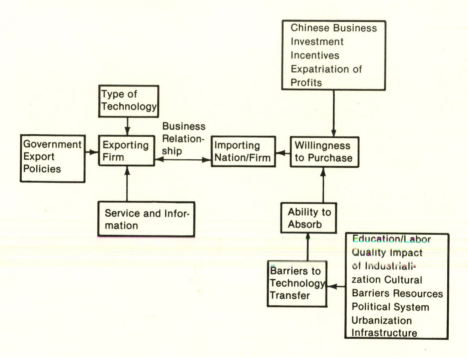

The Product/Technology

China's mission to transform the country from a predominantly rural to an industrial society is a complex one. Western technology is viewed as a key ingredient in the modernization recipe, yet the process of selecting the most appropriate technology is complicated by the myriad technologies that exist in the world and by Beijing's lack of expertise in selecting the appropriate technology.

China classifies technology on a functional basis. There is production technology (production hardware and know-how), consumption technology (product design, features, and performance), and managerial technology (the firm's planning, operating, and control systems) (35). All of these should be addressed in an integrated and controlled manner but have been approached in a willy-nilly manner. As a result, U.S. industrial firms will find themselves playing an extremely important role via the negotiation process in deciding what type and level of technology is to be sent to China. By understanding China's desire, commitment, and, more importantly, capacity for trade, the U.S. firm could inadvertently stifle a mutually beneficial relationship before it materialized. Thus, the necessity for awareness of market needs such that exported technology complements prevailing internal conditions on the part of U.S. industrialists cannot be ignored. Without this kind of understanding there is no basis for a mutually satisfactory relationship.

Jerry L. Roby clarifies the role of the negotiation process:

the quality and skills of the [executives] you send to investigate and negotiate in the PRC market will be crucial to your results. Ideally, your executive vice-president should speak fluent Mandarin Chinese, be your best detail technician, have the patience of Job, and have several months free to devote to the project. This is an uncommon combination indeed. . . . The Chinese are interested in facts and price, not marketing pizzazz (36).

If negotiations reach fruition, relationships can be long term. The Chinese are known to be honest and hold up more than their end in any bargain. Future dealings will be based on friendships and relationships. "As long as you remain true in your interactions with them, you've little fear of competitive replacement" (36).

Misunderstandings do occur. Inappropriate technology transfer as well as inadequate dissemination of imported technology information can become a prime area of conflict between trade participants. For example, Hughes Tool of the United States came under indirect attack by the Chinese press. They were accused of selling a product (drill bits) that China was presently producing at a higher level than could be used domestically (11). This and comparable situations can only contribute to domestic criticism that Western firms are inducing China to spend vital foreign exchange and to allocate scarce resources on technologies that are inappropriate to domestic needs (7).

Faced with situations where China is avidly seeking technology without regard to prevailing economic conditions, U.S. firms must incorporate within their technology transfer package a policy that could promote long-term transfers with China.

Service and Information Systems

One such policy would be to integrate service and information support with most sophisticated technology transfers. The higher the level of complexity of the technology under consideration, the greater the need for a clear understanding of the relationship between technological complexity, and information and service support.

Provisions for training operating personnel, appropriate operationalization, and maintenance of transfer technology will advance transaction success. If such provisions are neglected, the Chinese may fail to make the equipment operational, and future transactions between the parties could be jeopardized. As Phillipe, Lasserre astutely observes, "training activities are crucial to successful transfer of technology. . . . Technology transfer involves learning and learning can be improved by appropriate training methods" (37). Therefore, the ability to absorb production process-related technologies is closely wedded to the ability to absorb required institutional technology. Among plant management, there is a necessity for on-the-job training of production workers and clerical staff, and for improving the adaptation of rank-and-file workers to modern manufacturing production processes (38).

The importance of this approach cannot be overstated. It is believed that almost a quarter of the population is illiterate. In addition, there is a lack of a scientifically and technologically trained labor pool to allow for large infusions of technology. According to Beijing sources, there were 957,000 engineering and technical workers in 1980. But two-thirds of them were concentrated in metallurgy-oriented industries (39). Short-term gains are constrained by an anemic educational system for training technically competent personnel. There are only twenty-four colleges specializing in training personnel for light industry, only thirty-three technical institutes, and just seventeen technical middle schools. Therefore, the added burden of effectively operationalizing the technology is placed squarely on the shoulders of the transferor.

An additional factor to consider when transferring technology is the omnipresent feasibility study. Such studies not only can provide insight into China's ability to successfully implement transfers but also bring insight into the degree of service and information support needed. For example, China recently invited the Canadian Railways to study its needs for a computerized railways information control and telecommunications system. The purpose of the study is to determine requirements in terms of communications, and hardware and software (40).

Table 7.1 illustrates some of the major industrial agreements with China, Technology transfer is the core activity and includes the provisions for service and information support.

Although agreements continue to be signed and progress has been made on the road to modernization, China remains an LDC. Thus, firms likely to be involved in transferring technology to China will have to be concerned with two additional factors: (1) willingness to purchase and (2) ability to absorb.

Willingness to Purchase

After China announced its $350 billion long march to modernization, the country was willing and anxious to import the most modern technology and industrialize as quickly as possible. This anxiousness is an outgrowth of China's traditional political isolationist climate. Unlike the ultraconservative and nationalistic Maoist doctrine of self-reliance of the past, there is presently a more open and internationally oriented philosophy (12).

As a result of China's pragmatic importing policy, its trade with the United States has shown an astonishingly rapid growth. Two-way trade for the first five months of 1981 increased 47 percent over the same period of a year before (9). Nevertheless, there has been an overall leveling off in the rate of growth. Beijing officials have revamped their initial overambitious buying spree. A Chinese editorial of 1979 proclaimed two general rules: (1) halt or postpone a number of projects on the drawing board (those for which adequate fuel, power, or raw materials cannot be assured), and (2) concentrate on key projects (13, 14). Furthermore, the new "readjustment" of the national economy has witnessed substantial investment cuts in capital construction. The major reshaping policy has been directed at increasing demand for raw materials and semimanufacturers to boost production in China's export-oriented industries. While heavy industry and its concomitant import of machinery becomes the greatest loser, priorities will be concentrated in sectors that include energy, transportation, telecommunications, light industry textiles, and tourism (11).

Despite the cancellation of many projects, the "adjustment" policy has injected realism into their buying plans. Furthermore, the Chinese have liberalized the conditions under which foreign investment can operate. They have attempted to allay foreign concerns about legal language and commercial contracts, and investment incentives.

Language has been perceived as a major barrier to exporting technology. The Chinese language presents some fundamental problems in expressing technical terms or legal concepts generally accepted among Western nations. There is at present no codification of commercial law. Until legal codes do materialize, however, the Chinese are willing to grant by means of contracts the protection which the foreign investor would normally find in the legal systems of Western countries. This concern is manifested in the Chinese agreement to write all contracts in English; they are aware that Chinese-language contracts would be an insurmountable barrier for Western firms (41). This policy has not proved to be a panacea, however. When the Chinese sit down to negotiate any agreement (for example, a joint venture) they find some notions difficult to understand, especially the division of profits, goodwill, patents, and the taxation of an entity. Also consider the cautionary words of an experienced China hand:

Table 7.1
Selected Technology Transfer Contracts with China

Technology	Seller	Buyer	Provisions
Production of one- to five-ton folklift trucks	Mitsubishi Heavy Industries (Japan)	Beijing Folklifts Works	Provide technical know-how over a period of 5 years in production of folklifts, including production techniques, maintenance of quality standards, upgrading the plant, and training the Chinese engineers.
Supply of technology and parts for electric power plants	Combustion Engineering, Inc. (C-E) (United States)	China National, Technical Import Corp. (Tech import)	In this long-term licensing and technology transfer agreement, train Chinese personnel in designing and manufacturing the company's fossil-fuel burning steam generators.
Plant technology for aluminum foil plants	Kobe Steel Showa Aluminum of Japan	City of Peking	Furnish technical assistance to the Chinese on the design and plant layout of the foil-rolling machinery and foil separators. Dispatch engineers to give on-site assistance in the construction and start up of the plant as well as train Chinese technicians in Japan.

SOURCE: *Business China* (April 1980-February 1983).

The Chinese say a contract is not worth the paper it is written on because written characters can be interpreted many different ways, as can sentences and paragraphs. So they place tremendous importance on the handshake, on [trust] and on knowing who they are dealing with (42).

The Chinese have also opened their doors to outside investment, either on a wholly foreign-owned or joint venture basis. These policies enable China to accelerate its development program, and it is a process best suited to the infusion of Western technology. This policy brings into focus two issues: (1) expatriation of profits, and (2) investment incentives.

For any agreements, foreign investors can ship out, or sell in China, products they obtain as their share of dividends. Net profits after taxes may

Table 7.1 *(continued)*

Technology	Seller	Buyer	Provisions
Diesel Engineers Technology	Maschinen fabrik Angsburg-Nuerburg (MAN) [West Germany]	China Corp. of Ship-building Industry	Training Chinese technicians.
Steelworkers: service technology	Nippon Steel Corp. (Japan)	Paoshan Steelworks	Dispatch 300 engineers and technicians to aid in start-up operations. Also train over 1,000 Chinese workers in control and operation techniques at Nippon Steel's facilities in Japan.
Industrial equipment: sparkplugs	Smiths Industries (United Kingdom)	China National Technical Corp. (Tech import)	Provide design, machinery, technology, and train Chinese technicians. (This technical cooperative agreement will be in force for a period of 10 years.)
Agricultural machinery	International Harvester (United States)		Through this $7.5 million contract for farm equipment, furnish technical training for the Chinese in the United States as well as in China.

be remitted abroad from their foreign exchange deposit account. But the most intriguing policy is the establishment of Special Economic Zones (SEZs), which provide foreign investors with very favorable conditions.

There are four SEZs, and they are located in three provinces. Two are in Quangdone Province, one in Fugian, and one in Shenshen. The key tenet of the SEZ is that the foreign investor is offered special incentives to set up shop. For example, corporate tax rates are half the national rate in the SEZ: from 30 percent in the rest of China to just 15 percent in the SEZ. Property rents are also much lower (43). However, there is a caveat for all foreign investors—all investment risks are borne by the foreign investor. In addition, any costs associated with feasibility studies are the investor's responsibility.

These issues indicate the extent to which China's ruling party is willing to achieve its modernization program. However, the retrenchment policies and concentration on wholly owned subsidiaries and/or joint ventures may reflect China's *real* ability to absorb and pay for technology.

Ability to Absorb

China's initial overly ambitious buying spree indicates that the greatest barrier to fulfilling its economic goals is the country's ability to absorb technology. Quite often, in attempting to industrialize, LDCs maintain an unrealistic view of that ability (6).

The most vivid example of this dilemma can be seen in the case of Iran. The Shah, armed with billions of petrodollars, also embarked on a massive buying spree of technology. However, the rapid infusion of technology in a traditionally conservative society inadvertently disrupted the social fabric of the Islamic Republic and produced an upheaval that resulted in the overthrow of the Shah, disrupted the transfer of technology, and rendered previous technological advances useless.

China has not escaped the inherent problems associated with technology absorption. Unlike Iran, however, China has not at the same time been plagued by political and social upheaval, but rather by the path taken to industrialize.

Rawski (15) explores some of the problems facing developing countries. Successful implementation of technology transfer should focus on modernizing existing industrial facilities rather than a disproportionate allocation of investment on new turnkey operations. The role of the older, established firms of the importing country is to take the lead in introducing new technicians and modern technology. Typically, these firms are relatively smaller, more manageable, and efficient.

The new Shenyang Machine Tool Works, which employs 5,000 workers, is a case in point. The organization is

swollen and ineffective; technical control . . . [is] highly complicated. . . . The potentialities of the equipment and personnel cannot be fully developed and utilized, and production technology is not likely to advance and improve. On the other hand, strength lies in the older enterprises: with their skilled workers and experienced technical persons and superior development of interenterprise cooperation, . . . Old industry bases and old enterprises . . . find it easier to tackle . . . complicated technical problems than new enterprises and new industry (15).

Concentration on modernizing existing industrialized bases and adding new, large, modern facilities can lead to imbalanced economic growth. In China, local governments and enterprises were given greater authority to initiate new projects and allocate available investment capital. However, local authorities preferred the construction/modernization of small plants in raw materials-producing areas, and in processing and manufacturing sectors.

This construction policy was aimed at exploiting local comparative advantages. The projects were preferred because of their expected high profitability and quick returns. However, the resource requirements of these small plants cut into the supply of raw materials for the traditional production centers, causing larger, modern plants to operate below capacity. The competition of smaller firms resulted in a net economic loss for the nation since the modern plants had advanced technology and produced better quality goods at lower costs. This orientation also increased the prevailing pressures on energy, transportation, and building materials (28).

These economic imbalances and threats to China's economic growth and stability stem from (1) excessive ambition in terms of rapid industrialization (a common denominator in most LDCs), and (2) the apparent inability to assess the internal barriers that inhibit absorbing technology efficiently.

Barriers to Technology Transfer

The ability to absorb is largely a function of barriers to technology transfer. Thus, it is extremely important for U.S. exporting firms to understand the specific factors that are causing these barriers. There are at least seven factors, as depicted in Figure 7.1. Education, industrialization, culture, availability of natural resources, political structure, state of urbanization, and extensiveness of the infrastructure can impede or promote any industrialization program.

Education

Without the availability of a certain level of intellectual capital, a Third World country will have difficulty absorbing high-level technology. In China the education issue is an acute problem. The Great Cultural Revolution of 1966-76, which involved major revolutionary social reforms in the areas of economic policy, foreign trade, and science/education, has left China with a severe shortage of technical manpower: technicians, skilled workers, and so on. From 1966 to 1970, no colleges or universities enrolled students. When they did enroll students, revolutionary education (stressing political consciousness) replaced conventional academics (16). As a frame of reference, the Chinese have attempted to operationalize computer or nuclear technology with a pool of workers from an educational system in which few of the 200,000 university student admissions actually qualify academically.

China has taken steps to increase its skilled labor force externally. The major strategy is patriotic appeal. Graduates, particularly college graduates and people of Chinese heritage working in advanced-level studies, are induced by offers of attractive material awards to return permanently to work in China. As a result, an initial batch of 400 scientists from the United States alone have responded to this call (17). This involvement of overseas Chinese in China's national recovery and development could well give cause to reflect on the extent and level of technology that can be absorbed.

The bleak portrait painted above does have its bright side. College students are now being recruited on the basis of competitive exams, and academic subjects have replaced political ideology as the mainstream of university life. Professors, relieved of the ideology albatross, are being paid for imparting scientific and technological knowledge. In the short run, however, the academically oriented graduates will not make major contributions to modernization goals (10).

The paucity of a technically equipped labor pool is glaringly evident. No less compelling is the shortage of competent managerial personnel. Traditionally, managers were selected on the basis of political orientation, not organizational skills. Furthermore, many firms were staffed by managers who were selected by the employees from a pool of acceptable candidates. These positions, too, were often rotated routinely. Thus, management skills were seldom hewed.

The extent of this problem is revealed by China's insatiable appetite for learning Western management techniques. The Chinese are busy learning everything through contracts with major Western universities around the world, as well as through contacts with Western consulting and accounting firms.

The task of gaining expertise is staggering. Take, for example, determining and measuring industrial firm accountability. China has about 200 auditors for approximately 20,000 production enterprises. They hope to train an additional 300,000 in the future. However, the trainees have little experience with Western accounting techniques and literally must start from scratch (42).

Socialist bureaucrats are earnestly studying capitalist techniques through their own business school. Located at the Dalian Institute of Technology, the B-school acquaints seasoned Chinese managers with the lessons of American business. Faculty are borrowed from major U.S. universities and corporations.

Chinese faculty members are also being retooled to meet the challenges of the modernization program. The orientation is uniquely Chinese, however. "We are not asking them to tell us how to manage our enterprises. Rather, through digestion of their experience, we decide how we want to manage our enterprises." This reflects the Chinese road to industrialization. Professors have been resurrected. Bonuses are paid for absorbing and diffusing scientific and technological knowledge. The bonuses are paid by length rather than by manuscript quality (10).

Industrialization

The actual level of prevailing industrialization, rather than the intent to industrialize, is perhaps the chief determinant of the ability to absorb. When a severe gap exists between the present industrial base and the advanced technology being imported, it may become very difficult to absorb this technology.

Wenlee Ting proposed that, while a nation may encourage

a wide spectrum of transfers, an optimum match between technology transfers and the recipient is governed by the existing technology structure and level of the recipient environment. A technology to be efficiently operational, must be completed by a whole array of supportive and facilitating systems in the environment and such external economics may be absent at the receiving end (18).

China's *People's Daily* underscored this issue recently. It brought attention to the problem of imported technology by asking rhetorically, "must we proceed from China's actual conditions in adapting new technology" (when some big plants without adequate fuel for operation are being left exposed to the elements and are nothing more than showpieces and a major drain on hard currency) (11). The party organ proclaimed that "some comrades" felt it was important to take as a starting point the actual state of international technology and to bring in only the most modern equipment (without regard to China's ability to operate and maintain the equipment) to help modernize Chinese industry. "The practice of the past two years and more has proved that this will not work" (11). (For additional comments on industrialization, see Problems of Technology Transfer.)

The party's vociferous comments on the right road to industrialization is manifest in the cultural barriers.

Cultural Barriers

Coming out of a labor-intensive work culture and going into a proposed capital-intensive work culture poses a readily understandable cultural shock for the indigenous population.

Rapid technology transfer can open up a Pandora's box of cultural, socioeconomic, and ecological problems. Brown has stressed the extent of the cultural and social trauma. "Facing rapid industrialization, centuries of technological progress are being compressed into decades and, in some extreme cases, into years. Herein lies the trauma of the . . . (industrialization process)" (19). Moreover, as Toffler states, the concomitant acceleration or change inevitably subjects individuals to a shattering stress and disorientation (20). Thus, as part of the self-preservation instinct, individuals continue to cling to old cultural values and, therefore, establish artificial barriers to technology transfer and inhibit the modernization process.

Victor Nee has stressed that the Chinese people have not been docile—a legacy of the Maoist emphasis on mass mobilization. Instead of continual class struggle and individual but directed activism, the new emphasis is on social unity and harmony (21). The Chinese leadership is counting on various societal forces to develop strong vested interests that are tied to the success of the modernization program. If the Four Modernizations is successful, it will change the social/cultural face of China. If it fails, Baum suggests that a severe "backlash in the form of a revolution of rising frustration," which emanates from a "revolution of rising expectations," *could* occur, for once expectations are developed by the society they must be met or unrest will result (10).

Revolutionary economic reforms which were instituted to meet rising expectations and develop strong vested interests have backfired. This is because a free enterprise, free-market, profit-oriented policy has been grafted onto the slow-moving, debilitating bureaucracy of central planning. The two systems do not mesh. For example, state pricing, which sets ceiling prices on certain material inputs and low prices for finished products, creates a situation where a poorly managed firm can be profitable. Managers are encouraged to produce high-priced, high-profit goods which consumers cannot afford. At the same time low-priced everyday goods are discontinued because they provide low margins. Therefore, there is no way for prices to reflect real shortages and surpluses. And management behavior is predetermined by economic policy (30).

Labor and labor incentive policies have been tarnished by cultural and social factors. The "right to fire" is inimical to the socialist dictum. Lazy and incompetent workers not only are retained but also are rewarded with bonuses. Factories are rewarded on the basis of percentage increases in profits. As such, the older firms get higher rewards because they grow faster than newer firms. In addition, there is resistance to implementing modern technological equipment since it is the firm's profits which are used to modernize its plants. There are three possible reasons for this behavior: (1) most advanced plants have to import raw material to operate at capacity and thus are open to criticism for draining hard currency, (2) the more advanced the technology adapted, the less manpower the unit making the investment will employ, which gives rise to serious contradictions between increasing labor productivity and full employment, and (3) it reduces the capital available for the workers' bonus pool (45).

Bonuses were instituted to improve labor productivity, but they have not achieved this goal. For example, in 1981 bonuses in heavy industry increased despite a corresponding 3.2 percent decrease in labor productivity (30).

The bonus system has evoked a disconcerting reaction from labor. Workers are more interested in high bonuses without regard to output. Workers at the Shouder Brewery refused to overhaul fermentation tanks on overtime unless their demands for "exorbitant bonuses" were met. But managers also have contributed to the dilution of the stimulative effect of bonuses. The egalitarian notion, a legacy of Maoist China, has caused managers to distribute bonuses equally among workers regardless of contribution.

Firm profitability may please planning officials but may cause turmoil within the firm. For example, a taxi firm that hired six new managers increased the firm's income by 144 percent in just six months. Yet, the firm's old guard made it difficult for the new management team to such an extent that Beijing officials had to intervene to save their jobs (30).

Another and deleterious effect of rapid industrial growth on social/cultural factors is inflation. For three decades inflation has been controlled by maintaining general price stability. However, firms have increased consumer prices, despite the introduction of technology which was to improve quality and cost efficiency. The action has offset increases in consumer income and has stagnated growth in the standard of living. Both are major societal concerns.

Resources

Perhaps the most obvious barrier to technology transfer is related to resource availability. Most imported technology is energy-intensive. If China selects, as it has, technology that makes excessive demands on the available energy sources, that technology is rendered idle.

Chinese officials have admitted to chronic power shortages. This is largely the result of poor management, outdated equipment and know-how, and usage patterns that have led to energy waste (22). These power shortages have impeded the absorption of industrial technology and can be considered a "weak link" to industrialization.

As late as 1977, the Chinese admitted to inadequate generating capacity. Output for 1977 rose nearly 10 percent from 1976 levels, but was due to the start-up of more than forty large- and medium-sized hydro- and thermo-electric-generating units. The Chinese should maintain high rates of growth, but production of electric power will be hardpressed to keep pace with demand (1, 47).

Power-generating units, industry, and mechanization all demand energy sources. And coal and oil are the major energy sources.

Raw coal output in 1977 increased by 10.2 percent compared to 1976. An increase of 19.3 percent was registered for the first half of 1978. But the Chinese plan calls for a doubling of production to 1 billion tons by 1985. This would require coal output to expand at a compounded rate of 7 percent annually. But it seems that the Chinese are setting themselves an extremely ambitious goal. The industry itself is plagued with notoriously low labor productivity levels and technical backwardness. Moreover, one-third of the total output is produced at small mines and pits (46, 47).

Mechanization and the opening of larger mines certainly will increase production, but China is not immune to the ills suffered by the two largest producers of coal—the USSR and the United States. These two giants are finding out that costs, logistics, and the environmental problems of mining more than 500 million tons of coal a year are keeping growth rates much lower. Since passing the 500 million-ton mark, U.S. coal production has increased by only 2.1 percent annually; Soviet production is increasing by 1.4 percent per year (46).

Generating power per ton of coal is extremely low in China. In 1975 (the last year for which reliable figures are available), the United States produced just over 800 kilowatt hours of electricity for each ton of coal consumed. The Soviet ratio was 740, and the Indian about 640. But Chinese generation was just below 300 kilowatt hours of power per ton of coal. Thus, with large increases in production, and the energy demands on it, coal alone cannot supply energy-generating capacity to match the needs of energy-intensive industries (46).

The original blueprint for modernization envisaged oil as an important source of energy for domestic needs and as a source of financing technology imports. Planners have reassessed their initial estimates, however, and have concluded that China's oil potential was too optimistic. Crude oil production decreased over the 1980-82 period rather than increased. Subsequently, the high levels of internal consumption requirements created by energy-intensive technologies have taken their toll on limiting certain technology transfers. They have also reduced anticipated hard currency earnings from exports—a major source of financing modernization.

A prominent example of the extent of China's resource problem concerns the showcase Wuhan Iron and Steel mill complex. After the mill began operations, it operated at only half of its production capacity. This was because of raw material and power supply shortages that were discovered only after construction was completed (24). Other modern production facilities, nicknamed "tigers," because of their high consumption of oil, coal, and power, have remained idle and are good only as high-priced showpieces.

Political System

In China, the political system is, of course, not a barrier to technology transfer, since the modernization program does have the support of the government. Still, the stability or instability and the continuity of a government's policies are concerns for the exporting firm. It could determine the extent of the firm's overseas commitment (25).

For China, political stability is firmly in the hands of the architect of the modernization policy—Deng Hsiao-Ping. To ensure the long-term stability and continuity of these policies, Deng has successfully placed his political associates and cadres in leadership positions throughout the country. Nevertheless, there are rumors of internal discontent with Deng's economic programs (10, 28). One Chinese source told a Western correspondent that "nearly every effort to revise economic, diplomatic and educational policy has encountered opposition from avowed Maoists on the Politburo"(49).

If the struggle over the direction and pace of Deng's modernization plan continues, it could lead to an explosion inside the Politburo, wrecking the party's leadership and unity and inflicting damage on China's foreign and domestic programs. Deng's defeat would mean a return to square one, and possibly a return to Mao's dogma—self-sufficiency (49).

The political scenario cannot neglect the People's Liberation Army (PLA). To restore the prestige of the political organs necessitates the realities of Mao's concept of party control: "Who has the guns and at whom are they pointed" (50). But Deng, by his attacks on Lin Piao, thinks that the army needs to be persuaded of the dangers of conspiratorial activity resulting from too much emphasis on politics. Hua Kuo-feng, however, clings to the Maoist view that the PLA can never be too disassociated from politics. The final confrontation will resolve the issue and determine the life span of the Four Modernizations program.

The question of how best to tackle this problem is paramount. Deng is aware that the PLA commanders have an important role in the formation of national policy and the leadership succession. The Sino-Soviet border conflicts on the Ussuri River, the Sino-Vietnamese debacle, and the instability of Southeast Asia will harden the PLA's stance. Surely, the PLA's demands for the modernization of the army will require not a slice but a wedge of the investment pie. Such a situation will lead to unpleasant ramifications for economic planning and for the extent of technology purchased.

This political scenario reveals the essence of China's internal problems. Any measure of successful modernization (forget the arithmetic of Chinese goals) is predicated on unity of purpose—not on splits on matters of principle and priority.

Even with a strong and stable political system, U.S. firms should be cognizant of the backlash of foreign policy decisions. Amicable relationships can deteriorate quickly as a result of the actions of one of the trading parties. For example, China recently canceled a high-priority port facility expansion project with Holland because of Holland's trading policies with Taiwan (27). This example is atypical, however.

To the Beijing leadership's chagrin, the United States still fosters the two-China policy. However, even with continued arms sales to Taiwan, the recent granting of political asylum to a tennis star and a diplomat, and the imposition of import quotas on some Chinese textiles, Beijing's reaction has been surprisingly mild. The chill created by these actions has not resulted in a boycott or curtailment of any U.S. technology.

Urbanization

The urbanization dilemma is quite real in all LDCs. Transfer of technology and its successful implementation are almost by definition urban undertakings. Thus, if the country does not have a certain level of urbanization and/or does not have the necessary conditions for the urbanization process, it may not be able to absorb the technology successfully.

China's heavy infusions of modern technology into a predominantly rural society can precipitate conflict and tension. One of the problems is the potential of a rural-urban conflict engendered by income discrepancies. This has produced a situation where urban workers have a 20 to 25 percent higher standard of living than the peasants (10).

Mechanization of agriculture creates multiple problems. China has 25 percent of the world's population on 8 percent of the world's arable land. The agrarian villages are overcrowded with unemployed peasants. Mechanization would not produce more on the arable land and would only add to the country's unemployment woes. Thus, large numbers of unskilled peasants would be released into already tight labor markets in the urban sectors. These problems are complicated by the serious political contradiction of an economic policy that stresses labor productivity and full employment (10).

The alienation of the young has also created problems. During the Cultural Revolution up to seventeen million intellectual youths were sent to communes. They have been left out of the modernization program and have been told to stay in the countryside. Moreover, many young people who were promoted to local leadership during that period have been demoted and replaced by the old cadre. The actions have resulted in mass protest demonstrations. These conditions will make it extremely difficult, if not impossible, to transfer technology to thousands of communities that are not equipped or will resist the use of newly transferred technology and will fail to benefit from it.

Infrastructure

Very closely related to the urbanization structure is the infrastructure. The infrastructure means the necessary institutional makeup as well as the necessary physical conditions for transferring technology. For instance, if the country wants to import first-generation communications systems but does not have the necessary institutional structure to generate and disaggregate the information, the transfer of such technology will be impeded. Moreover, if the country is considering importing automotive technology but has neither the roads nor the necessary fuel to operate the vehicles produced, that transfer will again be unsuccessful.

China's infrastructure is backward. The Yinhau news agency has admitted the need for improvements in internal air, rail, road, power, water, and pipeline transport networks before China can adequately absorb substantial levels of new technology (1). Not only is the internal movement of goods and services affected, but also the external system. Past facilities are inadequate. Material handling and storage facilities continue to depress the efficiency of port operations. The railroad system has traditionally been designed as a defense and strategic system, rather than as a commercial system, and this approach is not likely to change. Moreover, without the means for moving resources, industrial development will be slowed. If bottlenecks are to be avoided, the infrastructure will require a massive improvement and expansion program. In addition, China must link the internal system with the external system.

In the present state, the infrastructure is anemic. However, U.S. firms can anticipate the inherent problems manifest in the weak infrastructure, and, possibly, propose a proper remedy within the context of China's goals.

THE TASK AHEAD

U.S. firms can do little about the existing barriers to technology transfer, nor can they change the ability to absorb or willingness to buy. However, American firms are in charge of a most important catalyst, one that is likely to make it possible for them to transfer technology—service and information support. This particular support, at least in the short run, could ease the most obvious absorption problems, such as education, industrialization, and infrastructure. (And it seems China is aware of its deficiencies.)

Although the American firm is not going to educate the Chinese population, it can bridge the gap by providing special information and skills to make up for the deficiency. While a service support system developed in China by the exporting American firm is obviously a stopgap measure and answers only short-run problems, it at least provides the basis for a smooth transition of the technology and its effective utilization for some period of time. During this period the recipient country is also responsible for making some adjustments so that the newly transferred technology will be internally accepted by the populace.

The crux of the thesis presented here is that the American firm can and should take a very active role in transferring the technology. This is much more than just selling highly technical equipment. The U.S. firm must become more cognizant of its capability in providing a smooth transition in the technology transfer process. The support service system of the American firm that can enable China to absorb very complicated technology, albeit temporarily, is extremely valuable. If the transfer, with the aid of the American firm, has been smooth, the recipient country (that is, China) can overcome the temporary nature of this process by deliberate action. This deliberate action involves the Chinese alleviating the barriers to technology transfer.

Given the fact that both parties, that is, the American and Chinese, understand the importance of overcoming the technology transfer barriers and further understand how these barriers can be overcome makes it possible for the technology transfer to endure. This, of course, is the paramount objective in the whole process. In order to cope with the Chinese dilemma, U.S. firms must carefully develop a service and information policy specifically tailored to the needs of the Chinese. Figure 7.2 illustrates the components and the flow of progression of such a system.

Figure 7.2 emphasizes the fact that the support service system has two major components—product and personnel. The system has to keep these two components in proper perspective and effectively balanced.

If the Chinese were to import high-level technology and were not able to utilize it properly, then the whole purpose of exporting would be lost. Thus, the Chinese should not only know how to utilize the newly imported technology but should also develop expertise for the sake of continuity.

Very closely related to the proper maintenance concept is product usage.

Figure 7.2
Industrial Marketing Support Service System

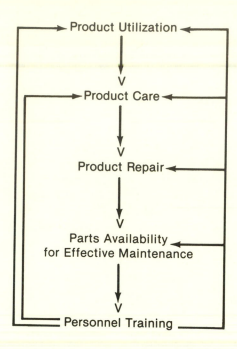

If in the product-use process necessary maintenance is disregarded, the benefits of the technology transfer activity are likely to be nullified. Product care or maintenance has two subcomponents: repair and parts inventory. As the technological product is properly maintained, it will have to be serviced and repaired periodically. In both cases, not only the technical know-how, but also the availability of necessary parts and components to perform the task is extremely important. As maintenance and repair activities take place, the need for parts occurs accordingly. Naturally, without critical spare parts, a highly complex piece of machinery cannot last indefinitely.

Training personnel in order to make the transfer of technology effective is a necessary condition for the total process of transferring technology. As mentioned in the above discussion, in order to utilize, maintain, and repair the highly technical products that are being exported to China, it is of utmost importance that a pool of intelligent and well-trained workers be made available. By definition, such a pool must be developed by the American marketers who aspire to capture a good portion of the vast Chinese market.

SUMMARY AND CONCLUSIONS

While China is still a developing country, it shows vast potential for American industrial exports. In order to be successful in capturing this market, the American marketing professional should understand not only the needs of the Chinese market, but, more importantly, the desire of the existing authority as well.

In order to deliver what the Chinese officials want and to be successful, the American industrial marketer must ensure that a market support system be made fully functional as the technology is being transferred. Without such a system, it will be difficult, if not impossible, to capture a substantial portion of the Chinese industrial market. Development of a marketing support system is a very involved activity; therefore, before American firms make a commitment to China in terms of transferring high-level technology, they will have to develop the details of a fully operational industrial marketing support service system.

REFERENCES

1. Central Intelligence Agency (CIA). *China: In Pursuit of Economic Modernization*. Washington, D.C.: Foreign Assessment Center, December 1978.

2. "China's Chant: Yankee Comeback." *U.S. News & World Report* (December 11, 1978): 35.

3. *Business America* 4, No. 4 (February 1981): 3-4.

4. Angelopoulous, Angelos. *The Third World and the Rich Countries: Prospects for the Year 2000*. New York: Praeger, 1972.

5. Coates, Joseph F. "Technology Assessment: The Benefits . . . The Costs . . . The Consequences." *The Futurist* (December 5, 1971): 33-37.

6. Swannock-Nunn, Susan. "U.S. Business and Transfer of Intermediate Technology: Agricultural Equipment and the Developing Nations." *Journal of Interntional Business Studies* 9, No. 3 (Winter 1978): 63-66.

7. Khera, Inder P. "A Two-Tier Technology Choice Model for Developing Countries." *Proceedings of the Academy of International Business: Asia-Pacific Dimensions of International Business* (December 18-20, 1979): 280.

8. Spencer, Daniel L., and Alexander, Woroniak. *The Transfer of Technology to Developing Countries*. New York: Praeger, 1967.

9. Lee, Jeffrey L. "China-U.S. Trade Growth Slows; New Policies Guide Investment: Prospects Bright for Raw Material and Technology Exports." *Business America* 4, no. 15 (July 27, 1981): 16.

10. Baum, Richard. "A Political Perspective on China's Four Modernizations." *Columbia Journal of World Business* 7, No. 2 (Summer 1979): 33-36.

11. *China Trade Report* 19 (February 1981): 2-9.

12. "China—The Start of a $350 Billion Long March." *Business Week* 2559 (November 6, 1978): 76-78.

13. "An untied, cautious borrower be." *The Economist* (April 7, 1979, p. 271): 112.

14. *Business China* 5, No. 5 (March 7, 1979): 33-38.

15. Rawski, Thomas G. *Problems of Technology Absorption in Chinese Industry. American Economic Review* 65 (May 1975): 383-388.

16. Chen, H. E. "Changes in Chinese Education." *Current History* 75 (September 1978): 74-80.

17. Fitzgerald, Stephen. "Peking's New Pull at the Purse-Strings." *Far-Eastern Economic Review* 100 (June 1978): 100-104.

18. Ting, Wenlee. "Transfer of Intermediate Technology by Third-World Multinationals." *Proceedings of the Academy of International Business: Asia-Pacific Dimensions of International Business* (December 18-20, 1979): 276.

19. Brown, Lester R. "The Social Impact of the Green Revolution." *International Conciliation* (January 1971): 6-8.

20. Toffler, Alvin. *Future Shock.* New York: Bantam Books, 1971.

21. Nee, Victor. "The Political and Social Bases of China's Modernizations." *Columbia Journal of World Business* 7, No. 2 (Summer 1979): 8-15.

22. *Business America* 3, No. 16 (November 11, 1980): 6.

23. *Business America* 4, No. 3 (February 1981): 3-4.

24. *China Trade Report* XIX (January 1981): 8.

25. Cateora, Philip R., and John M. Hess. *International Marketing.* 4th ed. Homewood, Ill.: Richard D. Irwin, 1979.

26. "Some Answers on the China Trade." *Columbia Journal of World Business* 7, No. 2 (Summer 1979): 43.

27. *Business America* 4, No. 5 (April 1981): 3.

28. Chen, Nai-Ruenn. " 'Readjustment' Remains Goal of China's Economic Policy." *Business America* 5, No. 6 (May 31, 1982): 18-21.

29. Quoted in Hill, John S., and Richard R. Still. "Cultural Effects of Technology Transfer by Multinational Corporations in Lesser Developed Countries." *Columbia Journal of World Business* 15, No. 2 (Summer 1980): 40-50.

30. "China Walks the Edge of the Capitalist Road." *Business Week* (October 18, 1982): 80-82.

31. "Official Chinese Output Figures, 1979-1980." *China Business Review* 7, No. 12 (June 17, 1981): 5.

32. "Technology Went Eastwards, But Some of It Was Misdirected." *Euro Money* (September 1982): 335-337.

33. "Technology Transfer: A Policy Nightmare." *Business Week* (April 4, 1983): 94-100.

34. "How Washington Put the Squeeze on Austria." *Business Week* (April 4, 1983): 99.

35. Ting, Wenlee. "A Comparative Analysis of the Management Technology and Performance of Firms in Newly Industrialized Countries." *Columbia Journal of World Business* 15, No. 3 (Fall 1980): 83-90.

36. Roby, Jerry L. "Is the China Market for You?" *Harvard Business Review* (January-February 1980): 150-158.

37. Lasserre, Phillippe. "Training: Key to Technology Transfer." *Long Range Planning* 15, No. 3 (1982): 51-60.

38. Tsurami, Yoshi. "Two Models of Corporation and Internal Transfer of Technology." *Columbia Journal of World Business* 10, No. 2 (Summer 1979): 43-50.

39. Sanders, Sol W. "For China, Another Great Leap Nowhere." *Business Week* (May 23, 1983): 77.

40. "CN to Do China Rail Study." *Spectator*, November 16, 1983, D2.

41. Li, Victor H. "Reflections on the Current Drive Toward Greater Legalization in China." *Georgia Journal of International and Comparative Law* 10 (1980): 71-74.

42. Herbert, Thomas, quoted in Silvesides, Ann, "Chinese Study Techniques of Capitalism." *The Globe and Mail* and *Financial Post*, November 19, 1983, C1.

43. MacDonald, Donald D. "China: The Challenges and the Changes." *Toronto Star*, September 14, 1983, B1-3.

44. "A U.S. Style B-School for Communist Managers." *Business Week* (October 28, 1982): 82.

45. "Peking Watch." *Far Eastern Economic Review* 19 (February 1981): 2.

46. Smil, Vaclav. "Peking Sets Ambitious Targets." *Far Eastern Economic Review* 100 (May 5, 1978): 50-51.

47. CIA, *China*.

48. "Deng Strips Six Maoists of Power to End Reform Opposition." *Phoenix Gazette*, April 25, 1979, F1.

49. Bonavia, David. "Hint of Distant Drums." *Far Eastern Economic Review* 100, No. 25 (June 23, 1978): 19-20.

50. Liu, Leo Y. "The Chinese People's Liberation Army." *Current History* 75 (September 1978): 87.

8

Reverse Technology Transfer: Demarketing Lessons from Less Developed Countries

A. C. SAMLI AND UGUR YAVAS

One aspect of reverse technology transfer is learning how less developed countries (LDCs) manage scarce resources. This chapter explores some of those demarketing lessons. Because there is no precedence for such an undertaking, the authors propose that reverse technology transfer is likely to be resisted by the American public; hence, a regular diffusion process is not likely to succeed. It is, therefore, necessary to devise procedures for reverse technology transfer that are likely to be beneficial to American society.

BACKGROUND

Over the last thirty years the United States and other industrialized countries have been involved in technology transfer to LDCs. During this period, there have been several attempts to develop theoretical models as well as to experiment with specific technology transfer issues.[1] Paralleling these efforts has been a growing interest by the marketing scholars in the diffusion of marketing innovations,[2] such as new products,[3] retailing techniques,[4] branding policies,[5] and advanced marketing expertise,[6] from the United States to other countries. As a result, substantial literature and information bases have been created. In all cases, much has been learned about transferring information from the United States to LDCs.

Now, because of changes in America's economy, some of the information and experience gained in LDCs may be coming back to the United States. The American economy has been going through dramatic changes since the mid-seventies—high costs of energy and food, shortages in a wide variety of goods and materials, and double-digit inflation. These call for changes in the life-styles of American consumers. Americans who had been accustomed to cheap energy to maintain an "energy-affluent" life-style must reorient their thinking about resources consumption, waste, and saving.

Kotler, in dealing with this needed reorientation, has suggested "demarketing."[7] The demarketing strategies to be used in the United States in order to exploit scarce resources more carefully and to eliminate excessive waste may be based on what can be learned from various developing countries whose people have had to exercise frugality throughout their existence. In other words, the recent economic order in the United States calls for a reverse technology transfer where the imparting countries are the LDC's and the recipient country is the United States. It should be noted that, while this chapter will deal only with reverse technology transfer to the United States, the discussion to be presented may have broader applicability because many other industrialized nations are facing similar economic crises due to shortages.[8]

Some researchers have already acknowledged the possibility of transferring marketing innovations from other countries to the United States. As early as 1973, Abegglen and Givens discussed the functions of an innovative Japanese marketing institution, the general trading company, and suggested that establishment of similar institutions here would benefit the U.S. economy.[9]

Sorenson dealt with the reversal of the typical flow of the transfer of marketing know-how to illustrate specifically how American marketers could learn from their European counterparts in regard to new product development, market segmentation, mass merchandising, and speciality retailing.[10] Other marketing innovations which have been exported to the United States include the two retailing institutions of the box store[11] and the hypermarket.[12]

In each of the previous cases, the innovation has come from another industrialized country. No scholar has yet advocated the exploration of reverse technology transfer from underdeveloped countries to the United States. This chapter, therefore, explores two major issues: first, the key lessons to be learned from LDCs in regard to dealing with shortages and the resulting demand-supply imbalances through marketing; and second, the implementation of reverse technology transfer.

LESSONS TO BE LEARNED FROM DEVELOPING COUNTRIES

When Kotler wrote that the year 1973 marked the end of the Glorious Age of Abundance and that shortages were the new byline of the seventies, he set the tone for the problems to be faced.[13] The imbalance between the demand and supply in industries such as oil, chemicals, and natural gas has substantially worsened because producers have reacted by raising their prices. The fact that producers have gained more power indicates that the American market has shifted from being a buyers' market to being a sellers' market. In economies where sellers' markets prevail, the contention is that the role of marketing considerably lessens.[14] However, in the American marketing scene, marketing's role is not decreased. On the contrary, the presence of a sellers' market because of the widespread shortages has necessitated more pointed and efficient marketing and distribution strategies.[15]

This is where the practices and experiences of developing nations may be of value to Americans. In those countries, a sellers' market is the rule rather than the exception. Therefore, both the governments and industrial concerns constantly seek ways to bring demand in line with supply. In essence, their major task is demarketing.[16]

The following illustrations drawn from the authors' teaching and research in developing countries highlight some of the demarketing strategies used in these countries.

EXAMPLES OF SELECTED DEMARKETING STRATEGIES

The Turkish pharmaceutical industry is heavily dependent on the import of raw materials from other countries. Any time there is a decrease or delay in the amount of imported raw materials due to a shortage of foreign exchange and/or government-imposed restrictions, there is naturally a decline in the production of ethical drugs. Consequently, the manufacturers of such items find it impossible to keep up with the demand. Since the prices are set and monitored by the state and since the advertising of ethical drugs is prohibited by law, manufacturers turn to other elements of marketing to curb the demand and/or allocate the existing supply to drugstores.

The most commonly used method involves allocation of supply based on past purchases. This method, in addition to being very simple to operate, is deemed very fair by the drugstores. A few of the manufacturers operating in the Turkish pharmaceutical industry also employ a tying strategy. They limit their sales of scarce ethical drugs only to those drugstores that agree to buy other commodities such as soaps (certain brands) which are not well received by the consumers and thus are not in demand by the drugstores.

The latter strategy has also been used extensively by Turkish companies operating in the foods and beverages industry. For instance, to curb the demand for margarine, one company required that grocery stores buy canned tomato paste. Knowing that tomato paste is a slow selling item, a substantial proportion of grocery stores canceled their orders for margarine. Similarly, especially during the summer months, manufacturers of soft drinks make it imperative that grocery stores and supermarkets buy fruit drinks (slow selling items) before they are allocated cola-type drinks for which a scarcity exists.

Turkish companies operating in glass, glassware, and ceramics industries try to bring supply in line with demand by concentrating on salesmen-related strategies. Their basic strategy is to reduce the size of the sales force either by firing or by forcing some to quit through the restriction of bonuses, premiums, or pay raises. The reduced sales force makes fewer contacts and is able to spend less time with the customers. In addition to stabilizing and balancing demand with supply, companies benefit from this strategy by paying lower compensation to their salesmen.

A different demarketing application is observed in the Turkish motor vehicle industry. To curb the excessive demand for cars, buses, and trucks, dealers require that customers pay anywhere between 30 to 60 percent of the full price of a vehicle in cash as downpayment in order to get on a waiting list. In addition, some dealers do not allow the customers to pay in cash the remaining portion of their debts when their turn comes. Upon delivery, they require the buyer to make the payments in monthly installments at high interest rates. Furthermore, most car dealers require that the customers buy accessories that may amount to almost 25 percent of the base price of a car. These practices certainly help curb demand. However, without the indirect price increases, waiting periods of two or even three years would not be uncommon in this country.

In East European countries, such as Romania, it is necessary to pay the full price before buying an automobile. In Poland the payment must be in hard foreign currency; otherwise, the waiting period becomes very long. Greece has the following practices which make a significant dent in reducing electricity consumption: (1) closing stores, business, and entertainment places during certain hours; (2) turning off street lights during early morning hours; (3) giving preferential rates for electricity used for basic necessities as opposed to luxury consumption; and (4) encouraging the production and distribution of low energy-consuming products.

In East European countries, economic development plans deliberately create supply shortages of consumer goods. On the basis of industrial development and consumer need priorities, these countries deliberately and decisively limit the supply. Consumers are totally conditioned to forming queues in front of businesses and to waiting their turn.

In East European countries there is also a constant monitoring of new products. Thus, products that are too wasteful of energy or too resource-demanding are not allowed to be produced.

A number of other demarketing techniques have been in use in the Turkish textile industry for a long time. In an attempt not to deal with un-profitable small retailers, a majority of the large textile manufacturers in Turkey have diminished place utility by giving priority to those retailers who provide their own transport services. In addition, increasing minimum order sizes has proven successful in the past. This strategy not only permits the manufacturers to handle and process fewer, yet larger, orders but also discourages small retailers who could not afford to buy substantial quantities.

Increasing the price is a logical and probably the easiest method of reducing demand for a product/service. One way to increase price is to charge a fee. For example, a method used to curtail demand for telephone service in Turkey is to charge application fees. There is normally a five- to ten-year waiting period between application for a telephone and installation of the phone in the applicant's residence. Many applicants desiring telephone service turn out to be newborn babies. The application fee, however, has been successful in reducing the demand.

From the foregoing discussion it can be inferred that some specific demarketing strategies are applicable to specific problem areas. Table 8.1 presents the problem areas in which certain demarketing strategies are particularly applicable.

In summary, it should be noted that, while most of these strategies are reasonable and have been field-tested, they all require consumers "to tighten their belts." The key question, therefore, remains—how can these strategies be popularized in the United States? In other words, the format of the reverse technology transfer needs to be determined.

Table 8.1
Demarketing Strategies and Problem Areas Where They Are Most Applicable

Demarketing Strategy	Problem Areas		
	Product Shortages	*Energy Conservation*	*Excessive (overfull) Demand*
Tying agreements	+	−	−
Restricting distribution	−	−	+
Sales force reductions	+	−	+
Price increases	+	+	+
Allocation of supply	+	+	−
Monitoring new products	+	+	−

Key +: Applicable
        −: Not applicable

FORMAT OF REVERSE TECHNOLOGY TRANSFER

Because the United States has had experience with only one-sided technology transfer, namely, from the United States to other countries, there is no information regarding the format of the reverse technology transfer. However, it is logical to hypothesize that the immediate reaction in America will be one of resistance and anger. This reaction stems from what the authors of this chapter call "the permanent consumption hypothesis." The permanent consumption hypothesis is an extension of Milton Friedman's permanent income hypothesis,[17] which purports that, while people have upward flexibilty, they have downward inflexibility. As their income goes up, they very quickly and proficiently adjust to it; however, when their income goes down, they resist the changes and do not adjust readily.

Naturally, the adjustment process is primarily related to consumption patterns and life-styles. Thus, the *permanent consumption hypothesis* could be formulated as follows: individuals aspire to achieve higher standards of living and, hence, easily adjust to having more. However, they resist pressures to lower their standards of living or to having less.

The proposed practices of the reverse technology transfer at first sight may require that consumers give up their higher standards of living. This being the case, there will be great resistance to the reverse technology transfer strategies. Thus, it can be deduced that a standard technology transfer model is not likely to work in the case of reverse technology transfer. Before we begin a discussion of the reverse technology transfer model, a brief explanation of the salient features of the standard technology transfer model is in order.

Standard Technology Transfer Model

Although it may be a misnomer to call any model a standard technology transfer model, most technology transfer models used for LDCs share certain similarities. Such a model is likely to have four stages: search, adaptation, implementation, and maintenance.[18]

In the search stage, ideas and techniques that can be fruitfully employed for the existing problems are explored. The adaptation level involves a consideration of what is needed to apply these techniques in the local environment. The techniques may have to be changed to cater to local needs. The third stage, implementation, deals with the ways and the means that the techniques will be applied. Finally, maintenance is concerned with the necessary continuity in the technology transfer activity. The importance of this stage cannot be overemphasized because without continuity technology is, in essence, not transferred.

The success of a standard technology transfer model lies in the close co-operation of the donor and the recipient. If the policies and priorities of both parties do not match, the chances for a successful transfer are slim. The joint effort between the donor and the recipient has been the key to the success of past applications in transferring technology to developing countries.

The premise that a standard technology transfer model is not likely to work in the case of reverse technology stems from the belief that demarketing practices used in developing countries will receive little, if any, support from the recipients (U.S. consuming public). When the tactics and techniques used in bringing demand in line with supply in developing countries are used in the United States, certain sacrifices and hardships on the part of U.S. consumers will be required. There will naturally be a resistance to such new ideas. Therefore, a model of reverse technology transfer has to begin with efforts to alleviate the inherent resistance. Hendon's[19] model of social adaptation to any innovation is not likely to hold here since this model deals with a slow buildup of resistance. In the case of reverse technology transfer, resistance is expected to be almost instantaneous.

COPING WITH RESISTANCE

Three specific ways of alleviating the initial resistance can be identified: utilizing social institutions; working with individuals themselves; and enacting government regulation.

With regard to the utilization of social institutions, two separate types of institutions can be identified: formal and informal. Formal institutions can be any of the existing institutions such as planning commissions, local offices of consumer affairs, or churches. They can play an important role in passing on the information and in being a part of the attitude adjustment process, both of which are necessary requirements of the reverse technology transfer. Informal institutions, on the other hand, are spontaneously organized groups of people whose specific aim is to facilitate the reverse technology transfer process. It is quite possible and even necessary that certain citizens' groups be organized just for the purpose of spreading information about reverse technology transfer strategies.

Instead of using institutions, people may be influenced individually. Here opinion leaders can play a very significant role. The third option, government regulation or fiat, would obviously be the last resort. If the other two approaches failed, it would be necessary for the government to specify what to do so that the reverse technology transfer would work. This situation would be somewhat similar to the Swedish experience where the government specifically indicates, for instance, the upper limit of the quantity of liquor an individual can purchase at a given time.

Figure 8.1 presents the conceptual framework for a proposed format that may be employed in reverse technology. The format is essentially a variation of Roger's diffusion model.[20] The major modification incorporated here is the inclusion of opinion leaders at every stage of the diffusion process.

It is necessary to reiterate that these three ways of alleviating the original resistance to the reverse technology transfer are not mutually exclusive. They can all be utilized at the same time just as each can be used separately. However, if formal and informal institutional pressures are utilized as the strategy, it may be rather difficult and too costly to influence late majority and laggard groups. Hence, it may be necessary to use certain government

Figure 8.1
A Model for Successful Reverse Technology Transfer

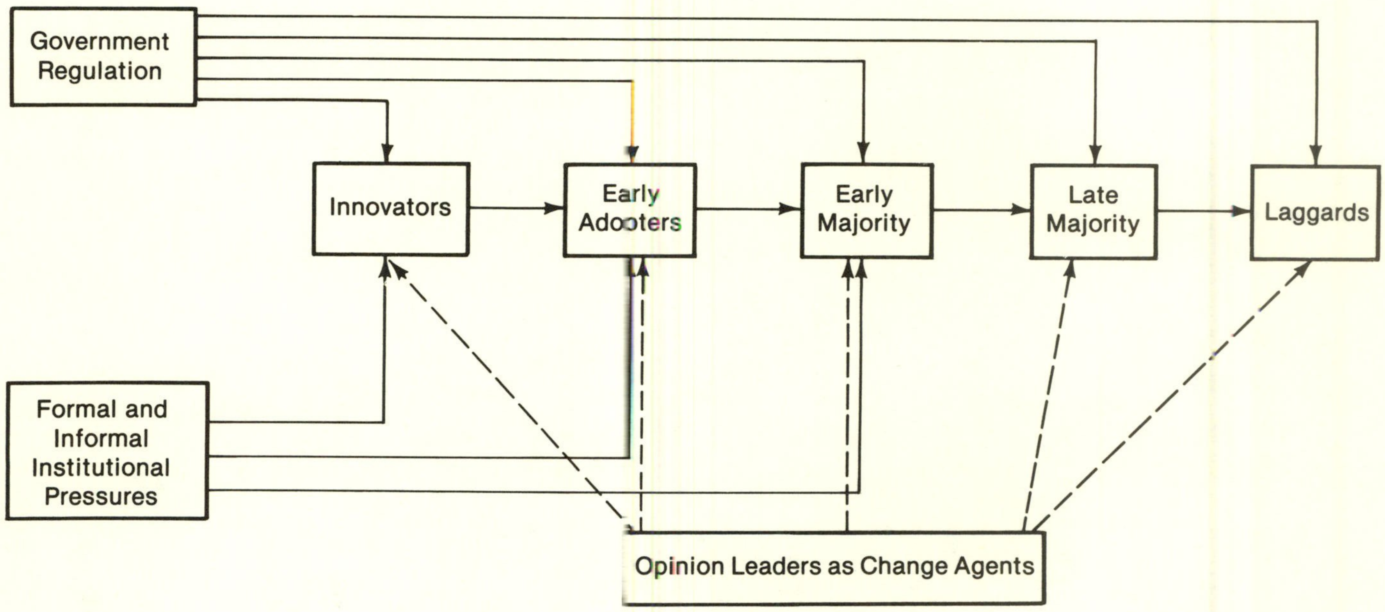

sanctions in order to overcome the resistance. The role that is attributed to opinion leaders in influencing late majority and laggard groups is particularly significant. Opinion leaders will have to function with expertise as change agents in order to overcome particularly strong resistance exerted by these groups. This way government functions could be kept to a minimum.

SUMMARY AND CONCLUSIONS

There is much to be learned from the experience of LDCs that have utilized different demarketing strategies in conserving key resources and streamlining their economic systems.

It is expected that in using a reverse technology transfer process, the permanent consumption hypothesis will be in effect. Hence, the American public wil exhibit substantial resistance to the demarketing strategies. It is necessary, therefore, to consider an atypical technology transfer model. By using the model presented in this chapter reverse technology transfer can be accomplished.

There are many other demarketing areas and many more techniques, but the objective in this chapter is to show that reverse technology transfer is a necessity and that with proper modifications it can be achieved. Much research is needed in the area of demarketing experiences of other countries and how those experiences can be adopted to the American scene because America is going to need reverse technology transfer for its economic future.

NOTES

1. See, for example, Denis Goulet, "Dynamics of International Technology Flows," *Technology Review* (May 1979): 32-39; Simon Teitel, "On the Concept of Appropriate Technology for Less Industrialized Countries," *Technological Forecasting and Social Change* (January-February 1978): 349-369; Jerry R. Ladman, "Technology Transfer to Less Developed Countries," in Subhash C. Jain and Lewis R. Tucker, Jr., eds., *International Marketing* (Boston, Mass.: CBI Publishing Co., 1979).

2. The term *innovation* here is used to mean any thought, behavior, or thing that is new because it is qualitatively different from existing norms. See H. G. Barnett, *Innovation: The Basis of Cultural Change* (New York: McGraw-Hill, 1953), p. 7.

3. See, for example, Phillippe d'Anton. "The Nestlé Product Manager as Demigod," *European Business* (Spring 1971): 44-49; Warren J. Keegan, "Multinational Product Planning: Strategic Alternatives," *Journal of Marketing* (January 1969): 58-62.

4. Edward W. Cundiff, "Concepts in Comparative Retailing," *Journal of Marketing* (July 1965): 47.

5. David Carson, "Marketing in Italy Today," *Journal of Marketing* (January 1966): 14.

6. See, for example, A. Coskun Samli, "Exportability of American Marketing Knowledge," *MSU Business Topics* (Autumn 1965): 39; V. H. Kirpalani, "Oppor-

tunities/Problems in the International Transfer of Marketing Skills/Technology to the Third World," in Edward Mazze, ed., *Combined Proceedings* (Chicago: American Marketing Association, 1975), pp. 285-288; A. Greame Cranch, "Modern Marketing Techniques Applied to Developing Countries," in Boris Becker and Helmut Becker, eds., *Marketing Education and the Real World and Dynamic Marketing in a Changing World* (Chicago: American Marketing Association, 1973), p. 183; Ugur Yavas and W. Daniel Rountree, "The Transfer of Management Know-How to Turkey Through Graduate Business Education: Some Empirical Findings," *Management International Review*, No. 2 (1980): 71-79.

7. Philip Kotler, "Marketing During Periods of Shortages," *Journal of Marketing* (July 1974): 20-29.

8. Ugur Yavas and Glen Riecken, "Exploring Relations Between Cognition and Behavior in Marketing: The Case of Energy Conservation," *Der Markt*, No. 1 (1981): 16-20.

9. James C. Abegglen and William L. Givens, "What Can We Learn from Far East Innovations," in Boris Becker and Helmut Becker, eds., *Marketing Education*, pp. 187-190.

10. Ralph Sorenson, "U.S. Marketers Can Learn from European Innovators," *Harvard Business Review* (September-October 1972): 89-90. Also see Walter Weir, "What Americans Can Learn from Europe-Market Segmentation," *Advertising Age* (February 16, 1976): 41.

11. William Bishop, "Limited-Assortment Stores Multiply, Sell to Cost-Aware Market Segment," *Marketing News*, No. 13 (1978): 1, 3.

12. Barry J. Mason and Morris L. Moyer, *Modern Retailing* (Dallas, Tex.: Business Publications, 1978), pp. 52-53; William R. Davidson, "To Understand Retailing in 1980's, Analyze Firms' Responses to Trends," *Marketing News*, No. 18 (1980): 12.

13. Kotler, "Marketing," p. 20.

14. Saddik Saddik, "An Analysis of the Status of Marketing in Egypt," *European Journal of Marketing*, No. 2 (1973): 77-79.

15. David Cullwick, "Positioning Demarketing Strategy," *Journal of Marketing* (April 1975): 51-57; Nessim Hanna, A. H. Kizilbash,. and Albert Smart, "Marketing Strategy Under Conditions of Economic Scarcity," *Journal of Marketing* (January 1975): 63-66.

16. Ugur Yavas, "The Turkish Marketing Scene: A First Hand Report," *Journal of International Marketing and Marketing Research* (October 1981): 83-95.

17. Milton Friedman, *A Theory of the Consumption Function* (Princeton, N.J.: Princeton University Press, 1957).

18. Samuel N. Bar-Zakay, "Technology Transfer from the Defense to the Civilian Sector in Israel—Methodology and Findings," *Technological Forecasting and Social Change* 10 (1977): 143-158.

19. Donald W. Hendon, "Toward a Theory of Consumerism," *Business Horizons* (August 1975): 16-23.

20. Everette M. Roger, *Diffusion of Innovations* (New York: Free Press, 1962).

9
Technology Transfer from Japan to Southeast Asia

*BRUCE D. HIENEMAN, CHARLES JOHNSON,
ASHOK PAMANI, AND HUN JOON PARK**

Nowhere in the world is the impact of imported Japanese technology greater than in the developing nations of Southeast Asia. Because of its relative proximity and greater cultural similarity (at least as perceived by the West), Japan has often been called the "natural source" of technology for this region. However, the great inroads which Japanese technology has made in Southeast Asia have been due more to their careful effort to adapt the means of transfer and the technology itself to the needs of Southeast Asian nations than to any cultural, geographic, or linguistic advantages. This chapter traces the development of this transfer, and examines its nature and the motivations behind it.

OVERVIEW

Japan is a relatively new face in the realm of technology transfer. For some time the Japanese were more an object than a source of transferable technology. The early 1950s saw the first postwar export of technology by Japan. This export was primarily to the developing countries of Asia and grew throughout the fifties. During the 1960s the export of technology to Asia and beyond grew dramatically.[1] The growth trend, with the exception of some oil shock related slowing, continued into the seventies. Currently, Japan is transferring technology to developing countries as well as to the more advanced nations.[2] In 1979, Japan sent one-half of its technology exports to Asia. Southeast Asia was the major object of this transfer.[3]

The trade structure between Japan and Southeast Asia is highly asymmetrical. Indonesia is a prime example of this relationship, with 27.1% of that country's 1977 imports originating in Japan. In contrast, these imports accounted for only 2.2% of Japan's 1977 exports. Like relationships for the Philippines, Thailand, Malaysia, and Singapore are, respectively, 25.1% / 1.4%, 32.4% / 1.1%, 23.4% / 1.1%, and 1.5% / 2.1%.[4]

*Charles Johnson, Ashok Pamani, and Hun Joon Park were advanced graduate students in international marketing at the University of Hawaii at the time this chapter was written.

THE NATURE OF JAPAN'S TECHNOLOGY
TRANSFER TO SOUTHEAST ASIA

Substantial differences exist between the nature of the technology that Japan transfers to the advanced countries and that which is transferred to the developing countries of Southeast Asia. Technology transferred to the advanced countries generally consists of patented high-level technology. The technology transferred to the developing countries, however, is largely modernization experience and skills associated with standardized production methods.[5] The scope of a typical contract extends to production, management, and, frequently, marketing.[6] The wide variety of production activities transferred to Southeast Asia includes: assembly methods, material selection, machine operation, maintenance techniques, provision of technical data, training of personnel, plant layout, selection and installation of equipment, quality and cost controls, and inventory management.[7]

THE CHANNELS FOR JAPAN'S TECHNOLOGY TRANSFER

Direct investment is the channel through which most of Japan's technology reaches the developing nations of Southeast Asia. The emphasis on direct investment is in contrast to the licensing agreements Japan employs in transferring technology to the advanced nations outside Asia.

In Southeast Asia, the joint venture appears to be the preferred means of entry to the host country. The Japanese prefer to see both parties to the venture involved in the common pursuit of profit, showing responsibilities, and solving managerial and technical problems as they arise.[8] Moves by Southeast Asian countries to restrict imports in favor of local production have also served to promote direct investment and joint venture activity.[9] Moreover, there is a common feeling among Japanese managers that joint ventures are less vulnerable to political risk.[10]

A principal motive for Japan's selection of direct investment as a transfer vehicle is the previously discussed nature of the transferred technology. The Japanese primarily transfer general know-how and industrial experience. Technology of this type requires long-term involvement by the transferor in the production and management activities in the host country. Furthermore, host country recipients often require foreign capital and skilled workers to begin production. In general, however, developing countries do not recognize the economic value of industrial expertise. Expertise is considered a free or normal service that accompanies the purchase of machinery or equipment. The Japanese thus seek compensation for their technology through capital ownership and management of foreign ventures. Compensation is obtained through a long-run strategy that eventually leads to a share of corporate profits.[11]

Generally, Japan's direct investment in Southeast Asia is relatively small in scale compared to that originating in the United States and Europe. The above-mentioned situation may be seen as a reflection of the relatively shorter distance between Japan and the Southeast Asian countries. The suitability of small business to local host country environments is also an important determinant.[12] Furthermore, Japanese investment in the area tends to involve relatively small shares of capital ownership and small-scale or less capital-intensive operations. Overall, the pattern reflects the desire of host countries to participate in ownership and the tendency of the Japanese to invest in labor-intensive industries. This tendency has its origin in the Japanese desire to make use of relatively cheap Southeast Asian labor.[13]

THE ROLE OF LABOR TRAINING IN
JAPAN'S TECHNOLOGY TRANSFER

Since most technology transferred by Japanese firms to Southeast Asia is directed toward labor-intensive industries, labor training is uniquely important in the Japanese strategy of technology transfer. In fact, labor traiing has been called Japan's "inner mechanism of technology transfer."[14]

For the most part, the technologies transmitted in this fashion take the form of know-how or experience with standard, well-proven production techniques. Such technology cannot easily be transferred in the form of capital equipment or transmitted through blueprints or operating sheets. Rather, it lends itself best to personal communication between workers and managers at all levels.

Furthermore, for Japanese firms language problems constitute a particularly difficult barrier to communication. This fact may partially acccount for the Japanese preference for the "learning by doing" approach to technology transfer, as opposed to relying on voluminous printed instructions that may be directed toward a largely illiterate workforce.

The greater reliance of Japanese firms on "transfer through people" is closely connected to their preference for direct foreign investments or joint ventures. A strong correlation has been shown to exist between a donor firm's willingness to become involved in the training of the local firm's employees and the donor's financial interest in the recipient.[15] Training programs are far less extensive in the case of purely technical collaboration agreements. In Table 9.1 the five Asian countries that account for more than half of the total number of trainees sent to Japan (Republic of China, Thailand, Republic of Korea, India, and Malaysia) are also the countries in which Japan's direct investments in manufacturing are greatest.[16]

Trainees are sent to Japan for technical instruction under programs arranged through the Japanese International Cooperation Agency (JICA), a semigovernmental organization. Although the majority of the foreign employees invited by Japanese firms go through these programs, some do not. Hence, these numbers understate the true situation.

Table 9.1
Number of Foreign Trainees Sponsored by Japanese Firms, August 1954–March 1969

Industry	I. Southeast Asia	Okinawa	Republic of Korea	China (Taiwan)	Hong Kong	Philippines	Thailand	Malaysia	Singapore	Indonesia	Burma	India	Ceylon	Pakistan	Others	II. Middle East and Africa	III. Latin America	IV. Other regions	Total
Electrical machinery	438	3	76	105	22	11	42	8	4	13	2	137	3	7	5	5	42	5	490
Communication equipment	188	4	5	14	3	4	40	6	5	19	31	18	1	30	8	25	64	1	278
Home electrical appliances	231	32	20	41	8	5	27	29	5	4	5	33	1	13	8	25	24	4	284
Industrial machinery	315	8	52	67	9	16	48	9	1	63		34		5	3	18	14	3	350
Agricultural machinery	229	19	38	21		29	17	36	2	22	2	16	5	20	2	14	13	4	260
Tool-making machinery	51		13	7		1	9					18		2	1	2	1		54
Textile machinery	37		1	8	4					8	1	3	6	3	3	12			49
Precision instruments	72	2	9	13	2	3	6	8		1	4	23	2	1		6	10	1	89
Other machinery	97	4	21	19	4	3	12	4	1	4	1	19	6	2	2		5	1	103
Automobiles	517	187	32	23	6	22	162	19		13	24			9	13	35	46	6	604
Shipbuilding	95		9	17	13	1	4	12	21	2		5		11		6	22		123
Construction	148		34	63	1		4	9		7		10		4	16	2	23		173
Steel and iron	171	1	9	3		42	19	66	2	2		7		20			2	1	174

Industry \ Region	I. Southeast Asia	Okinawa	Republic of Korea	China (Taiwan)	Hong Kong	Philippines	Thailand	Malaysia	Singapore	Indonesia	Burma	India	Ceylon	Pakistan	Others	II. Middle East and Africa	III. Latin America	IV. Other regions	Total
Nonferrous metals	95		78			1	2	3	1			7	2	1		1	2		98
Chemicals	75		10	21	2	1	3	1	2	7	3	7	3	13	2		7		81
Electric batteries	32		1	2			5	3	1	7		6	7		6	4			36
Stone, clay, and glass	33		8	4		4	1		3		5		1	1	2				33
Mining	32		3	18			1			7	1								32
Textiles	184		14	48	3	7	61	5		5	2	6	17	12	4	53	31		268
Rubber products	99			36			26	30		1					6	2			101
Paper products	30			4		3				1				20	2		1		31
Printing	73		17	30		1	4	10		5				2	4	7			80
Food processing	126		3	16		9	35	43	8	13		1	2	2	2	3	10		140
Railroad stock	14			6			2					6					8		22
Others	89		25	11	2		4	9	8	10	1	3	3	6	7	1	2		92
Total	3,471	260	478	597	79	163	534	310	56	214	82	359	59	184	96	221	327	26	4,045

SOURCE: Japan, Ministry of International Trade and Industry, Trade Promotion Bureau, *Keizai Kyoryoku no Genjoh to Mondaiten* [The Present Status and Problems of Economic Cooperation] (Tokyo, 1969), pp. 490–491.

In addition, the Japanese government is committed to a policy of encouraging and supporting technical training within these developing countries. The following excerpt from its report to the 1977 Colombo Plan Bureau for Co-Operative Economic and Social Development in Asia and the Pacific summarizes the Japanese government's position:

The training of a large number of middle-level technicians is indispensable as an immediate step, not to mention the need for raising the general educational and technological standard. A mere increase in the number of college or university graduates does not adequately serve the purpose. As there are quantitative limits to developed countries' capacity for dispatching experts and accepting trainees, developing countries are obliged to foster locally a great number of middle-level technicians to cope with the increasing demand for technicians. Hence the cooperation of the government of Japan in establishing technical training centres in many developing countries. At present (1977) Japan is cooperating at 22 such centres through the Japan International Cooperation Agency (JICA).[17]

Recently, such Japanese government-sponsored training has focused mainly on agriculture and medicine. The training centers accept trainees not only from the host country, but also from neighboring countries. For example, the Korat Central Research and Training Centre, established by JICA in Thailand, receives trainees from Laos as well as Thailand.[18]

One of the problems the Japanese have encountered with their labor training programs has been the high rate of turnover of the trainees once they return to their respective firms in their home countries. The problem results from the generally severe lack of trained workers in these developing countries. When skilled workers return home, they usually find that they are in high demand and often find more lucrative offers by changing firms. This situation is particularly troubling to the Japanese who are accustomed to a system of lifelong employment with the same firm. Some Japanese firms have countered this problem by sending abroad only trainees who are under contract to work for the sponsoring company a minimum of three years upon their return.[19]

THE REASONS BEHIND JAPAN'S
TECHNOLOGY TRANSFER

The Japanese government has strongly supported technology transfer. Three governmental measures are significant to that transfer. Encouragement has come by way of technology export financing, export insurance, and tax credits on income from technology exports.

Technology export financing is one factor contributing to technology transfer. The Export-Import Bank of Japan gives loans to firms at relatively low interest rates. Rates tend to be in the area of 4 to 7 percent, with maturities ranging from five to fifteen years. The exporting firm's commercial bank is required to lend a minimum of 20 percent of a requested loan. The

Export-Import Bank can conversely provide only 80 percent of a given loan.[20]

Export insurance is a second factor in promoting technology transfer. The Export Insurance Law of 1950 is applicable to technology exports. Exporting firms are protected from default by an importer in return for an insurance premium paid to the Ministry of International Trade and Industry (MITI).[21]

Tax credits on income from technology exports have also served to promote technology transfer. The Japanese have established a system under which 70 percent of corporate profits earned from technology exports are excluded from taxable income. The right to use this tax shield is granted by MITI.[22]

The importance of the private sector in promoting technology transfer should not be overlooked. The Japan External Trade Organization (JETRO) was established in 1958, and the Japan Plant Export Association was created in 1955. Promotion of exports through overseas market research, trade centers, and advertisement is the goal of both MITI and JETRO.[23]

Japan has been called a "museum of materials." The country is endowed with almost every variety of mineral. Quantities, however, are sufficient only for a museum display. The above geological fact is a key reason behind Japan's technology transfer to Southeast Asia.[24]

Postwar economic growth and resulting changes in the industrial structure have led to a rapid growth in Japan's need for critical resources. Japan depends on foreign sources for 88 percent of its needed iron ore, 76 percent of its copper, and 70 percent of its coking coal. Foreign sources also provide 100 percent of the nation's needed petroleum, aluminum, and uranium.[25]

Until recently, Japan experienced little difficulty in obtaining needed resources from abroad. During the 1960s, however, the Japanese demand for raw materials grew to account for a significant share of world consumption. This development prompted Japanese resource industries to expand investment in exploration and development of natural resources overseas. Technology naturally followed this search for a dependable resource base.[26]

Since the 1960s and for the first time in Japan's history, Japan has been experiencing a severe labor shortage. A steady rise in wages, especially among young female workers, has followed this tightness in the labor market.[27] The Japanese, however, decided against following the example set by Switzerland and Germany, that is, importing labor from countries with an abundant labor supply. The Japanese have chosen instead to export industry and technology to the labor-rich areas of Southeast Asia.[28]

THE ROLE OF TRADING COMPANIES IN JAPAN'S TECHNOLOGY TRANSFER

The "Big Ten" trading companies play a major role in Japan's transfer of technology to Southeast Asia. The so-called Big Ten are Mitsubishi,

Mitsui, Marubeni-Iida, C. Itoh, Nissho-Iwai, Toyo Menka, Sumitomo, Nichimen, Kanemat-su-Gosho, and Ataka. The worldwide sales and purchasing networks of the trading companies are of great importance to Japan's trade with Southeast Asia and the world.

Traditionally, the role of the trading companies was to assist Japanese manufacturers in exporting and importing. More recently, however, the companies have begun to perform the same function for developing nations in Southeast Asia which do not have strong international marketing capabilities. Given their extensive worldwide activities, the trading companies are the first to obtain information on demand for Japanese technology. Furthermore, the companies have the best access to detailed information on the supply side of Japanese technology. In general, the trading companies are more interested in the long-term profits associated with direct foreign investment than in brokers' fees for arranging licensing contracts.[29]

PROBLEMS OF JAPAN'S TECHNOLOGY TRANSFER

The transfer of technology from Japan to Southeast Asia has not been without its problems. The sheer size of Japanese investment in the area is a source of conflict and concern. Moreover, cultural and business styles have likewise created problems for the Japanese.

The use of traditional Japanese management techniques in the developing nations of Southeast Asia has often created difficulties. Permanent employment, seniority-based wage scales, and other aspects of the lifetime employment system serve to generate strong cooperation among Japanese workers and substantial loyalty to the firm. Strong group identification, however, also serves to isolate host country personnel. As a result, local management is often denied sufficient responsibility and control.[30]

The isolation of expatriate Japanese has also caused conflicts in technology transfer to Southeast Asia. Because of the culture and cohesiveness of Japanese society, Japanese personnel tend to isolate themselves from local activities. The language barrier is also a problem that cannot be overlooked. Moreover, even if a Japanese manager makes an attempt to overcome the language and cultural barriers in Southeast Asia, he is likely to be rotated out of his post in two to three years. Any desire to mix or become a contributing member of the local society is thus discouraged.[31]

DEALING WITH THE PROBLEMS OF
TECHNOLOGY TRANSFER TO SOUTHEAST ASIA

The Japanese have made an effort to deal with the problems accompanying their export of technology to Southeast Asia. On June 1, 1973, five leading business organizations jointly announced the "Guidelines for Investment Activities in Developing Countries," as follows:

In the world economy of the 1970's, international business activities in all their many aspects, including investments, are bound to grow and expand with increasing vigor. But as the degree of interdependence among nations grows stronger and the interplay of needs and requirements becomes increasingly complex, the time honored theories of economic liberalism are inadequate to meet the demands of the new times. New approaches, though within the context of free enterprise and free competition, are called for in order to maintain world peace and to ensure stability in the lives of all people. It is in this tide of the world economy that the overseas economic activities of Japanese enterprises will unfold themselves on varied fronts. In the developing nations, especially, investments must be promoted in a manner acceptable to the host country under the improved investment environment created by it to the end of contributing to its long-term development and and to the enhancement of the well-being of its people. It is incumbent on each investing enterprise to observe local conditions, conventions and practices and to endeavor to cultivate and establish the entrepreneur spirit founded on the principle of self-responsibility.[32]

A portion of the guidelines established for technology transfer to the developing countries concerns the basic posture of direct investment. Investments should be undertaken in a manner that will insure the long-term growth and benefit of the investor and the host country. The investor should seek to become an integral part of the community.

The guidelines for developing countries also make reference to employment and promotion in the host country. The investor is expected to make an effort to employ and promote host company personnel. Working conditions and the health and safety of local workers are also of concern.

The Japanese have also established guidelines dealing with education and training. In order to insure the successful transfer of technology, local personnel must be given the opportunity to acquire knowledge and skills. As detailed earlier, the Japanese commitment to this point is made through on-the-job training and training in Japan.

The Japanese have also made a commitment to fostering related industries. The desire is to foster the international division of labor, improve the balance of payments for the host country, and develop local industry. To this end, the investor is encouraged to use the machinery, parts, and equipment of the host country whenever possible. The extension of necessary technical guidance is also an expectation.

Cooperation with host industries is also a part of Japan's foreign investment policy. Coordination with host country firms is considered essential to prevent concentration in specific industries and areas that could cause local economic problems. The commercial practices and distribution channels of the host are to be respected to the extent possible.[33]

SUMMARY AND CONCLUSIONS

Japan is currently the major source of technology for Southeast Asia. The Japanese have been highly successful in packaging mature technology for export to the developing countries. Industrial know-how and expertise are the primary exports, and direct investment is the most commonly used channel for delivery. The extensive development of local labor is also a vital link in the process. Government incentives, desire for a secure resource base, and the need for an industrial labor pool will continue to encourage technology transfer by the Japanese. The giant trading companies will remain an important force in that transfer.

Japan is in a unique position in regard to technology transfer. Japanese economic development was largely accomplished through imported technology from the advanced nations. Japan has had many recent years of experience in training workers and adapting processes in order to work with and build on foreign technology. The Japanese are thus in an excellent position to aid the developing nations of Southeast Asia in their quest for economic development.

The current economic "stars" of the Third World include Singapore, Taiwan, Hong Kong, and South Korea. These countries have to a large extent developed with technology imported from Japan. John Naisbitt, in his book *Megatrends*, points out that the Third World has begun to take up most of the world's industrial tasks. Naisbitt also points out that the Japanese are getting out of basic industries such as steel and shipbuilding. The Japanese recognize that in the future the South Koreans will make better steel and the Brazilians better ships.[34] Japan is thus a party to world-wide specialization and evolution. Japan developed its industrial base while the then advanced nations moved into high-technology, service-based economies. The industrial base has now begun to shift to the Third World, with a significant portion in Southeast Asia.

This trend is clearly going to continue, with Japan as the major supplier of technology and industrial know-how. From a longer term perspective, it seems likely—or perhaps inevitable—that Japan will one day be a major purchaser of industrial products from these very countries whose industrialization it helped so greatly to bring about.

NOTES

1. Terutomo Ozawa, *Transfer of Technology from Japan to Developing Countries* (New York: UNITAR, 1981), p. 3.

2. Mitsuhiko Yamada, "Japan's Direct Overseas Investment," *Journal of Japanese Trade and Industry* 5 (September 20, 1982): 18-23.

3. "Japan's Technology Trade," *Focus Japan* 58 (September 1981): 558-563.

4. Saburo Okita, *The Developing Economies and Japan* (Tokyo: University of Tokyo, 1980), pp. 264-265.

5. Ozawa, *Transfer of Technology*, pp. 3-6.

6. Ibid., p. 40.

7. Ibid., pp. 3-6.

8. Ibid., p. 10.

9. Ibid., p. 35.

10. M. Y. Yoshino, "Japanese Foreign Direct Investment," in Isaiah Frank, ed., *The Japanese Economy in International Perspective* (Baltimore: Johns Hopkins University Press, 1975), pp. 261-262.

11. Ozawa, *Transfer of Technology*, p. 40.

12. Saburo Okito, *Japan in the World Economy* (Tokyo: Japan Foundation, 1975), p. 146.

13. Ozawa, *Transfer of Technology*, pp. 7-10.

14. Ibid., p. 35.

15. V. N. Balasubramanyan, *International Transfer of Technology to India* (New York: Praeger, 1973), p. 72.

16. Ozawa, *Transfer of Technology*, p. 36.

17. Colombo Plan Bureau, *The Colombo Plan* (Colombo: Colombo Plan Bureau, 1978), p. 100.

18. Ibid., p. 102.

19. Ozawa, *Transfer of Technology*, p. 36.

20. Ibid., p. 42.

21. Ibid.

22. Ibid.

23. Yoichi Okita, "Japan's Fiscal Incentives for Export," in Frank, *The Japanese Economy*, pp. 225-226.

24. Yoshino, "Japanese Foreign Direct Investment," p. 252.

25. Ibid.

26. Ibid.

27. Ibid., p. 263.

28. Okita, *The Developing Economies*, p. 145.

29. Ozawa, *Transfer of Technology*, pp. 31-32.

30. Okita, *The Developing Economies*, pp. 147-148.

31. Ibid., p. 148.

32. Ibid., p. 152.

33. Ibid., pp. 153-156.

34. John Naisbitt, *Megatrends* (New York: Warner Books, 1982), pp. 60-62.

10

Transfer of Technology from Developed to Developing Countries: Some Insights from Turkey

ERDENER KAYNAK

The years following the Second World War brought a major change in the evolution of economic thought. Dynamic and controversial problems of economic growth received increased attention from economists, as nations faced the problem of reconstruction and, at the same time, of diversifying their economies.[1] An important aspect of the international economic order that followed has been the extensive flow of technology between industrialized countries. However, the technological gap between industrialized and developing countries has continued to widen.

The developing countries have been struggling with the problem of increasing the rate of their economic growth. Developing countries, as part of the solution, have looked to the transfer of technology from developed countries. Thus, technology transfer is now taking place at a rapid pace between enterprises (public and private sector) in industrialized countries and developing countries. Technology transfer involves a number of problems. One set of problems concerns countries with an adequate and technical base, who are therefore capable of absorbing and building on the introduced technology. Another set involves some underdeveloped countries which require a different analytical approach because of their limited technical capability.

In developing countries the inflow of technology is often achieved through foreign investment. Modern industrial and technological techniques and processes can, however, be acquired independently of foreign investment. Technology is now being transferred increasingly through joint ventures with minority foreign equity and through licensing agreements.[2]

DEFINITIONS

The term *transfer of technology* can be broadly defined as the transmission of know-how to suit local conditions, with effective absorption and diffusion both within a country and from one country to another. Technology denotes the sum of knowledge, experience, and skills necessary for manufacturing products and for establishing an enterprise. The term *technology license agreement* refers to communication on technology according to agreed commercial terms. Such agreements usually cover license rights and could also include the provision of various technical services and supply of materials. In developing countries technology covers not only the specific process of manufacturing technology but also knowledge and expertise necessary for setting up a plant. The term *composite technology* is used here when various types of knowledge and expertise are involved.

TRANSFER OF TECHNOLOGY BETWEEN INDUSTRIALIZED COUNTRIES

Technology license has been the major form through which transfer of technology between enterprises in industrialized countries has taken place. It confers the right to use patented technology for a manufacturer and to communicate related know-how on mutually agreed terms. In most cases, technology license is the result of a transaction between two enterprises with little or no interference by governments. An exception is Japan where contracts providing for technology payments beyond a certain level require government approval.

Recipient enterprises in developed countries normally have an established infrastructure and technological base, and their objective in acquiring technology is to cover specific gaps in their technological knowledge. The licensee is enabled to use new techniques and processes it would otherwise have not been able to employ either because of lack of knowledge of specialized techniques or because of patent or trademark protection. For the licensors of technology the advantages of license receipts consist of downpayments, periodic cash royalties, and dividend returns. Technology payments take the form of capital, sales of prototypes, and components. The licensor receives income without additional capital expenditure.

The greatest outflow of technology has been from the United States largely because its large multinational corporations are so advanced technologically. As a result, the United States has been the main recipient of payments for technology, to the extent of over 50 percent of all such payments in the last two decades. At the same time, technology has also flowed into the United States, mainly from Western European countries. Although there has been extensive inflow of technology to enterprises in Western European countries, Japan accounts for the most significant increase in payments for technology. Japanese payments have risen at the rapid rate of about 15 to 18 percent per annum since 1957. Table 10.1 provides the values of such technological transactions between U.S. and Western European countries.

Table 10.1
Value of Transactions Between the United States
and Western Europe, 1957-73

License & royalty payments	$ 264 million
Investments by U.S. affiliates	1,860 million
Sales of U.S. affiliates	14,357 million
Import of produced goods into Europe	5,311 million

SOURCE: "The Impact of Changes of the International Environment on International Business," *Journal of Business Administration* 7, No. 1 (Fall 1975): 1-21.

Similarly, Table 10.2 provides the details of payment made to monopolies in the United States for patents, licenses, and so on, as well as payments made by American institutions to monopolies in other countries.

Table 10.2
Payments to Monopolies in the United States
and Other Countries, 1966-73

Year	Payments to Monopolies in United States	Payments from United States to Monopolies in Other Countries
	Million $	Million $
1966	1,383	140
1967	1,534	166
1968	1,700	186
1969	1,894	221
1970	2,203	225
1971	2,491	241
1972	2,760	276
1973	3,200	335

SOURCE: S. Turnbull, "Multinationals, Fading Out with a Profit," *Development Forum* 2, No. 5 (June 1974): 3.

Table 10.2 makes it abundantly clear that the United States has received a larger share of payments from abroad than its payments to other countries.

TECHNOLOGY TRANSFER TO DEVELOPING COUNTRIES

The rate at which technology is actually transferred from developed to developing countries falls far short of what is needed.[3] Direct payments from these countries for the right to use patents, license know-how, and trademarks represent only a small proportion of total payments for technology. Nevertheless, the flow of technology is expected to increase substantially in the coming years.

Developing countries have a greater awareness of the possibilities of acquiring technology and know-how from abroad, and of the need to acquire this technology in order to produce on an internationally competitive basis. With the growth of manufacturing enterprises in these countries, an increased flow of specialized knowledge through technology licenses can be assumed. In India, for example, annual payments for technology averaged over $140 million from 1967 to 1975, while payments made by certain Latin American countries such as Mexico, Brazil, and Argentina were even higher. A similar increase took place in most developing countries with a substantial rate of industrial growth.[4]

Traditionally, technology transfer to developing countries, largely in the form of direct foreign investment, has taken place in the extractive sectors like petroleum, mining, and export agriculture. Until the end of the 1960s, the share of stock of foreign investment was quite high, being as high as one-half, compared with about 30 percent in manufacturing. In recent years, additions to this stock have been dominated by manufacturing, partly because of policies adopted by the developing countries.[5] Table 10.3 shows the stock of foreign capital investment for developed and developing countries.

Table 10.3

Foreign Capital Investment for Developed and Developing Countries

	Developing Countries		Developed Countries		Total	
	Mil $	*Pct.*	*Mil $*	*Pct.*	*Mil $*	*Pct.*
Foreign capital stock	39	25	114	75	153	100
Foreign trade volume	123	20	490	80	613	100
G.S.M.H.[a]	435	18	1,937	82	2,372	100
Foreign capital as percentage of GSMH		9		5		
Foreign capital volume as percentage of foreign trade volume		31		23		

SOURCE: J. K. Freeman, "Channelling Funds for Development," *Columbia Journal of World Business* (Spring 1973): 66-71.

[a]GSMH—Goods sold that are manufactured at home country.

Having looked at the overall status of the foreign investment stock, let us evaluate the inflow of foreign capital and profit transfers from Turkey (see Table 10.4).

Table 10.4
Inflow of Foreign Capital and Profit Transfers, 1970–75 (Million US $)

	1970	1971	1972	1973	1974	1975
Foreign capital	58	45	43	79	88.1	304.8
Profit transfers	33	36	35	35	71.1	36.3
Relative rate (%)	56.9	80.0	81.4	44.3	80.2	11.2

SOURCE: "Treatment of Foreign Capital in Turkey," Unpublished paper by Recep Yuksel Altug, Istanbul, 1976.

The total amount of inflow for 1970-75 was $617 million, while the amount of profit transfers was $245 million. The inflow after 1973 shows a relative annual increase. However, the foreign capital inflow into Turkey has not made a satisfactory contribution, closing the resource deficits in the financing and development-oriented investments.

THE TECHNOLOGY REQUIREMENTS OF DEVELOPING COUNTRIES

The form of technology transfer to developing countries is different from that between the industrialized countries. Enterprises in developing countries acquire composite or package technology rather than specific know-how covered by patents or trademarks, which is the usual form of technology transfer between industrialized countries. The reason is that the internal level of knowledge and expertise in manufacturing is usually lower in developing countries; consequently, the transfer of any specific process or product technology must often be accompanied by technical assistance. Thus, technology transfer to developing countries relates both to the establishment and the operation of an industrial enterprise. A manufacturing enterprise in a developing country is normally established through the following stages:

1. Preinvestment studies. including preparation of a feasibility study.
2. Basic and detailed engineering, including preparation of machinery specifications, plant design, and factory layout.

3. Selection of equipment, plant construction, erection and installation of machinery, and start-up of plants.

4. Acquisition of process on manufacturing technology.

5. Technical assistance during the postinstallation period, including training programs and management assistance.[6]

Some of these stages overlap, but it is necessary to define very clearly the various functions and reponsibilities at each stage. Foreign technological expertise is required at more than one of the stages. In many cases, feasibility studies have to be done by foreign agencies, while basic engineering services, and even relatively conventional process technology, must usually be obtained from abroad. In some cases, local expertise is nonexistent, even at the construction stage, and so plant and equipment are installed by foreigners.

CHANNELS FOR INFLOW OF TECHNOLOGY

The Third World countries need capital as much as technology and management know-how. Direct foreign investment, which offers the prospect of all three in one complete package, appears most attractive to some, while in other cases, the country may only need some elements of the package. In the latter case, the cost of the domestic resources that must be allocated to supply the replaced elements needs to be considered.[7] There is ample evidence of this practice in the computer and microelectronics industries.[8]

Before we proceed further, we should look at the global technical balance of payments in 1977 (see Table 10.5)

Table 10.5
World Technical Balance of Payments, 1977 (by percentage)

World Technical Exports		World Technical Imports		Percentage Difference
United States	57	United States	12	+45
England	12	England	11	+ 1
West Germany	6	West Germany	14	− 8
France	5	France	5	− 6
Other West European countries	18	Other West European countries	25	− 7
Japan	1	Japan	13	−12
Other developed countries	X[a]	Other developed countries	6	− 6
Developing countries	X[a]	Developing countries	8	− 8

SOURCE: *Turkish Engineering News* (January 1977): 34.

[a]Less than 1 percent.

Foreign Investment

The flow of technology to developing countries has been an integral part of direct foreign investment. A significant flow of new techniques and processes has followed in the wake of foreign capital investments made largely by multinational corporations which prefer a more capital-intensive technology. These corporations have invested in developing countries in order to protect the existing market, to create new markets, to bypass prohibitive barriers and import restrictions, to take advantage of cheap labor and skills, and to discover or protect raw material sources. Table 10.6 shows the number of affiliates for multinational corporations of various countries operating in both undeveloped and developing countries. Within the group of developing countries, a breakdown is given according to the region.

Table 10.6
Multinational Corporations of Selected Developed Market Economies:
Number of Affiliates and Distribution by Area, 1968–1969

| | | Distribution of Affiliates by Area | | | | |
| | | World (in %) | | Developing countries (in %) | | |
Home Countries	Minimum Number of Affiliates	Developed Market Economies	Developing Countries	Africa	Western Hemisphere	Asia
United States	9,691	74.7	25.3	8.3	72.8	18.8
United Kingdom	7,116	68.2	31.8	40.0	28.5	31.5
Federal Federal Republic of Germany	2,916	82.2	17.8	21.8	49.9	28.3
France	2,023	59.7	40.3	66.6	24.1	9.2
Switzerland	1,456	85.7	14.4	15.8	60.3	23.9
Sweden	1,159	83.4	16.6	10.4	66.7	22.9
Netherlands	1,118	72.6	27.4	27.8	47.4	24.8
Belgium	594	69.7	30.3	69.4	21.7	8.9
Italy	459	67.3	32.7	30.0	56.0	14.0
Denmark	354	84.8	15.2	27.8	35.2	37.0
Norway	220	84.6	15.5	47.1	26.5	26.5
Austria	105	81.0	19.0	5.0	50.0	45.0
Luxembourg	55	85.5	14.5	37.5	62.5	—
Spain	26	73.1	26.9	14.3	85.7	—
Portugal	8	50.0	50.0	75.0	25.0	—
Total	27,300	73.6	26.4	29.3	47.9	22.8

SOURCE: Centre for Development Planning, Planning, Projection and Policies, Department of Economic and Social Affairs of the United Nations Secretariat, based on *Yearbook of International Organizations*, 13th ed., 1970-71.

Many developing countries have been becoming increasingly aware of the total cost of investments by foreign multinational corporations which normally operate through their branches and/or wholly owned subsidiaries. The outflow of profits and dividends, together with the fees, royalties, and other remittances to patent companies and payments for goods and components imported, have been of a very high order. There has also been a growing feeling in these countries that ownership and control should be with the nationals of the country. Consequently, foreign equity holdings are often limited to a certain percentage. In countries like India, Iran, and Mexico, foreign majority ownership is not usually permitted with respect to new investment. In India, foreign technology is permitted for certain industrial sectors, but without any foreign capital participation. In underdeveloped countries, heavy restrictions have been imposed on foreign investments as the permissible pattern for foreign investment differs from country to country.

A country's policies with respect to foreign investment have considerable impact on the form of technology acquired. In cases where foreign investment in industry is regulated and local entrepreneurship exists, technology licensing is increasingly being used. Experience in both Japan and India corroborates this trend. The flow of technology is often treated as an integral part of investment in foreign branches or wholly owned subsidiaries.

In many cases a substantial degree of foreign capital ownership is a prerequisite for technology transfer. Highly technical processes and techniques, such as for the manufacture of computers, electronic products, sophisticated electrical equipment, or certain chemical products, may not be available to developing countries unless the owner is allowed at least controlling capital ownership of the enterprise. The method for technology transfer between the parent company and the branch or subsidiaries may differ considerably. When the parent company has full control over the branch or subsidiary, it makes no specific charge for supplying technology. It ensures a technology flow which is considered adequate to meet the latest requirements. In other cases, the foreign subsidiary is required to contribute to the parent company's research and development activities by making a small percentage payment against total turnover. Such payments, which are not often covered by normal license agreements, should be viewed differently from technology agreements between enterprises that do not have a close investment relationship because the licensee enterprise lacks the element of choice.

Research and Development (R&D)

Some developing countries undertake R&D in some form, but few have well-defined and properly organized institutions for the management and coordination of such work. R&D has of late been recognized as an essential tool for the expansion of the national economy. Developing countries spend a very small portion (from 0.2 to 0.5 percent) of their respective GNPs on R&D and not much more than that on the followthrough activities required to reap the benefits. However, the question of building up an R&D structure should be considered seriously, and an appraisal should be made of what is required of it, what it is expected to do, and how. Nevertheless, it is essential that R&D institutions be properly planned and operated. For a description of the types of R&D organization found to be most effective in various countries, see Table 10.7.

Technology License Agreements and Joint Ventures

Foreign direct investment in developing countries has generally been in the form of wholly owned subsidiary corporations. Recently, however, an increasing number of new investments have been joint ventures involving shared ownership between local and foreign partners. There are various factors contributing to the growth of joint ventures. Developing countries may pass legislation either prohibiting total foreign ownership or making incentives conditional upon a certain degree of local ownership. But many foreign investors have become increasingly aware of the advantages of sharing ownership with local partners, be they private or governmental. These advantages include tangible contributions such as land, capital, trained personnel, and familiarity with local markets, suppliers, and conditions of doing business. Some intangible benefits include the goodwill engendered with employees, customers, and the government, and the resultant decreased likelihood of nationalization or any discriminatory legislation. Thus, the number of joint ventures with minority foreign holdings is growing fairly rapidly.

Depending on the overall investment capital in a developing country and on the size and profitability of the market, foreign investors are becoming increasingly willing to participate in equity capital on a majority basis *if* majority foreign ownership is not permitted. Joint ventures with a foreign capital participation of less than 51 percent assumes considerable significance. Majority capital ownership by nationals ensures that various commercial aspects of acquisition of technology will be considered from the point of view of the licensee enterprise. To avoid any possible conflicts, it is highly desirable that both partners enter into a formal agreement for the transfer of technology. Such an agreement should describe the responsibilities, rights, and liabilities of both parties, the details of the technology to be transferred, and the terms and conditions of the transfer. The level of foreign equity participation in a joint venture will depend on the amount of technical assistance that may be required from the foreign licensor in production, management, and marketing including exports. The extent of foreign investment should be reflected clearly in the terms of the agreement.

Table 10.7
Principal Types of Industrial R&D Organizations In Market-oriented Countries

Private Sector In-House R&D	Independent Contract Research Institutes	Research Associations (RA) Cooperative Research Organizations (CRO)	Quasi-governmental R&D Organizations Operating Mono-Industry Laboratories	Autonomous State-aided, Multidisciplinary Research Institutes	Government-controlled Industrial Research Institutes
North America	North America (Battelle, Stanford, A.D. Little, etc.)	Western Europe	Bangladesh-BCSIR	Iran-ISIRI South Korea-KIST	Indonesia, Thailard ministries of industry
Western Europe		230 RA	India-CSIR		
Asia Japan India Pakistan	Western Europe (Battelle, IRDS, Huntingdon, Fulmer IRDC, Inveresk, etc.)	150 CRO in 12 countries Also a few RA	Pakistan-PCSIR	Malasia-SIRIM Singapore-SISIR Sri Lanka-CISIR Thailand-ASRCT	Japan-AIST (mainly background R&D)
Latin America Argentina		and CRSs in India	Australia-CSIRO	Argentina-INTI (-IPT)	Egypt-National Research Centre
Brazil Mexico	India (Sri Ram)	South Africa	New Zealand-DSIR South Africa-DSIR	Brazil-CETEC Colombia-IIT Guatemala-ICAITI Trinidad-CARIRI Ghana-FPRI Nigeria-FIIR Sudan-IRI Turkey-TUBITAK	

SOURCE: "Guidelines for Development of Industrial Technology in Asia and the Pacific," 1974, United Nations, Bangkok.

Foreign investors argue that capital investment by the licensor and payments for technology should be considered separately as the first relates to capital, while the second represents payments for specific know-how. This argument, of course, is quite valid as it may not be appropriate to insist on substantial reduction in payments for technology on account of foreign equity participation as this attitude would discourage foreign investment.

METHODS FOR TRANSFERRING TECHNOLOGY

Transfer of technology (not necessarily involving foreign equity participation) can take different forms, depending on the kind of technological assistance needed.[9] Technology can be transferred through:

1. Employment of individual foreign experts.
2. Arrangements for supply of machinery.
3. Technology license agreements.
4. Technological expertise and assistance in different stages of project implementation.

A combination of two or more of these methods is often used, resulting in transfer of composite technology comprising various elements of technical knowledge for project implementation and manufacturing. The turnkey project is the most comprehensive of such combinations.

Individual Experts

This device is used quite often but is not sufficiently publicized. If a competent individual expert can be found, he or she will transfer technology at a relatively low cost. Enterprises in developing countries have been acquiring simple and unpatented manufacturing techniques and processes by employing an individual expert. This method is generally suitable only for small-scale and medium-sized projects in various industries.

Supply of Machinery

Contracts for supply of machinery and equipment normally provide for the transfer of operational technology pertaining to such equipment. This is normally quite adequate for manufacturing purposes, not only in small-scale projects but also in large-scale industries including cement, textiles, and labor where the nature of technology is not very complex and where no proprietary techniques or processes are involved. In some cases, provision is made even in machinery-supply contracts for preinvestment studies and for extensive training facilities for local personnel. Payments for such services are either provided for separately or are included in the machinery supply prices.

Technology License Agreements

Licensing covers the broad spectrum of permissions that are granted for the use of patents, technology, and trademarks, regardless of whether an equity relationship exists between the licensee and licensor.[10] Of the various systems of transmission of technology, licensing is the most versatile as it offers flexibility in the choice and opportunity for the source firm and the receiving institution to accommodate their individual needs through negotiation.

The transfer of manufacturing technology which forms the substance of technology license agreements between enterprises in industrialized countries is assuming increasing significance in many developing countries, particularly in those countries where the technological base is already fairly diversified. The need for diversified technical knowledge, much of which is patented, becomes more important at later stages of manufacture. Many enterprises wish to avail themselves of foreign trademarks that make products easier to market.

A technology agreement enables a foreign licensor who may be unwilling to risk his or her capital, or who is not allowed to invest on acceptable conditions, to reap substantial returns in the form of fees, royalties, and profits from assured sales of components and intermediate products. In such cases the developing country should carefully consider the provision of the technology agreement to ensure that the acquired technology is appropriate to needs, that the cost of acquisition is not disproportionately high, and that the licensee can absorb the technology within a reasonable period.

Entrepreneurs in developing countries who wish to acquire foreign technology have to approach the foreign manufacturer when the manufacturing technology is covered by patents or when know-how is confidentially held. Specialized technical processes are often linked with specific plant designs and engineering. In such cases, the entrepreneur from a developing country, who has only limited experience with licensing agreements and insufficient knowledge of the technical implications and cost of the various parts of the technological package, can find it difficult to arrive at a satisfactory arrangement at a reasonable cost.

International license agreements may be divided into the following major categories.[11]

1. Patent Licenses: Patent licenses are used for a specific process or method of manufacture, like a metal finishing process, or for a specific apparatus, product, or design coverage. A specific apparatus with an essential element which is patented or a refinement of a production process which is patented are more

saleable than those which are not. A patent license can be a combination of these two types and used to achieve a complete and marketable product.

2. Know-how Agreements: Such agreements cover information that may be classified and thus difficult to obtain. They may cover various processes, formulas, and industrial techniques. Those agreements are as important as patent agreements and often greater in value than trademark licenses.

3. Technical Assistance Agreements: These agreements involve supply of scientific assistance, engineering services, training, and management guidance to the licensee. These aspects are sometimes in the know-how agreements.

4. Trademark and/or Copyright Licenses: These licenses cover certain registered and proprietary identification creations, and such licenses can be realized without concurrent patent or know-how coverage.

5. Miscellaneous Agreements: This category includes basing, franchising, sales, and service representations. Their usefulness depends mainly on local laws and regulations.

Let us now appraise and compare licensing agreements in some of the developing countries. Table 10.8 compares licensing agreements in India, the Republic of Korea, the Philippines, Turkey, and Thailand. The comparison is provided on a sectoral basis and reveals that a large proportion of agreements are related to mechanical engineering industries in India (1,350 out of 3,731 contracts) and Korea (87 out of 337) because this sector is considered essential for self-sustaining growth. On the other hand, the emphasis in the Philippines was in beverages (69 out of 321) and pharmaceuticals (60 out of 321).[13]

Turnkey Contracts

Enterprises often enter into turnkey arrangements in the early stages of their country's industrialization, whereby one party is responsible for setting up a plant and putting it into operation. The turnkey contractor may be either the owner of the technology or the main supplier of machinery or even a consulting engineering organization. If the project is large like a steel plant or a major petrochemical plant, several foreign organizations combine to take up turnkey projects. Although it may be advantageous to deal with one party that is responsible for establishing a plant, the cost of a turnkey arrangement is often much higher than the cost of contracting separately for the various supplies and technological services.

In many developing countries, the tendency is to gradually replace turnkey contracts with technology license agreements for manufacturing technology and know-how. Included in these agreements are basic engineering services that cannot be performed by local agencies and with specific contracts for supply of machinery and its installation. This procedure is cheaper and encourages the development of indigenous technical services.

Table 10.8
Appraisal of Licensing Agreements in Selected Developing Countries

Industry	India (1946–73)	Republic of Korea (1962–73)	Philippines (1945–73)	Thailand 1972)	Turkey (1974)
Food, drinks, and tobacco	38	6	69	5	9
Textiles	126	9	5	29	3
Drugs and pharmaceuticals	155	23	60	12	—
Chemicals, paints, and fibers	377	75	35	8	25
Paper and pulp	66	3	2	—	1
Machinery, machine tools, and transportation	1,350	87	29	6	26
Electricals and electronics	538	69	23	11	16
Rubber products and tires	47	NSA	NSA	2	5
Cosmetics, toiletries, soaps	NSA	NAS	21	20	—
Plantations, mining petroleum	NSA	16	6	NSA	5
Others	1,034	49	71	62	19
TOTAL	3,731	337	321	155	109

SOURCE: "Guidelines for Development of Industrial Technology in Asia and the Pacific," United Nations, Bangkok, 1974, p. 100; and Erdener Kaynak, "Transfer of Technology to Turkey," *Management and Administration Journal* 13, No. 122 (October 1978): 16.

NSA = Not separately available.

DEVELOPMENT OF INDIGENOUS TECHNICAL SERVICES

The cost of total dependence on foreign agencies is normally much higher in the long run, particularly in industrial sectors.[13] It is, therefore, natural that some developing countries are making efforts to strengthen indigenous technical service facilities, particularly engineering and consulting organizations. In India, for example, where the growth of various forms of consulting services has been fairly rapid in recent years, the government has adopted the policy of restricting foreign consulting services to fields in which local facilities are considered inadequate. The greater the local participation in planning and implementing projects, even in the early stages of industrial development, the more rapid will be the rate of growth of service facilities.

Determining accurately the cost-benefit ratio to the economy for the use of local service facilities is a very difficult task. An assessment can be made only when such services have been developed over a long period and the savings, including saving in foreign exchange, resulting from the use of indigenous technical services can be set off against the possible additional cost for projects executed during the period when such facilities were being developed.

TECHNOLOGY TRANSFER MECHANISM IN TURKEY

Multinational corporations are important agents in transferring existing technologies across national boundaries, and in creating new technologies in the countries where their subsidiaries operate. Foreign capital and technology enter Turkey according to the following laws:

Foreign Capital Encouragement Law No. 6224.

Decree No. 17 Concerning the Protection of the Value of the Turkish Currency.

Petroleum Law No. 6326.

Law No. 7462 (established for the iron and steel factories in Eregli).

Foreign capital encouragement law (Law No. 6224) has been valid since 1954, and there has been no substantial change in its essence. The Ministry of Commerce is the competent authority for applying the provisions of this law. Procedures related to the foreign investments that are not included in the framework of Law No. 6224 are carried out by the Ministry of Finance and the Ministry of Natural Resources. According to Article 1 of this law, foreign capital is permitted into Turkey provided the enterprise will promote the country's economic development. In the planning period, this implies that the investment made should be in conformity with the objectives and the strategy of development plans and related yearly programs.

The Turkish government tends to use foreign private capital in those branches of industry where Turkish entrepreneurs have not been active for lack of sufficient technical knowledge, experience, and capital. Foreign capital is directed to those investments where large amounts of capital, wide organization, and superior technologies are required. It is believed that foreign private capital could contribute to the production and marketing of export goods which will enable indigenous firms to compete in international markets.

Incentives are given to foreign capital providing it is geared to the production of essential industrial products. Among those incentives are custom duty exemptions, tax refunds, and exemption of taxes on income of the joint venture companies for a substantial period of time. The intensity of government protection and promotion for the establishment of joint ventures varies from industry to industry. The government, at present, gives first priority, as far as the financial support of foreign investors is concerned, to the establishment of basic and strategic industries producing capital and intermediate goods.

Acceptance of foreign capital will depend on the assessment of various projects of the Department of Foreign Capital of the Ministry of Commerce. Generally, foreign investments are assessed on the basis of the following criteria:

1. Extent of projected increase in the country's income and production level.
2. Benefits of the investment to the less developed areas of the country.
3. Extent of competitive position with the industries of the Common Market.
4. Amount of superior technology and know-how provided by the investors.
5. Amount of employment created by the project.
6. Production capacity of the project.
7. The extent to which the investment may contribute to the growth of other industries as a part of an industrial complex.
8. The degree to which the idle resources of the country are utilized.
9. The net effect of foreign investments and of import substitution.

Foreign capital investments are assessed on the basis of the same criteria, and there are no preferences as far as the country of origin is concerned. While there are no legally determined levels of foreign shares in a joint venture project, there is a tendency to accept those projects with higher domestic shares. The full text of this law could be obtained from the Turkish Ministry of Commerce, whereas the evolution and approval procedure based on Law 6224 is shown in Figure 10.1. The diagram shown in Figure 10.2 shows the evolution and approval procedure based on Decree No. 17 for technology inflow in the form of simple licensing and know-how agreements. The diagram given in Figure 10.3 shows the preliminary layout of the central evaluating and approving agency for all technology transfer agreements. Figure 10.4 shows the evaluation and approval procedure based on the concept of the central evaluating and regulating agency within the Ministry of Industry and Technology.

SUMMARY AND CONCLUSIONS

During the process of technology transfer from developed to less developed countries, the aim should be to develop skills rapidly in all ancillary aspects of technology transfer. Over a period of time technology license agreements between enterprises in developing countries and enterprises in industrialized countries should be largely similar to agreements between enterprises in the industrialized countries.

If the developing countries are to raise their share of world manufacturing output significantly, new forms of partnerships must be devised with the developed countries and among developing countries themselves. Concerted efforts should be made to develop innovative mechanisms for acquiring the right technology at fair terms. For example, a system of technology preferences could be formulated similar to trade preferences schemes. Large commercial corporations could be set up with assistance from developed countries to lease complete plants and equipment with embodied technology at favorable rentals.

Technology and investment promotion consultants would be helpful in bringing "makers" and "takers" together. Alternately, technology negotiations could be added onto financial collaboration consultations.

A national institutional framework is necessary to establish a commercially oriented policy for regulating technology import; to provide assistance in selecting and negotiating for a technology; and to make arrangements for adapting imported technology to local needs and upgrading already existing local technologies.

So far as regulation of technology is concerned, its function should not be reduced to the static purpose of cutting down royalty payments. Its function should be a dynamic one: create a legal, technical, economic, and social framework within which correct decisions on technology transactions from the national point of view can be taken. Governmental scrutiny need not, however, necessarily inhibit the flow of technology. This can be ensured by a properly administered and unified system motivated by well-trained personnel. From the point of view of developing countries, the acquisition of foreign technology does present some problems with respect both to the technology itself and to the means of its transfer. The United Nations Conference on Trade and Development has been endeavoring to develop a code of conduct on transfer of technology, aimed at ending the restrictive business practices and increasing the access of developing countries to technology. Given understanding on both sides, transfer of technology could be

Figure 10.1
Evaluation and Approval Procedure Based on Decree 6/24

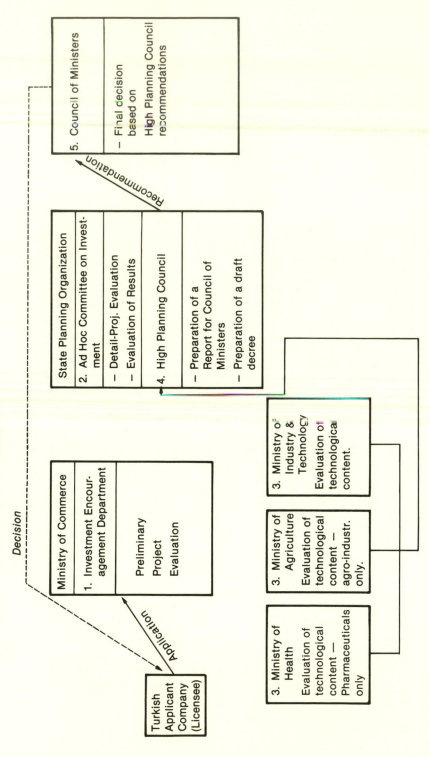

172

Figure 10.2
Evaluation and Approval Procedure Based on Decree No. 17 for Technology Inflow in the Form of Simple Licensing and Know-How Agreements

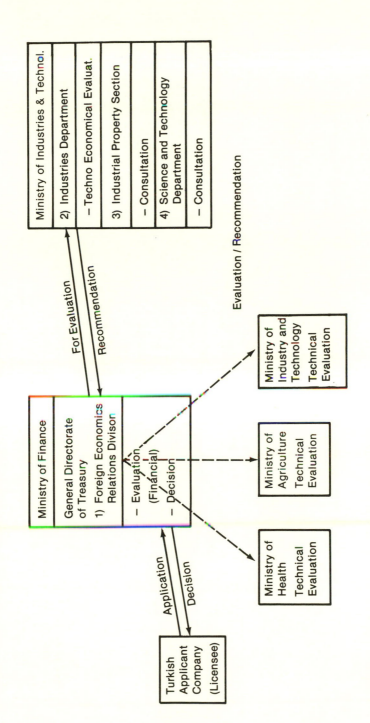

Figure 10.3
Preliminary Layout of Central Evaluating and Approving Agency
for All Technology Transfer Agreements

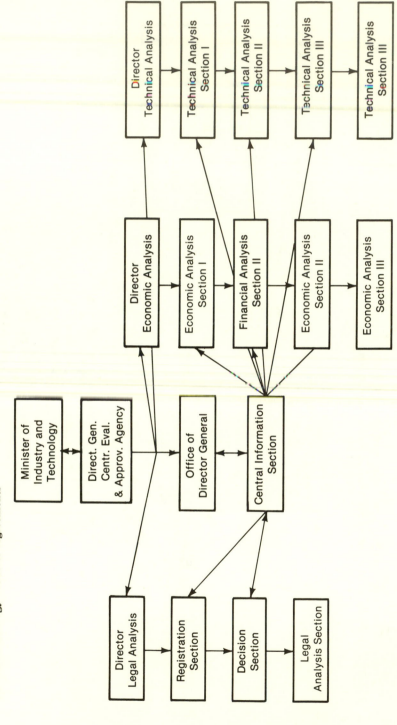

Figure 10.4
Evaluation and Approval Procedure Based on the Concept of Central
Evaluating and Regulating Agency Within the Ministry of Industry and Technology

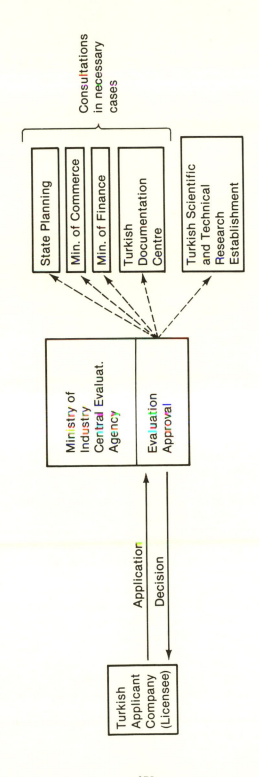

achieved effectively for the mutual benefit of both sides. Otherwise, the hope of achieving new international economic order will be further beyond reach. To achieve success in technology transfer programs, wide-ranging actions are required for a cooperative program of action. At the national level, action is required on the part of governments, enterprises, and research institutions. An effective triangular link needs to be established among them. Not only a heavy order of investment is required, but also effective attitudes, approaches, and policies. At the international level, action has to be innovative and catalytic.

NOTES

1. *Industrial Technologies for Developing Economies* (New York: Praeger, 1969); R. Vernon, *Sovereignty of Bay* (New York: Basic Books, 1971); and *Storm Over the Multinationals* (Cambridge, Mass.: Harvard University Press, 1977).

2. Hubert A. Janis Zewski, "Technology Transfer Policy," UNIDO/ICIS, No. 2, February 5, 1976.

3. H. W. Buttner, *Problems Encountered, Solutions Envisaged and Results Achieved with Respect to Transfer of Technology to Developing Countries* (Ankara: National Productivity Agency, November 1975).

4. *Impact of Multinational Enterprises on National Scientific and Technical Potentials*, OECD. DSTT/SPR/75—80, Paris, November 18, 1975.

5. *Technology and Employment in Industry* (Geneva: International Labour Organization, 1976).

6. *Guidelines for Development of Industrial Technology in Asia and the Pacific*, United Nations Publication, Bangkok, 1976; and J. Dunning and M. Gilman, "Alternative Police Prescriptions," in Curzon and Curzon, eds. *The Multinational Enterprise in a Hostile World* (London: Macmillan and Co., 1977).

7. William H. Gruber, *Factors in the Transfer of Technology*, William H. Gruber and Donald G. Marquis, eds. (Cambridge, Mass.: MIT Press, 1969), and J. Behrman and H. Wallender, *Transfers of Manufacturing Technology Within Multinational Enterprises* (Cambridge, Mass.: Ballinger, 1976).

8. For further information, see E. Sciberros, *Multinational Electronic Companies and National Economic Policies* (Greenwich, Conn.: JAI Press, 1977); and "International Business Machines: Can the Europeans Ever Compete?" *Multinational Business* (1973): 37-46.

9. A. Cilingiroglu, *Transfer of Technology for Pharmaceutical Chemicals* (Paris: OECD, 1975) and *Acquisition of Technology from Multinational Corporations by Developing Countries*, United Nations Publication (Geneva, 1974).

10. Thomas Rhymes, *On Concepts of Capital and Technical Change* (Cambridge, Mass.: University Press, 1971).

11. Edward P. Hawthorne, *The Transfer of Technology*, International Seminar, Istanbul, October 5-9, 1970.

12. *Manual on the Establishment of Joint-Venture Agreements*, United Nations Publication (Geneva, 1971).

13. Yves L. Doz, "Strategic Management in Multinational Companies," *Sloan Management Review* (Winter 1980): 27-46.

11

Personality, Culture, and Technology Transfer: A Parsonian Social System Perspective

*M. JOSEPH SIRGY, A. C. SAMLI,
AND KENNETH D. BAHN*

In order to assume a successful technology transfer, it is important to understand people's behavior patterns as individuals and as members of a culture. Without such an understanding it will be very difficult, if not impossible, to determine the specifics of the transfer process which will make the new technology adopted by the country and its people. This adoption can be particularly important if the planned technology transfer is expected to make a particularly strong impact on the economic development attempts of the less developed countries (LDCs).

PARSONS' SOCIAL SYSTEM THEORY

Talcott Parsons and Edward Shils (1962) introduced a general social systems theory that uses the concept of personality to explain the working dynamics of social systems. Stemming from social system dynamics, systems of symbolic patterns are created and manifested by individual members of social systems. These systems of symbolic patterns are known to make up the concept of *culture.*

To describe systems of symbolic patterns (that is, cultural orientations) and how these, in turn, affect technology transfer, we have to briefly explain the theoretical underpinnings of the concept of culture as developed by Talcott Parsons. In doing so, we will (1) introduce the concept of social behavior as "action"; (2) argue that culture is determined by personality and social system dynamics; (3) explain the concept of personality systems in terms of basic motives and allocation/integration mechanisms; (4) explain the concept of social systems in terms of roles and allocation/integration mechanisms; (5) describe the similarities between personality systems and social systems; and (6) present a taxonomy of cultural orientations based on personality systems and social systems patterns of orientation.

Social Behavior

Social behavior, according to Parsons, is goal-directed "action." Individuals engage in action to attain one or more goals. Action is situational, normatively regulated, and involves expenditure of energy or effort. For example, the statement "a consumer purchases an automobile" can be analyzed as follows: Purchase is the social behavior. This behavior is viewed in the context of a specific situation (for example, "at the dealer"). The purchase of an automobile is normatively regulated, meaning that it is an intelligent, rational way of attaining one or more goals (that is, the benefits associated with the automobile). The consumer, in doing so, expends energy to attain those goals by driving down to the dealer, seeking information, comparing, discussing, and so on. (See Figure 11.1.)

Given an object opportunity, goal-directed behavior can be directly induced by a need-disposition (for example, need for food, love, power, to name a few) or by an evaluation process of the object opportunity directed by cognitive, appreciative, and/or moral standards. Cognitive standards are beliefs that are regarded as "facts" by most people. Appreciative standards are evaluative beliefs of preference. Moral standards are standards directed to the individual self (that is, self-interest) or a particular collective (that is, collective interest).

An example of goal-directed behavior directed by a need-disposition may be a consumer who purchases toothpaste to satisfy his or her need-dispositions of having white teeth, fresh breath, and preventing tooth decay. An example of goal-directed behavior directed by an evaluation with a cognitive standard may be the purchase of a toothpaste that meets a scientifically established conception of "quality" toothpaste. An example of goal-directed behavior directed by an evaluation with an appreciative standard may be the purchase of a toothpaste that meets the consumer standards of nice color, nice texture, and good taste. An example of goal-directed behavior directed by an evaluation with a moral standard such as collective may be the purchase of toothpaste by homemakers to satisfy the family's (that is, collective) need for brushing teeth. (The reader should note that social behavior can be instigated by evaluative processes that involve more than one of the aforementioned standards.)

Personality, Social Systems, and Culture

Through action and learning, objects in the environment become cathected (that is, wanted or not wanted) to individuals. Consequently, each actor develops his or her own system of relations-to-objects involving a unique configuration of cathected relations. These cathected relations are not only learned but also modified to form a system of orientation. Personality is, therefore, a system of orientation of an individual which motivates and directs social behavior. A social system is also a system of orientation of

Figure 11.1
Parsons' Theory of Social Action

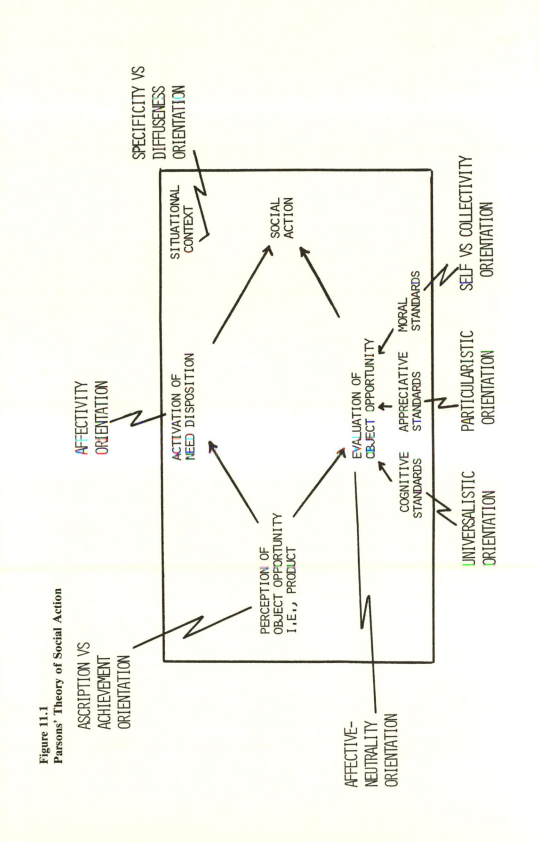

individuals' actions toward one another. Culture, on the other hand, is a system of symbolic patterns created or manifested by individual actors (personality system of orientation) and are transmitted among social systems by diffusion and among personalities by learning (social system of orientation). That is, culture or cultural orientation involves a set of symbolic patterns that are determined by personality and social system dynamics.

Personality

Parsons argued that the primary motives of personality systems are (1) the optimization of gratification (maximizing positive emotions and minimizing negative emotions), and (2) the maintenance of integrity (enhancement of consistency among cathected cognitions and reduction of intrapsychic conflict). For an individual to optimize gratification and maintain integrity, he or she has to engage in mechanisms of allocation and integration.

Personality Mechanisms of Allocation: Individuals allocate time to learn about their environment (that is, learning) and to take action to impact their environment (that is, performance) in an attempt to optimize their gratification and maintain the integrity of personality systems.

An example of allocation for learning involves individual perceiving their environment and distributing their attention to those objects/events that are related to their system of orientation. An example of allocation in performance involves individuals distributing time and action among the various units that they may accomplish their functions. A concrete example may be as follows: In order to purchase an automobile, a consumer allocates specific time/action to visit dealers x, y, and z, compare among brands m, n, and o, talk to a mechanic about a possible selection, return to one of the dealers, bargain with the dealer, and so on.

Personality Mechanisms of Integration: Integration also occurs in relation to learning and performance. With respect to learning, integration may occur in the form of generalization (that is, concept formation) and resolution of cognitive dissonance. Generalization in learning involves integrating two or more cognitions to form a supraordinate cognition. Resolution of cognitive dissonance involves learning as a result of conflict between two needs, two facts, or between a fact and a need. The individual here learns new ways to perceive and thus new ways to manipulate the situation. By doing so, the individual reduces or eliminates the conflict.

With respect to integration through performance, this process may occur through what Parsons calls "defense" and "adjustment" mechanisms. Defense mechanisms handle conflicts between different needs as in conflict resolution. Other defense mechanisms, such as rationalization, isolation, displacement, fixation, repression, reaction formation, and projection, are also defense mechanisms but involve learning, not performance. Adjustment mechanisms handle conflicts between facts or conflict between facts and needs. A fact, in this instance, may signal the deprivation of satisfaction of a need. Individuals adjust to these problems through (1) reality testing, (2) dependency as in dominance or submission, and/or (3) compulsive independence as in aggressiveness or withdrawal.

Value Components of Personality Systems: From the previous discussion of social behavior and personality mechanisms of allocation and integration in the context of both learning and performance, two value dimensions are derived. These are (1) affectivity versus affective-neutrality, and (2) specificity versus diffuseness.

Object opportunities present themselves or are sought by the individual to satisfy need-disposition. This is done through the allocation and integrative mechanisms of the personality system. However, the manner in which need-dispositions are met can be distinguished along the affectivity versus affective-neutrality dimension. An affectivity orientation involves an approach in which the individual engages in allocation and/or integration in which a need-disposition is directly involved. Conversely, an affective-neutrality orientation involves allocation and/or integration in which cognitive standards, appreciative standards, or moral standards are injected.

For example, certain need-dispositions such as need for food, affection, love, and friendship, among others, are need-dispositions that individuals strive to attain from object opportunities that present themselves to the individual and/or actively sought. On the other hand, needs such as approval and esteem are sought from object opportunities contingent on an evaluation of these objects along standards defining what approval is and what esteem is, in terms of cognitive, appreciative, and/or moral standards. Cognitive standards may be seen as scientific norms that the individual is cognizant of defining what approval is in specific terms. Appreciative standards may involve specific rules that are cathected for that individual, for example, "approval means when someone smiles to you." Moral standards are standards related to either self or the collective, that is, standards that are based on "self-interest" or "collective interest."

A specificity orientation (contrasted to a diffuseness orientation) involves allocation and/or integration mechanisms designed to attain one or more need-dispositions restricted to a specific situation. Conversely, a diffuseness orientation involves similar processes but is generalizable across a variety of situations. Thus, the benefits of a product may be restricted to a specific situation or may be applicable to several situations.

Social Systems

Parsons defined a social system as a system of the actions of individuals in which the principal units are roles and/or constellations of roles. As in personality systems, social systems have both allocative and integrative functions.

Social System Mechanisms of Allocation: Allocation in social systems is regulated to (1) roles, (2) facilities, and (3) rewards/punishments. In other words, social systems allocate roles, that is, what roles or division of labor should be institutionalized and who would occupy those roles; allocate facilities to roles, that is, what resources are needed for each role to carry out its function within the social system; and allocate sanctions and rewards to those role occupants for their role performance.

Allocation in social systems is based on three criteria: (1) Evaluative standards, that is, cognitive standards such as scientific specification of optimal role performance, appreciative standards such as values of taste, preference, and aesthetics, and/or moral standards such as self-interest or social welfare norms, (2) characteristics of ascription and/or achievement, for example, allocate rewards to those who attained prestige or social status (ascription) or to those who attained a level of performance based on achievement, and (3) distinction between self and collective, whereby the emphasis within the social system is the individual rather than the collective or vice versa.

Social System Mechanisms of Integration: Through the process of allocation, roles are differentiated in which certain roles are designed with integrative functions, that is, managerial, political roles. The social system integrates its roles to maintain an equilibrium state. The social system's own equilibrium is itself made up of many subequilibriums within that cut across one another such as kinship groups, social strata, churches, sects, economic enterprises, and governmental bodies. These subsystems, having their own equilibrium states (that is, subequilibriums) all enter into the overall social system's dynamic equilibrium. Instabilities in one subsystem are communicated to other subsystems, consequently disequilibrating the larger system or part of it. States of disequilibrium motivate the social system to re-equilibrate itself through a number of integration mechanisms. These mechanisms are socialization and social control.

Socialization functions as an integrative mechanism by having those individuals within a specific disequilibrated subsystem learn to bring the subsystem back to a steady state. This is usually done through learning mechanisms of generalization, imitation (modeling), and/or identification. Mechanisms of social control, on the other hand, are involved in the manipulation of rewards and deprivations as exercised by those roles and role incumbents in their integrative functions (for example, managerial/political roles). This is more specifically accomplished through (1) the allocation of roles, facilities, and rewards, (2) insulation, for example, incarceration, and/or (3) contingent re-integration, for example, treatment of deviance as illness.

Value Components of Social Systems: From the discussion of mechanisms of allocation and integration in social systems, three value dimensions are derived. These are (1) universalism versus particularism, (2) ascription versus achievement, and (3) self versus collective.

Universalism versus particularism involves the tendency of the social system to allocate roles, facilities, and rewards/sanctions based on cognitive versus appreciative standards. Given that the social system engages in allocation based on cognitive standards, it is said to have a universalistic orientation. Conversely, given that the social system engages in allocation based on appreciative standards, it is said to have a particularistic orientation. An example of a universalistic orientation of a social system may be role expectations that are based on universal norms of achievement.

Ascription versus achievement orientations involve the distinction between a social system allocation based on ascribed characteristics (for example, race, physical attractiveness, gender, power) or achievement characteristics (for example, performance, productivity, educational attainment). That is, evaluative standards that are used in allocation may be tilted toward valuing ascribed characteristics or achievement characteristics.

Similarly, self versus collectivity orientations involve the distinction between allocating roles, facilities, and/or rewards/sanctions based on outcome or opportunities that serve to meet individual goals (self) or goals of the collective.

Culture

As previously noted, culture is a system of value orientations that are determined by personality systems and transmitted among social systems by socialization and among personalities by learning. Parsons argued that the value orientations of cultures can be analyzed along five key dimensions that are derived from personality/social systems dynamics. These are (1) affectivity versus affective neutrality, (2) universalism versus particularism, (3) self-orientation versus collectivity orientation, (4) ascription versus achievement, and (5) diffuseness versus specificity.

Affectivity Versus Affective Neutrality: With regard to a specific need-disposition (for example, attainment of prestige and social status), a social system may be predisposed to act directly on those opportunities that may lead to the satisfaction of that need-disposition without engaging in an evaluation of the situation using cognitive, appreciative, or moral standards. For example, consumers who perceive air conditioners as a symbol of status/prestige may purchase an air conditioner without evaluating the product against other criteria. A social system that acts directly to satisfy a specific need-disposition without engaging in evaluation is said to be dominated by an affectivity orientation with regards to that particular need-disposition.

Conversely, when a social system acts to satisfy a specific need-disposition and, in doing so, evaluates the object opportunity along cognitive, appreciative, and/or moral standards, it is said to be dominated by an affective-neutrality orientation. Let us use the example of the air conditioner. Consumers of a social system may evaluate an air conditioner using cognitive

standards (for example, does it meet "quality" standards), using appreciative standards (for example, does it have specific features that are appealing
in terms of color, shape, size, among others), or using moral standards (for
example, to what extent does it benefit a collective that consumers belong to).

Universalism Versus Particularism: Given an affective neutrality mode of
action (that is, action based on evaluation), a social system is said to have a
universalistic orientation or a particularistic orientation. A universalistic
orientation is the tendency to use cognitive standards in evaluation, whereas
a particularistic orientation is viewed as the tendency to use appreciative
standards. Let us use the air conditioner as an example. Consumers of a
social system (for example, country), in evaluating an air conditioner, may
be predisposed to using cognitive standards such as technical reports defining "quality" air conditioners. This social system is viewed as having a
universalistic orientation.

Conversely, a social system having a particularistic orientation may be
exemplified by consumers who evaluate an air conditioner using appreciative standards such as color, style, and shape.

Self-Orientation Versus Collectivity Orientation: Whether or not evaluation occurs, actors of a social system may not give primacy to collective
moral standards, but instead to cognitive or appreciative standards that are
ego-integrative moral standards, or no standards are invoked. This is
viewed as the self-orientation of a social system. For example, consumers of
a social system may approach an air conditioner with a need-disposition
such as attainment of prestige and status within their community, or they
may evaluate the air conditioner along cognitive or appreciative standards
that are self-related, that is, to attain personal goals.

On the other hand, a collectivity orientation of a social system refers to
actors within that system engaging in evaluation of an object opportunity in
which the actors give primacy to collective moral standards. For example,
an air conditioner may be evaluated to see if it can increase the work
productivity and/or job satisfaction of a collective of organizational
employees.

Ascription Orientation Versus Achievement Orientation: A social system
that is ascription-oriented is a system with actors disposed to perceiving
social objects (that is, people) as a complex of ascribed qualities such as
gender, social status, race, dominance, and religion. A social system that is
achievement-oriented has actors that often perceive social objects as a
complex of achieved qualities such as educational attainment, occupational
attainment, and income attainment, among other performance factors.

With respect to object opportunities (for example, technological innovations) or a social system that is ascription-oriented may act to adopt the
object opportunity related to the ascribed need disposition. This behavior is
dependent on the object opportunity being perceived as meeting the need-
disposition. For example, a social system that is ascription-oriented involves
consumers who would adopt an air conditioner because they saw that it

would satisfy their need to attain an ascribed quality such as social prestige and status.

A social system may also evaluate object opportunities using cognitive and/or appreciative standards that have something to do with ascribed qualities such as "quality" and "color" defined by a reference group having an ascribed characteristic (for example, high social class group).

A social system that is achievement-oriented, on the other hand, may approach object opportunities with a tendency to examine the opportunity's potential to attain achievement-related goals such as educational and occupational goals. For example, does an air conditioner provide achievement-related benefits, does it help in studying, does it help in increasing efficiency at work, and so forth?

Diffuseness Orientation Versus Specificity Orientation: A diffuseness orientation of a social system reflects a perception of the object opportunity as having benefits that are generalizable or applicable to a variety of situations. Conversely, a social system having a specificity orientation is a system having actors perceiving the benefit(s) of an object opportunity as limited to a specific situation and not applicable beyond that situation.

For example, a social system may approach an air conditioner with a perception that it can provide comfort at home (a highly specific situation), or it can provide comfort at home, work, restaurants, and recreation places, among others. The former involves a specificity orientation and the latter a diffuseness orientation.

A MODEL OF TECHNOLOGY TRANSFER BASED ON PARSONS' CLASSIFICATION OF VALUE ORIENTATIONS

Technology transfer involves production of technological innovations and diffusion of these innovations. The model presented here involves diffusion of technological innovations. More specifically, the model establishes the relationship between the various components of value orientations (based on Parsons' taxonomy of value orientations of cultures) and product positioning. The use of the designated value orientations in the context of product positioning is referred to as "cultural product positioning." (See Figure 11.2.)

In the next section, each value orientation is applied in product positioning. As a result, a set of strategies are formulated to help technology transfer practitioners position their technological innovations to target social systems (that is, countries).

Affectivity Orientation and Cultural Product Positioning

Practitioners of technology transfer should conduct market research to assess the affectivity level of the target social system. This means that the practitioners should first try to identify those need-dispositions that the tech-

Figure 11.2
A Technology Transfer Model Based on Parsons' Cultural (Value) Orientations

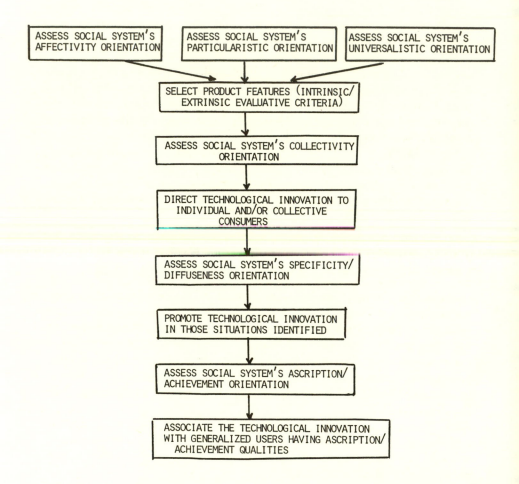

nological innovation may satisfy. Once these need-dispositions are identified (possibly through a focus group method), the technology transfer practitioner should use these need-dispositions in market survey (directed to a sample of respondents of the target social system) to assess the level of affectivity of the social system, that is, the extent to which the social system may adopt the technological innovation because the innovation is perceived to satisfy one or more need-dispositions.

For those who are familiar with marketing concepts, the concept of need-dispositions associated with a technological innovation can be equated to a specific category of evaluative criteria of a product, intrinsic evaluative criteria. Evaluative criteria are those benefit and cost factors that are used in consumer decision-making. For example, a brand of toothpaste can be seen to have the following evaluative criteria: breath freshener, teeth whitener, prevention of tooth decay, appealing color, appealing texture, appealing taste, and acceptable price. Note that the evaluative criteria of "breath freshener," "teeth whitener," and "prevention of tooth decay" are different from the "color," "texture," "taste," and "price" criteria. The former set can be viewed as designed to meet intrinsic goals, that is, need-dispositions. The latter set is made up of extrinsic goals that are designed to add to the product appeal to make it competitive with other products (Schiffman and Kanuk, 1983). If we use Parsons' terminology, intrinsic evaluative criteria are need-dispositions, whereas extrinsic evaluative criteria are appreciative standards.

Going back to the air conditioner example, we see that the technology transfer practitioner marketing air conditioners to a social system (for example, a less developed country) should identify the need-dispositions (that is, intrinsic evaluative criteria) associated with his or her brand of air conditioners and assess the extent to which consumers of the designated social system may adopt the air conditioner strictly, based on one or more need-dispositions such as provides physical comfort and symbolizes prestige and status.

Of course, since the social system scores highly on the affectivity orientation (that is, has a high tendency to adopt the air conditioner because of its intrinsic evaluative criteria), then the technology transfer practitioner should position his or her brand of air conditioner to that target social system along these attributes.

Particularistic Orientation and Cultural Product Positioning

As previously noted, a particularistic orientation of a social system involves a disposition by members of that system to use appreciative standards in evaluation. We have just mentioned that appreciative standards can be viewed as extrinsic evaluative criteria. Some marketers use the term *differentiating characteristics*, that is, those product features that are designed specifically to provide a relative advantage from its competition.

The practitioner of technology transfer first should identify the appreciative standards of his or her product and the extent to which members of the social system are disposed to using appreciative standards in their decision to adopt the technological innovation. This, of course, should be done through market survey research.

In the air conditioner example, the technology transfer of an air conditioner assesses the extent to which consumers of the target social system would focus on extrinsic evaluative criteria such as color shape, size, and noise level. Given that they do (that is, score highly on the particularistic orientation), the practitioner should focus his or her product design and promotional efforts on establishing and developing those features of the air conditioner.

Universalistic Orientation and Cultural Product Positioning

As previously discussed, a universalistic orientation of a social system refers to the tendency of the members of that system to use cognitive standards in their evaluation of object opportunities. Cognitive standards may be viewed as conceptions or beliefs that are derived from formal or informal education.

In marketing, cognitive standards may be viewed as information about evaluative criteria that are used in consumer decision-making. However, they are derived from less biased (independent or impartial) information sources. For example, in the United States, we have consumer reports, an information source about products, which most consumers believe provides "accurate" (or less biased) information about brands along a set of "performance criteria." For example, in evaluating air conditioners, performance criteria may include energy consumption in BTU, performance reliability, and safety aspects. Performance criteria are, of course, evaluative criteria (intrinsic and/or extrinsic) that are impartially derived by "scientific" means.

Many Western countries may be seen as having a universalistic orientation with regards to adoption of technological innovations. Less developed countries (LDCs), on the other hand, may score low in this value orientation. Given that a social system is found to have universalistic orientation, practitioners of technology transfer should concentrate on developing product design features that are likely to be rated highly by independent scientists and governmental agencies. In view of the high ratings by these "impartial" sources, technology transfer practitioners should use this information in their promotional endeavors.

Collectivity Orientation and Cultural Product Positioning

Up to now, we have made reference to three value orientations: affectivity, particularistic, and universalistic orientations. Implicit in our discussion of these value orientations is the notion of the self, that is, members of a social system may react to technological innovation to meet self-goals. A collectivity orientation involves evaluation of an object opportunity with reference to collective goals.

In marketing, this concept is usually treated in terms of making distinctions between consumer-buying behavior (self-orientation) and family and organizational buying behavior and international import behavior (collectivity orientation). In family and organizational-buying behavior, one or more members of the social system assume the role of the buyer for the collective (that is, family, organization, society).

This is an important concept to technology transfer practitioners since the evaluative criteria used in adopting a technological innovation by a social system may vary depending on whether the members of that system assume self- versus collective roles. Consequently, the technology transfer practitioner should investigate the potential of a social system to adopt a technological innovation for a collective within that system or for the system at large. Again, this could be done via market survey research. However, the practitioner should note that this assessment of the collectivity orientation has to be done *in the context of* assessing the other aforementioned value orientations, that is, affectivity, particularistic, and universalistic orientations.

For example, a practitioner who wants to transfer an air conditioner brand to an LDC should investigate the potential that air conditioners may be adopted by the government for large-scale use in both (or either) private and/or public sectors, or by specific private and/or public organizations, or by families or other groups. In doing so, the practitioner has to identify the member(s) who would assume the decider or buyer role. With respect to these individuals, the practitioner has to ascertain their affectivity, particularistic, and universalistic orientations. Only in this context would the practitioner be able to effectively position the air conditioner to the target social system.

Specificity/Diffuseness Orientation and Cultural Product Positioning

The specificity/diffuseness orientation refers to the extent to which an object opportunity is perceived to provide benefits that are highly specific to a given situation or diffused across a variety of situations. In other words, how extensive is the situational context?

Knowledge of how the social system perceives the situational context of the technological innovation is very important in product positioning. Of course, finding out the situational applicability of the technological innovation of a social system has to be done within the context of assessing the aforementioned affectivity, particularistic, universalistic, and collectivity orientations.

For example, air conditioners in one social system may be quite restricted to residential houses or mansions of the wealthy; in another social system, they may be used across a wide variety of situations such as in factories, offices, houses, apartments, and stadiums, to name a few.

Ascription/Achievement Orientation and Cultural Product Positioning

An ascription orientation is the tendency for a social system to perceive social objects in terms of ascribed qualities such as gender, social class, age, and race. Conversely, an achievement orientation is the tendency to perceive social objects in terms of achievement qualities such as occupational attainment and educational attainment.

In marketing, the distinction between the ascription and achievement characteristic is not as important as the distinction between utilitarian- and value-expressive attributes. Using Parsons' terminology, we should distinguish between need-dispositions/cognitive appreciative-moral standards of the actor and ascribed/achievement qualities of the social object. In marketing, recent research has concentrated on explaining and predicting the effects of value-expressive evaluative criteria on consumer decision-making (Sirgy, 1982, 1985; Solomon, 1984). Of course, the distinction between ascribed and achievement characteristics is a classification of value-expressive attributes that are directly associated with a technological innovation and may be quite useful in technology transfer to large-scale social systems such as LDCs

For example, given that a social system is ascription oriented (that is, tends to perceive social objects in terms of ascribed characteristics), then the practitioner working with a brand of air conditioner should promote the air conditioner to that social system by linking the object opportunity (that is, the air conditioner) with social objects (that is, people or generalized users of the air conditioner) *who have specific desirable ascribed qualities.* That is, the practitioner should create desirable product symbolism, or build an image of the generalized user of air conditioner as being a member of desirable ascribed groups. Of course, finding out what is a desirable ascribed quality should be examined within the context of that social system.

Similarly, since the social system is achievement oriented, then the technology transfer practitioner of air conditioners should strive to create an image of uses of air conditioners as achievement-oriented people and, as a result, may be in a better position to appeal to members of that social system.

SUMMARY AND CONCLUSIONS

This chapter reports a model of technology transfer based on Parsons' theory of social systems. This is done by providing an overview of Parsons' theory of social systems leading to a discussion of his classification of value orientations of cultures. This classificaiton includes five key dimensions: (1) affectivity versus affective neutrality, (2) universalism versus particularism, (3) self versus collectivity, (4) ascribed versus achieved qualities, and (5) specificity versus diffuseness. These value orientation dimensions are thus used to develop a model of technology transfer. The model develops the concept of cultural product positioning in which specific positioning strategies are discussed for social systems with different value orientations.

We have demonstrated that Parsons' taxonomy of value orientations can help technology transfer practitioners to better position their technological innovations to target social systems. Through market research, the technology transfer practitioner can identify the target social system's levels of affectivity, particularistic, universalistic, collectivity, ascription/achievement, and specificity/diffuseness orientations. Through this kind of assessment, practitioners would position their product more effectively by accomplishing the following tasks: (1) Select the precise product features (intrinsic/extrinsic evaluative criteria) that are highly appealing to the target social system as revealed from the assessment of the system's affectivity, particularistic, and universalistic orientations. (2) Direct the technological innovation to individual consumers or consumers who are assuming buying roles of specific collectives. This is directly revealed from the collectivity orientation of the target system. (3) Identify those situations to which the technological innovation is perceived to be applicable. The specificity /diffuseness orientation assessment is used to accomplish this task. (4) Identify those ascribed and/or achievement characteristics that can be associated with the technological innovation, thereby creating a desirable image of the generalized users of that technological innovation. This is done through an analysis of the target system's ascription/achievement orientation.

All in all, Parsons' classification of value orientations lends itself nicely to product positioning to target social systems.

REFERENCES

Parsons, Talcott, and Edward A. Shils (1962). *Toward a General Theory of Action.* Cambridge, Mass.: Harvard University Press, pp. 47-275.

Schiffman, Leon G., and Leslie L. Kanuk (1983). *Consumer Behavior.* Englewood Cliffs, N.J.: Prentice-Hall.

Sirgy, M. Joseph (1982). "Self-Concept in Consumer Behavior: A Critical Review." *Journal of Consumer Research* 9 (December): 287-300.

_____ (1985). "Self-Image/Product-Image Congruity and Consumer Decision-Making." *International Journal of Management,* forthcoming.

Solomon, Michael R. (1984). "The Role of Products as Social Stimuli, A Symbolic Interactionism Perspective." *Journal of Consumer Research* 10 (December): 319-330.

12

Achievement Motivation, Technology Transfer, and National Development: A System Model

M. JOSEPH SIRGY

Alex Inkeles (1978), and Inkeles and Larry Diamond (1980) argue that past research demonstrates the relationship between personality and social structures. They hypothesize that there is a relationship between personality development and national development. More specifically, they expect that individuals with the same education and occupation will manifest different degrees of selected personality characteristics, depending on their nation's level of development, that is, higher levels of national development (measured by per capita GNP) will be associated with higher levels of tolerance, efficacy, satisfaction, participation, interpersonal trust, and faith in science and technology. The meta-analysis results showed the following: (1) There is a strong inverse relationship between authoritarianism and national development (Meade and Whittaker, 1967; Gordon, 1967; Jordan, 1968; Torney, et al., 1975). (2) There is a strong positive relationship between efficacy sense of personal competence and national development (Lerner, 1958; Gillespie and Allport, 1955; Tannenbaum, et al., 1974; Inkeles, 1960; Ornauer, et al., 1976; Almond and Verba, 1963; Dennis, et al., 1968; Torney, et al., 1975; Husen, 1967). (3) There is a strong positive relationship between personal satisfaction and national development (Inkeles, 1960; Lerner, 1958; Cantril, 1965; Tannenbaum, et al., 1974; Liebman, et al., 1972; Haire, et al., 1966; Form, 1976; Ornauer, et al., 1976; Gallup, 1977). (4) The relationship between participation and national development is contradictory (Almond and Verba, 1963; Inglehart, 1977; Form, 1976; Havighurst, et al., 1969; Jacob and Teune, 1971; Gillespie and Allport, 1955; Igra, 1976). (5) There is a strong relationship between interpersonal trust and national development (Almond and Verba, 1963; Gordon, 1967; Jordan, 1968; Gillespie and Allport, 1955). (6) There is a strong inverse relationship between benevolence and national development (Jordan, 1968; Jacob and Teune, 1971). (7) There is a strong inverse relationship between optimism and national development (Cantril, 1965; Free, 1976; Gallup, 1977). And (8) there is a moderate inverse relationship between faith in science and national development (Ornauer, et al., 1976; Husen, 1967; Comber and Keeves, 1973).

The last three findings concerning benevolence, optimism, and faith in science in relation to national development led to the following conclusion:

Technical-economic development is not reinforced by growing optimism, but rather seems to lead to growing skepticism and pessimism. . . . People living in the most developed countries . . . seem to reflect a feeling of being at the end of something, of moving into a corner, without seeing any clear escape. . . . People in the less developed countries, socialist or not, have exactly the opposite conception: they seem to feel they are at the beginning of something, of an era full of promises, and meet the future with more confidence (Ornauer, et al., 1976, p. 73).

This chapter examines the relationship between personality variables associated with achievement motivation and national development (that is, economic development). More specifically, a systems model is developed showing how achievement motivation contributes to national development through technology transfer. It is a *systems* model because achievement motivation is seen as an input component, technology transfer as through-put, and national development as output. Feedback refers to the reinforcement/extinction properties of national development on achievement motivation.

Before describing the systems model, a number of other topics are covered:

1. How achievement motivation has been treated in the personality/social psychology literature and how achievement motivation theory may be viewed as a personality theory, and not merely as a personality variable.
2. Research involving the determinants of technology transfer and interpretation of the research findings in light of achievement motivation theory.
3. Research treating the effect of technology transfer on economic development.
4. The systems model linking achievement motivation, technology transfer, and national development.
5. The implications of this model in terms of policy making.

ACHIEVEMENT MOTIVATION

The achievement motivation construct can be traced back more than thirty years to the development of the Need for Achievement (n Ach) measure (McClelland, et al., 1953) and the test anxiety measure to avoid failure (Taylor, 1956). However, the historical roots of these measures lie in the work of Kurt Lewin (Lewin, et al., 1944) in the context of expectancy-value theory (Sirgy, 1981).

It would be most beneficial to classify achievement motivation research in terms of two major tracks: basic research and applied research. Hence, the major theoretical work in this area coming from the basic research track will be discussed, and then the focus will be directed to one specific applied research track, economic behavior. By doing so, the reader can become acquainted with the basic concepts of achievement motivation, and an attempt can be made to integrate these concepts and apply them in the area of economic behavior.

Basic Research in Achievement Motivation

This research track involves establishing relationships between achievement motivation and choice, performance level, and persistence in both laboratory and life situations (Atkinson and Feather, 1966). Atkinson and his colleagues introduced the following theoretical propositions: The tendency to achieve success (Ts) is postulated to be a multiplicative function of the motive to achieve success (Ms), the subjective probability of success (Ps), and the incentive value of success (Is). That is

$$Ts = Ms \times Ps \times Is$$

where the incentive value of success is inversely related to the subjective probability of success, or

$$Is = 1 - Ps$$

The tendency to avoid failure (Tf) is assumed to be a multiplicative function of the motive to avoid failure (Maf), the subjective probability of failure (Pf), and the negative incentive value of failure ($-If$), where

$$-If = (1 - Pf) \text{ or } -Ps$$

The resultant tendency to achieve (Tr) is assumed to be a function of the algebraic sum of Ts and Tf

$$Tr = Ts + Tf$$

All together, the Tr equation can be represented as

$$Tr = (Ms \times Ps \times Is) - (Maf \times Pf \times If)$$
$$\text{or } Tr = (Ms - Maf) [Ps(1 - Ps)]$$

The final strength of an action (Ta) is postulated to be influenced by extrinsic motivation (Text), which means

$$Ta = Tr + \text{Text}$$

From this research track, we have learned the following:

- $Ms > Maf$ individuals *prefer* achievement tasks of intermediate probabilities of success (that is, $Ps = 0.50$; or any moderately difficult task) to tasks of extreme probabilities (extremely difficult or extremely easy), whereas $Ms < Maf$ individuals prefer achievement tasks having extreme probabilities.

- $Ms > Maf$ individuals *persist* on an achievement task when the initial Ps is high ($Ps > 0.50$) more than $Ms < Maf$ individuals. Conversely, $Ms < Maf$ persist when the initial Ps is low ($Ps < 0.50$).

- $Ms > Maf$ individuals *perform* better on achievement tasks than $Ms < Maf$.

- $Ms > Maf$ individuals *expect to succeed* at achievement tasks more than $Ms < Maf$, and, conversely, $Ms < Maf$ *expect to fail* more than $Ms > Maf$.

- $Ms > Maf$ individuals' *success expectancy* decreases after failure and increases after success. Conversely, $Ms < Maf$ individuals' success expectancy increases after failure and decreases after success.

- $Ms > Maf$ individuals recall incompleted tasks (*Zeigarnik* effect) more than their $Ms < Maf$ counterparts.

Based on the initial conceptual work of Atkinson and Feather (1966), Raynor and his colleagues (Atkinson and Raynor, 1974, 1978; Raynor and Entin, 1982) extended the expectancy value formulation in the following manner. They argued that achievement on a particular activity can be studied more effectively in the context of an achievement path or goal hierarchy. A path consists of a series of steps. Each step represents an activity and its expected outcomes. The tendency to achieve success in an immediate activity (Ts) is postulated to be a function of the sum of the component tendencies to achieve (Tsn) in that path, each a multiplicative function of the motive to approach success (Ms), subjective probability of success (Ps) and incentive value of success (Is). That is,

$$Tsn = Ms \times P1sn \times Isn$$
$$Ts = Ts1 + Ts2 + \ldots + Tsn$$

where subscripts $1, 2, \ldots n$ represent the anticipated order of steps in a path. The tendency to avoid failure is similarly postulated

$$Tfn = Maf \times P1fn \times Ifn$$
$$Tf = Tf1 + Tf2 + \ldots + Tfn$$

The resultant achievement-oriented tendency (resultant achievement motivation) is postulated to be the summation of the Ts and Tf. Algebraically stated,

$$Tr = Ts - Tf$$
$$\text{where } P1sn = P1s1 \times P2s2 \times P3s3 \times \ldots \times Pnsn$$
$$\text{or } P1sn = Pisi$$
$$\text{and } Isn = 1 - P1sn$$

The major findings and conclusions from the Raynor and colleagues research can be summarized as follows:

- Resultant achievement motivation increases for $Ms > Maf$ individuals as they get closer to the goal in path contingent achievement tasks, while motivation decreases for $Ms > Maf$ individuals.
- Persistence increases for $Ms > Maf$ individuals when closer to goal than distant from goal, while persistence decreases for $Ms < Maf$ individuals.
- $Ms > Maf$ individuals perform better in a contingent path than a noncontingent one. Conversely, $Ms < Maf$ individuals perform better in a noncontingent path than a contingent one.
- $Ms > Maf$ individuals prefer easy tasks ($Ps > 0.50$) at the beginning of a goal path with increasing difficulty as they get closer to the goal. Conversely, $Ms < Maf$ individuals prefer difficult tasks ($Ps < 0.50$) at the beginning of a goal path with decreasing difficulty as they get closer to the goal.
- $Ms > Maf$ individuals anticipate positive self-evaluation in a test of competence, whereas $Ms < Maf$ individuals anticipate negative self-evaluation.

A parallel basic research track involves the work of Bernard Weiner (1972, 1974), which postulates a specific pattern of causal attributions of success/failure for high and low achievement-oriented individuals. Weiner and his colleagues postulate that $Ms > Maf$ individuals tend to attribute success to internal/stable causes such as high ability, and tend to attribute failure to internal/unstable causes such as lack of effort. $Ms < Maf$ individuals, on the other hand, tend to attribute success to good luck or task ease and failure to internal/stable factors such as lack of ability (Sirgy, 1977, 1980).

Elliot Entin and Norman Feather (1982) have demonstrated that $Ms > Maf$ individuals' attribution of success and failure may differ in contingent and noncontingent situations. That is, in a noncontingent task, high $Ms > Maf$ was found to attribute success to high ability and failure to bad luck or task difficulty rather than low effort. This finding is explained in terms of the "ego-defensive bias" in attribution. That is, individuals protect their egos by attributing failure to external circumstances. This is understandable in light of the ego-involving characteristics of contingent achievement paths.

Joel Raynor and Elliot Entin (1982) explain this behavioral phenomenon in terms of expectancy-value terms. They argue that $Ms > Maf$ individuals expect success and positive self-evaluation in undertaking achievement tasks that are path contingent. These positive expectations allow them to move forward in that path toward the goal state. Internal attributions given success in one step (and external attributions given failure) serve to increase the perceived probability of success in the next achievement step toward the goal, and therefore contribute to the attainment of the goal (positive self-evaluation of competence given goal attainment).

What have we learned from all of this? Basic research in achievement motivation points out that achievement-motivated individuals are more efficient in goal attainment and more adaptive to their environment. They set realistic goals to achieve and develop goal hierarchies (or contingent behavioral paths) that are efficient in attaining their goals. Successful attainment of goals allows them to evaluate their self-concept positively (positive self-evaluation), which, in turn, enhances their self-esteem. Self-esteem is the underlying motive of personality development and human action (Table 12.1)

In sum, achievement-motivated individuals (1) select realistic goals that they can achieve, (2) set up efficient paths leading to goal atainment, (3) act in a systematic way leading up to the superordinate goal, (4) persist in light of failure (persist more when the goal is closer and persist less when the goal is more distant), (5) think and become preoccupied with uncompleted tasks or contingent tasks that have not been successfully completed, (6) are confident about their ability to complete successfully the path leading to the goal, which, in turn, increases their expectancy of success in completing each contingent task, and (7) make causal attributions about success and failure of contingent tasks in such a way as to help attainment of the superordinate goal.

Achievement Motivation and Economic Behavior

J. N. Morgan (1964) has examined the relationship between the achievement motive and various facets of economic behavior. He provides data that show a positive relationship between achievement motivation and each of the following variables: level of education of the respondent, completed education of the respondent's children, plans for education of younger children, income from savings, hourly earnings, and planning ahead.

John W. Atkinson (1966) argues that $Ms > Maf$ individuals aspire to vocations and careers that are more difficult, up to a point. Charles H. Mahone (1960), on the other hand, shows that $Ms < Maf$ individuals set unrealistic vocational goals, goals that cannot be attained given the capabilities and resources of the individuals. Harry J. Crockett (1962) provides evidence supporting the hypothesis that $Ms > Maf$ individuals experience more upward social mobility than $Ms < Maf$ individuals.

David C. McClelland and David G. Winter (1971) have developed a general model of economic development. The essence of the model can be captured in the following theoretical proposition:

Table 12.1
Summary of Achievement Motivation Principles

Path Noncontingent	Path Contingent
$Tr = (Ms \times Ps \times Is) -$ $(Maf \times Pf \times If)$	$Tsn = (Ms \times P1sn \times Isn) -$ $(Maf \times P1fn \times Ifn)$
Risk Preference	
$Ms > Maf$ prefer $Ps = 0.50$	$Ms > Maf$ prefer $Ps > 0.50$ early in path and $Ps < 0.50$ closer to goal
$Ms < Maf$ Prefer $Ps \neq 0.50$	$Ms < Maf$ prefer $Ps < 0.50$ early in path and $Ps > 0.50$ closer to goal
Performance	
$Ms > Maf$ perform better than $Ms < Maf$	$Ms > Maf$ perform better than $Ms < Maf$
Persistence	
$Ms > Maf$ persist more than $Ms < Maf$ when initial $Ps > 0.50$	$Ms > Maf$ persist more than Ms $< Maf$ when closer to goal
$Ms < Maf$ persist more than $Ms > Maf$ when initial $Ps < 0.50$	$Ms < Maf$ persist more than $Ms > Maf$ when distant from goal
Attribution	
Ms $< Maf$ attribute success to ability and failure to lack of effort	$Ms > Maf$ attribute success to ability and failure to bad luck/task difficulty
Ms $< Maf$ attribute success to good luck/task ease and failure to lack of ability	$Ms < Maf$ attribute success to good luck/task ease and failure to lack of ability

Men act so as to maximize their interest(s) or return(s) over some time period, given the perceived constraints of the situation.

Interest/Return = goal as defined by the individual.

Maximization = a course of action that maximizes the likelihood of attaining the goal state with minimal cost.

Time perspective = short-term interest/return.

Perceived constraints of the situation = maximization of interest/return in the short term is dictated by how the individual perceives the situation.

McClelland and Winter (1971) argue effectively that differences in responsiveness to economic opportunities are due to achievement motivation. That is, only those who are achievement-oriented tend to be sensitive to economic opportunities, while those who are not achievement-oriented are not sensitive to the same opportunities (Papanek, 1962; Hagen, 1962; McClelland, 1961; Kolp, 1965).

This relationship explains (1) why people migrate from Third World countries where economic opportunities are perceived to be low to developed countries where economic opportunities are seen as high (Rogers and Neill, 1966), and (2) why some workers who are laid off start to look for work sooner and use better job-seeking techniques (those who are more achievement-oriented) than others (those who are not achievement-oriented) (Sheppard and Beltisky, 1966).

The relationship between achievement motivation and economic growth has been demonstrated by McClelland (1961). McClelland found that the n Ach content of popular literature increases prior to rapid economic growth at the national level and decreases prior to a slackening in the rate of growth.

McClelland (1961) and McClelland and Winter (1971) argue, with empirical evidence, that n Ach is a key factor in business success. Laboratory studies of individuals with high n Ach show that in general they behave like successful, rationalizing, business entrepreneurs. That is, (1) they set moderately difficult goals for themselves, (2) they seek concrete feedback on how well they are doing, (3) they assume personal responsibility for solving problems, and (4) they show more initiative and exploratory behavior. This pattern of behavior is argued to be highly similar to that of successful entrepreneurs (Kagan and Moss, 1962; Andrews, 1967; Kock, 1965; Wainer and Rubin, 1967).

TECHNOLOGY TRANSFER

William H. Gruber and Donald G. Marquis (1969) identified three *types* of technology transfer models: (1) science-technology-utilization models, (2) probabilistic technology transfer models, and (3) magnitude technology transfer models.

Models dealing with the science-technology-utilization typology (Model Type I) examine the relationship between science, technology, and the ultimate uses of science and technology. Loci of transfer are usually identified and examined. For example, the transfer can go from technology to use or from science to technology, or within science, technology, or use, and so on. Technology transfer may be viewed in a number of different ways such as transfer from science to technology, transfer of technology to initial use, and wide use of a given technology in a social system.

Models dealing with probability transfer (Model Type II) mostly involve predicting the probability that the idea of the technological innovation will be generated, researched, developed, produced, and diffused in a given social system.

The third type of model (Model Type III) deals with predicting the magnitude of transfer as a function of a set of factors such as source, nature of technological innovation to be transferred, structure of channels for transfer, and potential recipients (customers) of the innovation to be transferred.

The three models involving research in technology transfer focus on (1) invention, (2) innovation, and (3) diffusion (Gruber and Marquis, 1969). Although some investigators treat technology transfer from the perspective of invention, this author treats technology transfer as involving only innovation and diffusion. These two processes are most relevant to technology transfer because they can be treated directly in terms of economic value.

Based on the notion that technology transfer involves an innovation process (that is, a process relating to the producer of technological goods and services) and a diffusion process (that is, a process relating to the consumer of the same goods and services), the research literature can be categorized accordingly.

Research Involving Production of
Technological Products (Innovation)

Gruber and Marquis (1969) have identified the following set of achievement motivation-related factors influencing the production of technological innovations:

- Innovation is directly related to need for achievement.
- Innovation is inversely related to scientific research training and directly related to entrepreneurship. This may be explained through the mediating effects of achievement motivation, that is, achievement motivation determines entrepreneurship (Roberts, 1969).
- Innovation is directly related to demand recognition (recognition of a consumer demand that is not being satisfied by the technology currently in use) and technical feasibility (discovery that available technical information with perceived modifications would provide a new technical capability). This may be explained through the mediating effecs of achievement motivation, that is, achievement motivation increases demand recognition and technical feasibility.
- Innovation is directly related to management style. More specifically, the greater the management of R&D by a manager (compared to management by R&D personnel), the greater the rate of innovation. This is because R&D personnel are scientists who are trained to be meticulous and conservative in their work, whereas business-trained personnel are more daring in taking moderate risks and are more achievement-oriented (McClelland, 1969).
- Innovation is directly related to organizational mission. Innovation is said to occur most frequently in those organizations that define their mission in terms of discovering demand situations and the development of an organization system

that is capable of translating the demand recognition into organizational action. It can be argued that achievement-motivated executives tend to define organizational mission in terms of effective adaptation more than their nonachievement counterparts.

- Innovation is directly related to competition. The expectation that competition will innovate first increases efforts at ascertaining consumer demand that leads to demand recognition. Since competition is viewed as an important factor in organizational adaptation and effectiveness, it is postulated that this finding is due to the high achievement motivation strength of business executives.

- Innovation is directly related to reward structure. Organizations with a well-defined and visible reward structure tend to innovate more frequently than those with no reward structure. A well-defined reward structure functions to activate the achievement motive, especially in those who are highly achievement-oriented. Again, this finding may be explained in terms of achievement motivation.

These reported findings point to the possibility that innovation as an organizational phenomenon can be accounted for by achievement motivation. In other words, it can be stated that individuals occupying executive and managerial positions in the organizational structure tend to be more achievement-oriented than those who do not have entrepreneurial roles. Consequently, decisions related to organizational innovation are directly influenced by the achievement motivation characteristics of these individuals. In addition, as the evidence suggests, the greater the strength of achievement motivation of the individuals in a given organization, the greater is the rate of innovation in that organization. Achievement motivation in an organization is indicated by directly measuring n Ach and entrepreneurship, or by indirectly tapping causes and/or effects of achievement motivation such as demand recognition, management style, reward structure, organizational mission, and reaction to competition.

Research Involving Adoption of
Technological Products (Diffusion)

Gurprit S. Kindra (1983) has developed a model that illustrates the factors that affect diffusion of a new technology. The environment affecting the rate of diffusion is divided into three groups: governmental factors, conditional factors, and adopter characteristics. These are more distal factors that affect the more immediate (or proximal) factors related to the adoption of the new technology. *Governmental factors* include technology and developmental plans, barrier or incentive systems, communication structures, and financial access. *Conditional factors* include things such as existing and forecasted trade and economic conditions, political support, opinion leadership, and relative strength of existing indigenous technology. *Adopter characteristics* include factors such as education, innovativeness, sociocultural norms, professionalism, and conceptual skills.

These exogenous variables are postulated to influence a set of proximal (intervening) variables involving the following factors: (1) compatibility of the technology with domestic sociocultural norms, (2) relative complexity of the technology, (3) the extent to which the technology is trialable, (4) the perceived relative advantage of the technology, and (5) the communication system within the social structure of the potential adopters. More specifically, the following propositions were set forth:

- The more compatible the technology with domestic sociocultural norms, the greater the diffusion potential of the technology.
- The less complex the technology, the greater its diffusion potential.
- The greater the trialability of the technology, the greater its diffusion potential.
- The greater the perceived relative advantage, the greater its diffusion potential.
- The extent to which the benefits of the technology can be effectively displayed or demonstrated will enhance its diffusion potential.
- The more extensive the communication network with the adopters' social system, the greater the diffusion potential.

If we focus on Kindra's list of adopters' characteristics (education, innovativeness, sociocultural norm, professionalism, and conceptual skills), it can be argued that many of these personal factors are correlates of achievement motivation. An achievement-motivated adopter is very likely to be educated, professional, and have specific conceptual skills that permit him or her to engage in efficient and adaptive behavior.

Gerald Zaltman and Melanie Wallendorf (1983) have advanced several theoretical propositions related to factors affecting climate for change in adopting technological innovation in a given social system. They argue that the interaction between communication and achievement motivation influences the diffusion of technological innovations. More specifically, the following propositions were put forth.

- The larger the number and variety of communication channels (for example, mass media) in a society, the greater the communication exposure of consumers.
- The greater the communication exposure of consumers, the more favorable the climate for change.
- The greater the achievement motivation, the more favorable the climate for change in society.

A society with a more intensive formal communication network is said to have greater capability in disseminating information about a product to the members of that society, since the communication network serves to reach these members. However, communication is *not* adequate for creating a favorable climate for adopting technological innovation. Zaltman and Wallendorf state that communication exposure has to be accompanied by a high level of achievement motivation, or a desire for excellence in accomplishing the personal goals of the members of that society.

The effect of achievement motivation on diffusion of innovation has been studied in the context of technology transfer to developing countries (Rogers, 1973). The findings suggest that countries with high achievement-motivated citizens are more likely to establish institutions that create, diffuse, and utilize technological innovations.

Research Involving the Relationship Between Technology Transfer and Economic Development

Kindra (1983) argues that technological innovation and diffusion are limited to developed countries. This is because most innovations are labor-saving in nature, and consequently their payoff is highest in developed countries where expenditure of human time is valued more than in less developed countries (LDCs). Kindra demonstrates that LDCs are highly dependent on technology from developed countries. The factors contributing to technological dependence include (1) a high illiteracy rate (leading to lack of appreciation for technical knowledge), (2) lack of capital (accounting for 75 percent of the world population, but only 20 percent of its income), (3) lack of incentive (lack of perceived benefits from innovative activities), (4) lack of skills (few opportunities to acquire skills by learning-by-doing), and (5) lack of means of production (lack of an organizational infrastructure).

Economic growth is viewed to reflect increases in labor, capital, and productivity. However, Chen (1979) has demonstrated that economic growth is tied more to increases in productivity than to increases in labor and capital. His study indicates that four semi-industrialized LDCs (Hong Kong, Singapore, Korea, and Taiwan) followed a growth pattern that reflects increases in productivity rather than increases in labor or capital.

Kindra (1983) makes the point that increases in productivity are directly related to increases in technology acquisition and application in production. The Japanese experience demonstrates this relationship adequately. From 1950 to 1971, Japan spent approximately $3 billion on technology acquisition and currently enjoys the highest sustained rate of productivity increase. However, Kindra argues, for productivity increases to be translated into economic development, an increase in exports has to be sustained. Kindra demonstrates this point empirically.

Figure 12.1 shows a systems model that relates achievement motivation with technology transfer and economic development. The central theoretical propositions are as follows:

Figure 12.1
A System Model Involving Achievement Motivation,
Technology Transfer, and Economic Development

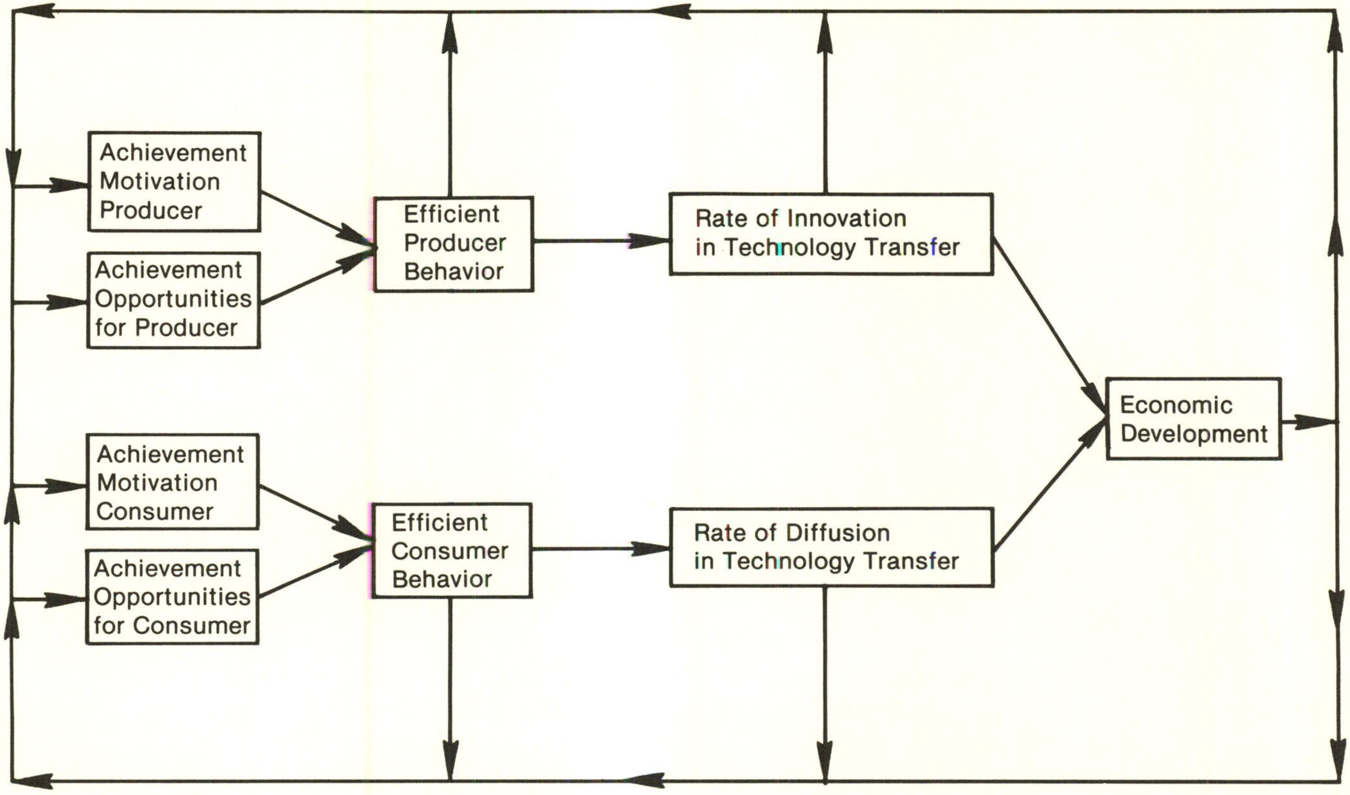

1. Individuals have social roles that serve specific functions, for example, a job role serving to attain goals such as personal income, social interaction, creativity, and self-esteem.

2. Two social roles concern us the most in the context of technology transfer: the producer role and the consumer role. The producer role is a role of an organizational executive who produces and markets an economic good to a designated consumer market for the purpose of satisfying one or more organizational needs (for example, profit, organizational growth). The consumer role is a role that an individual assumes to acquire an economic good from a producer for the purpose of satisfying one or more consumption needs of an individual, a family, or an organizational unit.

3. Individuals assuming producer or consumer roles vary in their achievement motivation tendency within the bounds of the designated role.

4. Given achievement opportunities, achievement-motivated producers engage in efficient organizational performance in producing and marketing their economic goods to prospective consumers. Efficiency is defined as maximizing the benefit/cost ratio, for example, maximizing profits.

5. Given achievement opportunities, achievement-motivated consumers engage in efficient consumption activities in the purchase, usage, and adoption of producers' goods. As in organizational efficiency, consumer efficiency is defined similarly as maximizing purchasing quality goods at the least cost.

6. Efficient producer behavior increases the likelihood of successful attainment of producer goals. Successful attainment of producer goals reinforces the behavior of those achievement motivation beliefs and values of the producer, which, in turn, strengthen the producer achievement motivation tendency. That is, high profit outcomes reinforce those achievement-related beliefs and values that initially determined the achievement behavior, thereby reinforcing the achievement motivation tendency.

7. Since adaptive behavior is mostly path contingent, the achievement-motivated producer seeks alternative courses of action to move closer to his or her superordinate goal given successful attainment of a subordinate goal. This motivation to seek *alternative courses of action* drives the achievement-motivated producer to not only capitalize on available courses of action, but also to generate new ones, therefore creating new achievement opportunities, that is, create and distribute innovations to new prospective markets more efficently.

8. Efficient consumer behavior increases the likelihood of successful attainment of consumer goals. Successful attainment of consumer goals reinforces the behavior of those achievement motivation beliefs and values of the consumer, which, in turn, strengthen the consumer achievement motivation tendency. That is, products generating maximum utility reinforce those achievement-related beliefs and values that initially determined the achievement behavior, thereby reinforcing the achievement motivation tendency.

9. Since adaptive behavior is mostly path contingent, the achievement-motivated consumer seeks alternative courses of action to move closer to his or her superordinate goal given successful attainment of a subordinate goal. This motivation to seek *alternative courses of action* drives the achievement-motivated consumer

not only to capitalize on available courses of action, but also to generate new ones, thereby creating new achievement opportunities, that is, adopt other innovations to meet consumption needs more efficiently.

10. Given efficient producer behavior at the aggregate societal level, a society's rate of innovation in technology transfer increases, that is, more technological innovations are produced and distributed to prospective markets.

11. Given efficient consumer behavior at the aggregate societal level, a society's rate of diffusion in technology transfer increases, that is, more consumption of technological innovations.

12. The greater the rate of innovation in technology transfer, the greater the reinforcement of producers' achievement motivation beliefs and values, and the greater the availability and generation of achievement opportunities for the producers. That is, the greater the success of a given industry in producing and distributing particular innovations to prospective markets, the greater the prosperity of that industry, which in turn reinforces the achievement behavioral patterns that are perceived to have determined this outcome.

13. The greater the rate of adoption of technological innovation, the greater the reinforcement of consumers' achievement motivation beliefs and values, and the greater the availability and generation of achievement opportunities for the consumers. That is, the greater the consumers feel that they have satisfied their consumption goals with minimal costs, the greater the likelihood that the achievement behavioral pattern perceived to have determined their satisfaction will be reinforced.

14. The greater the rate of technology transfer (innovation and diffusion), the greater the economic development of that society. In turn, economic development functions to reinforce the achievement personality through social and cultural norms and values. It also serves to create new opportunities for innovation and diffusion in exactly the same manner as discussed in the preceding points. The only difference is economic development is treated at a more macro or aggregate level.

CREATING SOCIAL CHANGE

To create social change in LDCs, two social change strategies may be undertaken. One strategy would be to (1) increase or strengthen the achievement motive of a collective in an LDC and (2) decrease or weaken competing motives that conflict with the achievement motive.

Strengthening the Achievement Motivation Tendency

McClelland (1965) has developed a theory of motive acquisition which posits that a motive is an affective toned network of expectancies arranged in a hierarchy of strength or importance in an individual. Changing motive strength then entails (1) reinforcing achievement-related expectancies, (2) tying the network to as many expectancies as possible in everyday life, and (3) insuring that other superordinate networks (for example, self-concept) do not block the train of achievement thoughts. These tactics of motive acquisition and change are laid out in propositional form as follows:

Proposition 1: The more reasons an individual has in advance to believe that he or she can, will, or should develop a motive, the more educational attempts designed to develop that motive are likely to succeed. That is, the target person or collective has to be made aware of the benefits associated with becoming achievement-oriented, for example, showing how achievement-oriented people are more successful and prosperous than nonachievement-oriented people.

Proposition 2: The more an individual perceives that developing a motive is consistent with the demands of reality (and reason), the more educational attempts designed to develop that motive are likely to succeed. In the context of the achievement motive, the target social system has to be made aware of the fact that not developing the achievement tendency will generate dire consequences such as poverty, loss of self-esteem, and loss of respect from significant others.

Proposition 3: The more thoroughly an individual develops and clearly conceptualizes the associative network defining the motive, the more likely he is to develop the motive. That is, the target system has to be well informed about those beliefs and values (for example, hard work, risk preference, goal setting, attribution of success and failure on achievement tasks) of the achievement personality.

Proposition 4: The more an individual can link the newly developed network to related actions, the more the change in both thought and action is likely to occur and endure. That is, the target system has to be taught how these achievement-related beliefs and values translate in career planning, running a business, schooling, and so on.

Proposition 5: The more an individual can link the newly conceptualized association-action complex (or motive) to events in his or her everyday life, the more likely the motive complex is to influence his or her thoughts and actions in situations outside the training experience. That is, in the context of achievement-related domains (for example, career planning, running a business, and/or schooling), specific concrete examples within the specified domains should be put forth.

Proposition 6: The more an individual can perceive the newly conceptualized motive as an improvement in the self-image, the more the motive is likely to influence his or her future thoughts and actions. That is, the target system has to be made aware that becoming achievement-oriented is a desirable ideal self-image, the attainment of which increases self-esteem and self-satisfaction.

Proposition 7: The more an individual can perceive and experience the newly conceptualized motive as an improvement on prevailing cultural values, the more the motive is likely to influence his or her future thought and actions. That is, it is important to bring out in the open the potential conflict between the achievement motive and other competing motives dominant in that culture (for example, need for power, need for affiliation, need for approval). This is to be followed by persuading the social system that behavior resulting from the achievement motive has greater benefits than outcomes related to other competing motives. (This subject is discussed again in a following section.)

Proposition 8: The more individuals commit themselves to achieving concrete goals in life related to the newly formed motive, the more the motive is likely to influence their future thoughts and actions. That is, it is important that the target social system be made to commit themselves to thinking, feeling, and acting as achievement-oriented.

Proposition 9: The more individuals keep a record of their progress toward achieving goals to which they are committed, the more the newly formed motive is likely to influence their future thoughts and actions. In an achievement context, this translates into getting feedback and monitoring progress toward goal attainment. Feedback is extremely important for the achievement-oriented person, since negative feedback signals further action or persistence.

Proposition 10: Changes in motives are more likely to occur in an interpersonal atmosphere in which individuals feel warmly but honestly supported and respected by others as persons capable of guiding and directing their own future behavior. This principle translates into the notion that target individuals should feel they can identify and obtain the support of significant others to help them adopt the achievement personality.

Proposition 11: Changes in motives are more likely to occur the more the setting dramatizes the importance of self-study and lifts it out of the routine of everyday life. This proposition points out that since adopting an achievement personality is an individual decision guided by self-study and self-evaluation, the educational environment that the target individuals are placed in has to facilitate these inner reflections.

Proposition 12: Changes in motives are more likely to occur and persist if the new motive is a sign of membership in a new reference group. In the context of the achievement motive, it is imperative to point out that successful adoption of the achievement personality may signify membership to key reference groups that identify directly with hard work and successful achievements, such as becoming a member of a board of a corporation, joining a business-related club, or joining a professional association, to name a few.

The achievement motivation of people in LDCs can be increased using a variety of means. These may include (1) conducting achievement motivation training seminars and workshops for business personnel to change directly their achievement-related cognitive-affective network, (2) changing the family structure through education, (3) changing the organizational reward structure, and (4) changing the government reward structure.

Changing the Individual Cognitive Structure: The practical implications of McClelland's ideas involve conducting achievement motivation training seminars and workshops in LDCs. Business personnel and potential business leaders are to be invited to participate in these workshops by public policymakers or other business leaders. In these workshops, the trainer or educator should do the following:

1. Cognitions: Educators (trainers) should help conceptualize the achievement motive associative network to the target persons. Educators should teach these "students" how a typical achievement-motivated person feels, thinks, and acts. The principles should relate to (1) the selection of realistic goals, (2) setting the contingent path to goal achievement, (3) selecting the most efficient paths, (4) feeling optimistic and expectant of goal attainment, (5) learning from trial and

error, (6) giving up a contingent path early on when confronted with failure and replacing that contingent path with a more efficient path, (7) persisting in a selected contingent path when getting closer to the goal, (8) making internal attributions given successful outcomes within the contingent path and external attributions given failure outcomes, (9) seeking feedback concerning outcome of achievement behavior within the contingent path, and (10) thinking about incompleted tasks (Zeigarnik effect).

2. Action: Educators should link the associative network to related actions and cases. They should use particular concrete actions and cases to demonstrate how an achievement-motivated person feels, thinks, and acts in these concrete situations.

3. Self-Interest: Educators should argue that the development of the achievement motive is beneficial to the individual, his or her family, and society in general. They should show how specific achievement-motivated people have managed to improve their lot, their family interest, and simultaneously have helped the community through direct/indirect social and economic means.

4. Application: Educators should have the students choose a particular goal important to them. The goal has to be assessed for its realism and potential attainment. Then the goal has to be translated in terms of a concrete, well-defined objective. The students should be shown how to evaluate, think, feel, and act like an achievement-motivated person within the chosen application problem.

5. Reinforcement: Not only goal attainment has to be reinforcement, but also the entire exercise has to be conducted in a psychological climate filled with interpersonal support.

Changing the Family Structure: Bernard Carl Rosen (1982) offers the theory that industrialization requires an achievement-oriented labor force to research human problems and present solutions, to produce innovations to meet consumer demands, to distribute these innovations, to communicate the benefits of these innovations to the consumers, and to manage the organizations dealing with these innovations, among other activities. Industrialization is said to involve those conditions that produce the achievement-oriented personality, which, in turn, reinforces the industrial momentum of a given society. This is said to occur in the following manner:

First, industrialization strengthens kinship ties in a developing society which values the extended family. This is usually done through an increase in education. Education helps give family members the skills to cope with kinship problems and provides interpersonal competence and empathy that ultimately strengthen kinship ties.

Second, with industrialization the relationship between husbands and wives becomes more egalitarian and communicative. This comes about through the education and employment of women, which, in turn, changes their value structure.

Third, liberal sex role attitudes enhance the wife's power in the family, which, in turn, depresses fertility in the industrial city. With women's greater independence, their motherhood experiences decline because women start to value other social skills to attain esteem and respect from others.

Fourth, industrialization eventually democratizes the relationships between parent and child, and increases the stress parents place on independence and achievement. That is, child-rearing in an industrial city changes to accommodate the demands of the industrial life-style.

Given that Rosen's theory is valid, industrialization or national development of LDCs can be accelerated by (1) creating conditions that encourage the development of industrial cities or townships, (2) increasing the education of family members, (3) promoting skills and strategies to help resolve family problems and, therefore, strengthen kinship ties through increasing communication and balancing power relations among family members, and (4) promoting child-rearing skills that involve the teaching of achievement-oriented values and beliefs to insure that the future generation will become responsible, achievement-oriented citizens who will strengthen the industrial society.

Changing the Organizational Structure: Since achievement-oriented individuals respond better to rewards, organizations should explicitly define their goals, translate them into concrete objectives, and reward the attainment of these objectives by extrinsic and/or intrinsic means. These would represent opportunities to the achievement-motivated workers. These opportunities serve to activate the achievement motive, which, in turn, determines performance efficiency in producing technological innovations and marketing them.

Changing the Government Structure: Government can control national development by creating conditions that can strengthen the achievement-motivation tendency of both producers and consumers of innovations. This can be accomplished by providing incentives and disincentives for certain actions. For example, several years back, the U.S. government (as well as some state governments) established an incentive program to facilitate the production and diffusion of solar energy devices. The government provided low-interest loans for those producers who were interested in producing solar energy innovations. In addition, the government provided incentives in the form of tax credits to those consumers who adopted solar energy-related devices. Achievement-motivated people view these incentives as opportunities to attain certain immediate or long-term benefits, and achievement-motivated people tend to respond more favorably to achievement-related opportunities.

Weakening Other Motivational Tendencies That Conflict with Achievement Motivation

Rosen (1982) argues that in many traditional societies (LDCs), achievement is not valued, for the following reasons:

1. *Image of Limited Good*: Many people in LDCs believe that society's goods are limited and that the achievement or attainment of more goods for one individual will have to come at a cost of the collective, that is, zero-sum game. In other words, they believe that personal advancement comes at the expense of others, and therefore should be discouraged.

2. *Belief That Achievement Is Not Rewarded*: Most people in LDCs believe that hard work such as weeding the field from dawn to dusk or standing long hours in a small shop is cruelly exhausting and meagerly rewarded.

3. *Belief in Power and Authority*: In LDCs, people believe that one way to insure survival and share of wealth is to flatter, ingratiate, and obey authority figures. Others strive to attain positions of authority to gain respect from people. This belief in power and authority overshadows belief in achievement and hard work.

These images and beliefs are responsible for behavioral tendencies that counteract the achievement motivation tendency, and therefore efforts have to be undertaken to weaken them. This can be done through direct or indirect educational means, such as in educational institutions, mass media programming, mass media advertising, and opinion-leadership communication networks.

SUMMARY AND CONCLUSIONS

A system model showing the theoretical connections among achievement motivation, technology transfer, and economic development is introduced in this chapter. The essence of the model involves individuals assuming producer and consumer roles. These individuals may vary in their achievement motivation tendency within a designated producer or consumer role. High achievement-oriented producers are said to engage in efficient production, thereby increasing the rate of innovation in technology transfer. Similarly, high achievement-oriented consumers are said to engage in efficient consumption of economic goods, therefore leading to increases in the rate of diffusion in technology transfer. The interaction of both innovation and diffusion of technological innovation in a given social system is postulated to determine the level of economic development of that social system. Outcomes resulting from the achievement behavior of producers and consumers are viewed to reinforce achievement-related beliefs and values within that social system, and to create additional economic opportunities for producers to increase the rate of producing technological innovations, and for consumers to increase the rate of adoption of these innovations.

The economic development of LDCs is therefore contingent on increasing the rate of producing and diffusing the technological innovations of those countries. Increasing the rate of technology transfer of LDCs, according to the system model introduced here, requires efficient producer and consumer behavior, which, in turn, can be attained by increasing the strength of the producer and consumer achievement motivation tendency. Therefore, economists, marketers, psychologists, sociologists, and public policymakers can create positive social change by focusing on creating conditions that facilitate the acquisition and reinforcement of the achievement motive in LDCs. Social change can occur by pursuing individual, family, organizational, and governmental change strategies, all directed to acquiring and strengthening the achievement motive.

REFERENCES

Almond, Gabriel A., and Sidney Verba (1963). *The Civic Culture*. Princeton, N.J.: Princeton University Press.

Andrews, J. D. (1967). "The Achievement Motive in Two Types of Organizations." *Journal of Personality and Social Psychology* 6: 163-168.

Atkinson, John W. (1966). "Notes on the Generality of the Theory of Achievement Motivation." In *A Theory of Achievement Motivation*, edited by John W. Atkinson and Norman T. Feather. Huntington, N.Y.: Robert E. Krieger Publishing.

_____, and Norman T. Feather (eds.) (1966). *A Theory of Achievement Motivation*. New York: John Wiley.

_____, and Joel O. Raynor (eds.) (1974). *Motivation and Achievement*. Washington, D.C.: Hemisphere Publishing Corp.

_____ (eds.) (1978). *Personality, Achievement, and Motivation*. Washington, D.C.: Hemisphere Publishing Corp.

Cantril, Hedley (1965). *The Pattern of Human Concerns*. New Brunswick, N.J.: Rutgers University Press.

Chen, Edward Ky (1979). *Hyper-Growth in Asian Economies: A Comparative Study of Hong Kong, Japan, Korea, Singapore, and Taiwan*. London: Macmillan.

Crockett, Harry J., Jr. (1962). "The Achievement Motive and Differential Occupational Mobility in the United States." *American Sociological Review* 27: 191-204.

Dennis, Jack, Leon Lindberg, Donald McCrone, and Rodney Stiefbold (1968). "Political Socialization to Democratic Orientation in Four Western Systems." *Comparative Political Studies* 1: 71-101.

Entin, Elliot E., and Norman T. Feather (1982). "Attribution to Success and Failure in Contingent and Noncontingent Paths." In *Motivation, Career Striving, and Aging*, edited by Joel O. Raynor and Elliot E. Entin. Washington, D.C.: Hemisphere Publishing Corp.

Form, William (1976). *Blue Collar Stratification*. Princeton, N.J.: Princeton University Press.

Free, Lloyd A. (1976). *How Others See Us*. Lexington, Mass.: D. C. Heath.

Gallup, George H. (1977). "Human Needs and Satisfactions: A Global Survey." *Public Opinion Quarterly* (Winter): 450-467.

Gillespie, James M., and Gordon W. Allport (1955). *Youth's Outlook on the Future*. Garden City, N.Y.: Doubleday.

Gordon, Leonard V. (1967). "Q-Typing of Oriental and American Youth: Initial and Clarifying Studies." *Journal of Social Psychology* 71: 185-195.

Gruber, William H., and Donald G. Marquis (1969). "Research on the Human Factor in the Transfer of Technology." In *Factors in the Transfer of Technology*, edited by William H. Gruber and Donald G. Marquis. Cambridge, Mass.: MIT Press, pp. 255-282.

Hagen, E. (1962). *On the Theory of Social Change*. Homewood, Ill.: Dorsey Press.

Haire, Mason, Edwin Ghiselli, and Lyman Porter (1966). *Managerial Thinking: An International Study*. New York: John Wiley.

Havighurst, Robert J., Joep M. Munnichs, Bernice Neugarten, and Hans Thomae (1969). *Adjustment to Retirement: A Cross National Study*. Assen, The Netherlands: Van Gorcum & Co.

Husen, Torsten (1967). *International Study of Achievement in Mathematics*, vols. 1 and 2. Stockholm: Almqvist and Wiksell.

Igra, Amnon (1976). "Social Mobilization, National Context, and Political Participation." Ph.D. dissertation, Department of Sociology, Stanford University.

Inglehart, Ronald (1977). *The Silent Revolution: Political Change Among Western Publics*. Princeton, N.J.: Princeton University Press.

Inkeles, Alex (1960). "Industrial Man: The Relation of Status to Experience, Perception and Value." *American Journal of Sociology* 66: 1-31.

_____ (1978). "National Differences in Individual Modernity." *Comparative Studies in Sociology*, Vol. 1. Greenwich, Conn.: JAI Press.

_____, and Larry Diamond (1980). "Personal Development and National Development: A Cross-National Perspective." In *The Quality of Life: Comparative Studies*, edited by Alexander Szalai and Frank M. Andrews. Beverly Hills, Calif.: Sage Publications, pp. 73-109.

Jacob, Philip E., and Henry Teune (1971). *Value and the Active Community: International Studies of Values in Politics*. New York: Free Press.

Jordan, John E. (1968). *Attitudes Toward Education and Physically Disabled Persons in Eleven Nations*. Ann Arbor, Mich.: Latin American Studies Center, University of Michigan.

Kagan, J., and H. A. Moss (1962). *Birth to Maturity*. New York: John Wiley.

Kindra, Gurprit S. (1983). "Technology Transfer and Export Marketing Strategies: The LDC Perspective," In *Multinationals and Technology Transfer: The Canadian Experience*, edited by Alan M. Rugman. New York: Praeger, pp. 142-164.

Kock, S. W. (1965). "Management and Motivation." Summary of a doctoral thesis presented at the Swedish School of Economics, Helsingfors, Finland.

Kolp, P. (1965). "Navaho Economic Change." Unpublished Ph.D. thesis, MIT.

Lerner, Daniel (1958). *Passing of Traditional Society*. Glencoe, Ill.: Free Press.

Lewin, K., T. Dembo, L. Festinger, and P. S. Sears (1944). "Level of Aspiration." In *Personality and Behavior Disorders*, vol. 1, edited by J. McV. Hunt. New York: Ronald Press.

Liebman, Arthur, Kenneth Walker, and Myron Glazer (1972). *Latin American Students: A Six Nation Study*. Cambridge, Mass.: Harvard University Press.

McClelland, David C. (1961). *The Achieving Society*. Princeton, N.J.: D. Van Nostrand.

_____ (1965). "Toward a Theory of Motive Acquisition." *American Psychologist* 20: 321-333.

_____ (1969). "The Role of Achievement Orientation in the Transfer of Technology." In *Factors in the Transfer of Technology*, edited by William H.

Gruber and Donald G. Marquis. Cambridge, Mass.: MIT Press, pp. 61-81.

_____, J. W. Atkinson, R. A. Clark, and E. L. Lowell (1953). *The Achievement Motive*. New York: Appleton-Century-Crofts.

_____, and David G. Winter (1971). *Motivating Economic Achievement*. New York: Free Press.

Mahone, Charles H. (1960). "Fear of Failure and Unrealistic Vocational Aspiration." *Journal of Abnormal and Social Psychology* 60: 253-261.

Meade, Robert D., and James O. Whittaker (1967). "A Cross-Cultural Study of Authoritarianism." *Journal of Social Psychology* 72: 3-7.

Morgan, J. N. (1964). "The Achievement Motive and Economic Behavior." *Economic Development and Cultural Change* 12: 243-267.

Ornauer, H., H. Wiberg, H. Sickinski, and J. Galtung (1976). *Images of the World in the Year 2000*. The Hague: Mouton.

Papanek, G. S. (1962). "The Development of Entrepreneurship." *American Economic Review* 52: 46-58.

Raynor, Joel O., and Elliot E. Entin (1982). *Motivation, Career Striving, and Aging*. Washington, D.C.: Hemisphere Publishing Corp.

Roberts, Edward B. (1969). "Entrepreneurship and Technology." In *Factors in the Transfer of Technology*, edited by William H. Gruber and Donald G. Marquis, Cambridge, Mass.: MIT Press, pp. 219-237.

Rogers, Evert M., and R. E. Neill (1966). *Achievement Motivation Among Colombian Peasants*. East Lansing, Mich.: Michigan State University, Department of Communication.

_____ (1973). "Social Structure and Social Change." In *Processes and Phenomena of Social Change*. New York: Wiley-Interscience, pp. 75-87.

Rosen, Bernard Carl (1982). *The Industrial Connection: Achievement and the Family in Developing Countries*. New York: Aldine Publishing Co.

Sheppard, H. L., and A. H. Beltisky (1966). *The Job Hunt*. Baltimore, Md.: Johns Hopkins University Press.

Sirgy, M. Joseph (1977). "Causal Attributions as a Function of Achievement Motivation, Outcome, and Post-Performance Expectancy." In *Proceedings of the 57th Annual Convention of the Western Psychological Association*, edited by Nathaniel Wagner. Seattle, Wash.: Western Psychological Association, p. 102.

_____ (1980). "A Path Analytic Validation Study of Weiner's Cognitive Model of Achievement Behavior." *JSAS Catalog of Selected Documents in Psychology* 10 (August): 63, Ms. 2071.

_____ (1981). "The Phenomenon of the Achievement Motive: A Review and Assessment of Its Various Conceptions and Measuring Instruments." *JSAS Catalog of Selected Documents in Psychology* 1 (May): 33, Ms. 2252.

Tannenbaum, Arnold S., Bogdan Kavcic, Menachem Rosner, Mino Vianello, and Greg Wiser (1974). *Hierarchy in Organizations*. San Francisco: Jossey-Bass.

Taylor, Janet A. (1956). "Drive Theory and Manifest Anxiety." *Psychological Bulletin* 53: 303-320.

Torney, Judith V., A. M. Oppenheim, and Russell F. Farnen (1975). *Civic Education in Ten Countries*. New York: John Wiley.

Wainer, H. A., and I. M. Rubin (1967). "Motivation of R&D Entrepreneurs: Determinants of Company Success." Unpublished paper, MIT, Alfred P. Sloan School of Management.

Weiner, Bernard (1972). *Theories of Motivation*. Chicago: Rand McNally.

(1974). *Achievement Motivation and Attribution Theory*. Morristown, N.J.: General Learning Press.

Zaltman, Gerald, and Melanie Wallendorf (1983). *Consumer Behavior: Basic Findings and Management Implications*. New York: John Wiley.

13

Multinational Corporations and the Management of Technology Transfers

S. TAMER CAVUSGIL

It is generally agreed that technology makes both positive and negative contributions to the present state of the world. It is not uncommon to hear criticisms of some of the unwanted and unforeseen effects of a new technology or mismanagement of an existing one. The majority of these criticisms are related to direct and visible effects, such as a technology's aesthetic, social, and economic implications. Those who take a philosophical perspective on technology argue that the villain is not technology per se, but is management. Since multinational corporations in developed countries are the principal forces behind the creation, management, and transfer of technology, most of the criticism is directed toward their corporate strategies. Their importance in this regard has increased as the less developed nations, unsuccessful in their attempts to create technology, have tried to catch up with their counterparts by means of technology transfer. These countries, with their huge profit potentials, have become attractive markets for multinational corporations.

It has long been recognized that these corporations, through direct foreign investment, have provided vital industrial inputs: capital, management skills, technical know-how, and other ingredients required for production. Management of technology transfer has become one of the distinguishing factors between successful and unsuccessful companies involved in technology transfer. In other words, the management of technology transfer has become a key element affecting organizational survival.

Only a few years ago, most multinational corporations were concerned with enlarging their activities abroad and showed keen interest in the development of Third World nations through the transfer of technology. At the same time, the host governments of these young and developing nations were competing with each other by offering various incentives to attract foreign investment. But in recent years, donors of technology have been accused of promoting social retardation, economic stagnation, conflicting interests, and environmental pollution. Critics of multinational corporations have charged them with social irresponsibility and have emphasized the importance of the social technology rather than advanced technology.

This chapter highlights the importance of the *management of technology transfers,* which, if not managed properly, could lead successful foreign operations to disinvestment and cause harm to the developing recipient nations.

CHARACTERISTICS OF A TECHNOLOGY TRANSFER

The transfer of technology has become an emotional issue in many developing countries. It is particularly sensitive in those countries where governments do not fully appreciate and understand the complexities of the transfer process. When the question is debated in international conferences, the advanced nations and the multinational corporations are often accused of narrow selfishness, charging exorbitant fees or royalties, enforcing a multitude of restrictive provisions, and completely neglecting the recipients' interests. The multinationals, while admitting some of the accusations, still assert that overall transfers have been successful. Their argument does not seem to have been very convincing, since, in a growing number of countries, restrictive legislation has been or is being enacted. These laws set rigid rules under which technology is to be transferred. Many consider this policy dangerous and self-defeating in the long run (Hill and Still, 1980).

The creation and expansion of technologically oriented societies is generally accepted as the best, if not the only, hope for sustained progress for the poor of the world. The initial step toward a technologically oriented society is to transfer technology, as many of the developing countries have been or are doing. However, dissatisfaction with the management of technology transfers in the past constitutes a serious problem. It is important to determine whether the criticisms are well founded and, if they are, to determine more satisfactory procedures.

The essence of a true transfer is extremely complex, and generalizations regarding it are dangerous. The following basic characteristics of a technology transfer are often forgotten by multinational corporations and recipient nations. These characteristics are potential sources of conflict and criticism and could result in failure of the technology transfer attempt.

To a great extent, the transfer is a people-oriented phenomenon. Its success depends on the existence of close interrelationships and direct, two-way communication between the parties involved. Drawings, specifications, processes, procedures, and patents are only some of the most obvious ingredients.

Technology transfer is a continuing activity, as demonstrated by the fact that many license relationships have been in effect for over fifty years. Although technology never stands still, emphasis changes as the relationship matures.

Technology transfer is a multifaceted, diversified, and constantly changing process. Variations exist from one industry or one company to another. In addition, it changes at different stages during the life of the association. Thus, it would be dangerous to try to police it through the enforcement of uniform rules and regulations.

The transfer of technology is an extremely costly operation. It is becoming increasingly expensive and difficult to develop, especially if the products incorporated into it are to be competitive in international markets. Technology transfer should build on past experience. Thus, in view of the urgent needs of today's world, it is criminally short-sighted to try continually to reinvent the wheel. Technology transfer bears little similarity to the dissemination of knowledge or pure science. Neither the U.S. government nor the U.S. universities have much practical technology to transmit. Nor do they have the techniques, experience, or organizational structure with which to do so effectively.

Buying technology can either be a useless outlay or a sound investment, depending on the ability of one party to relay it and the ability of the other party to make good use of it. The existence of a sound infrastructure is generally an essential ingredient for accomplishment.

Widespread confusion and misunderstanding exist as to the real meaning of the terms *patents*, *proprietary* and *nonproprietary manufacturing*, *process information*, *trademarks*, *brand names*, and so on. In a number of studies undertaken to analyze the cost of technology, the payments made for know-how and patents have been indiscriminantly added up with oil royalties, trademarks, franchise fees, and even interest on loans.

A real transfer of technology relates mainly to the information and services needed to produce something, plus the legal rights to use the information received. Commercial considerations involve trademarks, franchises, brand names, and so forth. They are legitimate services and have a definite value, but they are not germane to the subject under discussion (Hill and Still, 1980; Finnegan, 1979).

MEANS OF TECHNOLOGY TRANSFER

Many diversified means have been used to transfer technology from one country to another. The type of countries between which technology transfers occur and the means through which they often take place can be summarized as follows:

The Donor and the Recipient Countries	*Means of Technology Transfer*
Advanced to Advanced	Licensing

Advanced to Developing	Capital; Management; Technical know-how; R&D
Newly Industrializing to Less Developed	Managerial/Technical know-how through contracts
Less Developed to Less Developed	Capital; R&D; Technical know-how

No single method is perfectly suited to all circumstances; each has its advantages and shortcomings. However, even when the transfer is broadcast as being a generous gift, all of them have to be paid for eventually in one way or another.

The traditional pattern used frequently in the past includes technology as part of the investment package together with managerial, technical know-how, and capital. In many instances, especially during the early years of operation, this method has proved to be a workable and economical one for the host country. In a certain sense, the subsidiary becomes a hostage, ensuring the availability of the techniques thought best suited for the development plan of the nation. Regardless of these advantages and of the past record of performance, the concept of an investment package is being seriously questioned and has become politically unpalatable in many areas. Thus, an increasing number of governments are striving to find new ways to unbundle the package and are hoping to treat technology, managerial and technical know-how, and capital independently. Consequently, although foreign investment will continue to be one of the proven ways to transmit technology, other alternatives will have to be found which conform with the new written or unwritten laws (Wallender, 1980).

Naturally, technology can be purchased. Japan is an outstanding example of a nation whose industrial growth has been based primarily on acquiring American and European technology and paying for it in hard cash—an eminently profitable transaction. The Japanese seem to be the most successful in obtaining best results from technology transfer. They import more technology than they export, but they acquire properly trained people to select the necessary technologies and absorb and adopt them. They go one step further by improving the imported technologies and exporting them to other countries (even to those who originally exported it) in an improved form. However, to be successful through licensing only, the recipient country —like Japan—must have a well-developed infrastructure and a high degree of managerial and industrial receptivity. Unfortunately, these conditions may be lacking or in short supply in many developing areas. In addition, unless sizable territories can be served by the license, or unless the local market is completely protected, the straight buying of technology (know-how) can be a very expensive venture. The cost may be especially prohibitive if the industry involved is an advanced or a fast-moving one, or if a high ratio of local integration required for political or economic reasons. The license system presents another shortcoming for the local government in that, if a dispute were to occur, the authorities could not really exert much pressure on the licensor, as the licensor has no local assets to protect and can easily slow up the transfer process or even walk away from the whole deal without suffering appreciable losses (Wallender, 1980).

Another method of technology transfer is to give technology away without accepting payments from the users. Many emerging nations have urged the adoption of this philosophy as a practical way to catch up and achieve self-sufficiency. They argue that the technology they need already exists in the industrialized countries and that those rich societies have a moral debt toward the poor ones which they can pay in part by a free technological transfer. In a number of very significant fields such as health, education, and food production, technology has been and should be transferred without payment. However, it would be cruelly unfair to the struggling developing countries to give the impression that under prevailing conditions it would be feasible to extend a free transfer of the techniques they urgently need. It is not realistic to expect that owners of technology would agree to give their commodities away without some recompense. Furthermore, as stated before, a continuing process is involved which consists of more than a single shipment of plans and specifications. This ongoing process requires the establishment of human relationships and the spirit of pragmatic industrial cooperation. These are not on-the-shelf items to be mailed out at no charge by some government bureaucrat (Green and Lutz, 1980a).

CREATORS AND OWNERS OF THE
TRANSFERRED TECHNOLOGY

It is important at this point to determine where the technology to be transferred originates and who owns it. Different exchange means can then be devised, depending on the nature of the parties involved. In the United States, as a matter of national policy, most technology is developed by the private sector. Thus, the private sector alone is in a position to transfer it. West Germany, Japan, Switzerland, Belgium, and Holland have adopted similar patterns, while in the increasingly mixed economies of the United Kingdom, France, and Italy, technology is created in both the private and public sectors. In the countries of the Eastern Bloc and in the People's Republic of China, technology is the sole responsibility of the government. It is the government, then, that decides whether to sell, exchange, or give technology away. On the other hand, as foreign investments do not fit into the Marxist philosophy, these countries have not and cannot use the investment package approach (Green and Lutz, 1980b). These comments refer mainly to industrial activities; they do not necessarily apply to public services utilities, pure science, or basic knowledge, which generally comes within the scope of governments or public institutions.

By definition, investor-owned corporations should, and generally do, base their policy decisions on earning a fair return on the stockholders' equity. This philosophy permeates all levels of management in a well-run company. Since the sale of technology to a developing country is an economic transaction, its transfer must result in an advantage to the transferor. It must eventually generate an acceptable return for the division which developed, owns, and transmits it; for the corporation of which that division is a part; and ultimately for the men and women who hold the stock of the corporation (Edfelt, 1980).

The policy of transferring technology abroad is being harshly criticized by certain U.S. senators, congressmen, and union leaders who accuse the multinational corporations of exporting jobs, giving away valuable assets, and increasing the relative strength of foreign competition. It is also interesting to remember that the U.S. multinational corporations in the past have been considerably more open-handed, unrestricted, and generous in transferring technology than have their European and Japanese counterparts. Stripped down to its essentials, the issue now appears clearly defined. On one side are the owners of most of the available technology insisting on a fair return on their technological capital. On the other are the governments of the developing nations, intent on acquiring these essential tools as cheaply and with as few restrictions as possible (Salomon, 1981).

POTENTIAL PROBLEMS IN TECHNOLOGY TRANSFERS

The quality and adequacy of the technology transferred by U.S. multinationals to the developing world are causes for growing concern in international circles. Here again, broad generalizations should be avoided, and much more detailed research and cost/benefit analyses are needed before fair conclusions can be reached. The following listing merely highlights some of the basic problem areas:

The technology transferred does not take into account the social costs that may be incurred. Alien technology is accused of a multitude of sins, including pollution, urban giantism, slum proliferation, social discontent, the breakdown of traditional family patterns, and unemployment. It is certainly recognized that technology has an important impact on the social system, in both developed and developing nations. Recently, a great deal of thought has been dedicated to this problem at the highest corporate executive levels in the United States. As a result, many companies have develped the philosophy of a social balance sheet, and specific responsibilities have been assigned.

The general feeling prevails, however, that additional analysis is needed on all aspects of the issue, especially its international implications. What can be stated is that when governments establish guidelines for development, it would appear that decisions regarding what constitutes acceptable social costs should be made by the local authorities. The responsibility of the transferors of technology would thus be limited to following the established rules and to providing the basic information to facilitate sound decision-making. In addition, the social costs resulting from imported technology should always be weighed against those that would result if the technology were not available (Salomon, 1981; Sangster, 1979).

The technology transferred is obsolescent or obsolete. This is a serious accusation, as no one, least of all a poor country, can afford to buy inferior products. Furthermore, acquiring up-to-date technology is particularly important to a nation planning to compete in world markets. Unfortunately, the determination of what constitutes an obsolete technology is fraught with theoretical and practical difficulties. The explosive changes in the prices of energy and raw materials, along with the current high interest rates, have made traditional theories on technological obsolescence obsolete. Geography must also be considered, because a technology that has become obsolete in one part of the world may be better suited to the needs of another.

Analysis indicates that the most highly respected multinationals experiment at home and abstain from exporting designs, processes, and techniques until they have been thoroughly tested in familiar environments. This is a wise policy and is amply justified by sad examples of what happens when it is not followed. It is realized, however, that this is an area in which imaginative innovation might pay valuable dividends. The very long lead times required for introducing new technologies may also result in the potential recipients' considering the inevitable delays as examples of the nearsighted efforts by licensors to retain a competitive edge as long as possible. In reality, they are a consequence of the practical laws of industrial development. In other instances, operating in restricted markets may be the reason for not exporting a new technology. Foreign subsidiaries or licensees may not yet have been able to amortize the costs incurred to produce the last development and cannot justify appropriating funds for the newest development. This is a particularly difficult and serious problem in rapidly changing technological activities (Johnson, 1970).

The technology transferred is not suited to local needs. On closer examination the conclusion is that either this policy may be unfairly criticized or unavoidable. The following aspects may help clarify the issue:

1. The buyers of technology are becoming increasingly aware that they have a number of sources from which to select. They can also obtain reliable advice from an increasing number of competent consultants, their own government or that of the United States.

2. Most well-established owners of technology do not knowingly sell a product, a process, or a production system that is completely unsuited to the environment in which it will be applied. They have a valuable reputation to protect.

3. For industrial reasons, it is uneconomical in most cases for a developing country to create completely new products exactly suited to their restricted markets and parochial particularities. Experience proves that it is usually much wiser and cheaper to adopt a proven apparatus and modify it to conform to the local requirements.

4. The accusation often leveled against the multinationals of building up capital-intensive industries in developing countries instead of promoting labor-intensive ones, does not stand up under close examination, especially in the medium- and large-sized manufacturing industries. In many fields, plentiful cheap labor can rarely be an acceptable long-term substitute for high-efficiency machines and modern production methods. However, it certainly can, and, it is hoped, will, give a valuable competititve edge to those countries where these conditions exist along with a forward-looking policy for sensible capital investments. There is an urgent need for much more unemotional research on this and related issues (Johnson, 1970; Lewis, 1980).

The technology transferred is a lemon. Although U.S. industry is still the world leader in most fields, a number of U.S. technological failures have occurred overseas. It is not known whether they were caused by faulty application, inadequate transfer, untested processes, or just plain inefficiency.

There is a lack of understanding in the transfer process. Many U.S. corporations are accused of failing to cooperate with others and of following inflexible corporate guidelines. This is certainly an area in which much work is needed, and the multinationals must concentrate on becoming more sensitive to the feedback from their subsidiaries and licensees. On the other hand, foreign governments must remember that rationalization of production, coordination of marketing, and other such plans promoted by developing countries may create serious U.S. antitrust problems for some corporations. There is a great need for clarification by all parties concerned (Green and Lutz, 1980b; Green and Lutz, 1980a).

PRODUCT POLICY ISSUES IN INTERNATIONAL MARKETS

The question of what products to sell in foreign markets is the essence of product policy in international marketing. Should we sell the same products we sell domestically, or should they be adapted to local conditions? Will our product line be the same abroad as at home, or should we sell a different mix of products in foreign markets? For each company and industry the answers to these questions may be different. Most theories of foreign direct investment do not address these questions. They seek to explain why the firm will invest and produce in foreign markets without asking what products or businesses the firm will be in. They implicitly assume that the firm will be producing the same products abroad as at home. This is especially clear in the Product Life Cycle Theory which states that the firm begins foreign production when a product has reached the mature stage of its life cycle at home. The general answer to the product policy questions raised above is that the firm should sell those products abroad that best help it to meet its objectives, such as market share, growth, and profit maximization. The practical experience of most companies suggests that the products and product lines sold in foreign markets to meet these goals will not be identical to those sold domestically, although there will be a strong similarity (Anderson, 1979).

International marketing would be easier, of course, if a firm's products and product lines were identical in all countries. However, most multinational corporations are forced to modify both product and product lines in foreign markets. Many different factors combine to induce such modifications. Among them are differences in use conditions, technical specifications, government regulations, competitive opportunities and consumer tastes and purchasing power. Because the firm cannot usually automatically extend its domestic products to foreign markets, it faces a critical question in international marketing: how can the multinationals adapt, develop, or acquire the products appropriate to foreign markets? (See Teece, 1976.)

When firms first enter international markets, they usually market their domestic products with minimal adaptation to foreign conditions. Another approach is to acquire a foreign firm that has products designed for its own markets. Each of these approaches may be satisfactory as an initial method of internationalization. For the long run, however, a more sophisticated business and product development plan is desirable. In its planning process, the firm must decide what businesses and what markets it wants to pursue. Ideally, this planning and scanning should be on a global basis. Product strategy is an important part of this plan and includes a strategy of product development.

It is possible for a firm to get products without itself developing them. One way is to copy products developed successfully by others. Many firms follow this strategy with some success. Obviously, however, it is not the strategy of a market leader. Another way of getting products for world markets is shown by Colgate's approach. Colgate has chosen to market internationally several products that have been successfully developed and introduced nationally by other firms. This strategy seems to work well for Colgate, but it is not followed by many other firms. Most multinational corporations do not follow either of the strategies just mentioned. That is, they do not rely on imitation to develop their new products, nor do they market internationally products developed and introduced by others. The primary way firms get their products for world markets is through internal product development, with acquisition as a secondary method (Teece, 1976).

CONDUCTING R&D ABROAD

For American firms, foreign R&D amounts to about 10 percent of the total, or over $1 billion annually since 1971. IBM alone spent over $200 million annually on foreign R&D in the early 1970s. There are a variety of external pressures and company motivations for conducting R&D abroad. In the transfer of technology among the large U.S. multinationals, we find that the major initial corporate motivation is to aid in the production of existing company products rather than in the development of new products abroad. However, the evolution of these units was in the direction of new product development for local or even regional or global markets (Teece, 1976).

Multinationals also often conduct R&D abroad because of subsidiary pressures. For example, local staff might become restive if they remain just a factory operation instead of a full-fledged member of the multinational family. In this way, Sperry-Vickers acceded to the demands of European subsidiaries for a fair share of R&D. Granting R&D to local operations thus reduces discontent and improves morale in the subsidiary.

There are both incentives and pressures by host governments to conduct local R&D. For example, Canada offers financial rewards, which encouraged National Cash Register to begin a new research program in Canada and helped IBM and Control Data expand their Canadian R&D. Host governments also try to require multinationals to conduct R&D locally to maximize the technology fallout from their operations. While governments have difficulty in pressuring foreign firms to initiate R&D, they have more success in getting multinationals to continue R&D in the local companies they acquire. For example, Britain feared that Chrysler's acquisition of Rootes would lead to a brain drain to the United States. To counter this, the government required as a condition of purchase that Chrysler maintain Rootes' existing R&D activity. Corning Glass maintained and expanded an R&D operation in a French acquisition to keep a promise made to the French government (Gruber, 1967).

In addition to improved subsidiary morale and compliance with host governments, there is often a public relations reward in conducting R&D locally. For example, IBM has gained favorable publicity as a result of having its R&D efforts in Europe, just as Hoechst did in India—a very different environment. Conversely, a firm that refuses to conduct R&D in foreign markets may suffer from bad public relations.

Encouraging R&D abroad can be a way of utilizing personnel who have sophisticated research talent and specialized product skills, but who are unwilling to leave their home countries. This has been important to firms in such science-based industries as electronics, computers, chemicals, and pharmaceuticals. For example, even an advanced company like Hewlett-Packard found it advantageous to locate R&D facilities near the Universities of Edinburgh and Stuttgart which exercised world research leadership in certain products of interest to the company. The U.S. Manufacturing Chemists Association claims that only three of the world's top ten chemical research organizations belong to U.S. companies and that eleven of the nineteen great chemical innovations of the past thirty years were based on foreign discoveries (Blumenthal, 1979).

A further incentive to establish local R&D is potential cost savings in many countries where scientific and technical personnel are paid less than U.S. personnel. This trend appears to be changing, however. A country like India offers technical skills at moderate remuneration compared to Europe or the United States. The Conference Board study found strong evidence that the performance of R&D is less costly overseas than in the United States.

With R&D in more than one country, a greater and more varied flow of new ideas and products may be possible. There are theoretical arguments to support this position on decentralized R&D, a few examples of which can be given here. R&D personnel in any one country are subject to one set of environmental constraints and influences, while those in other countries are subject to a different set. Monroe Auto Equipment, for example, set up an R&D facility in the Netherlands because American R&D in auto parts is so dominated by General Motors that no one dares to innovate very far from GM design. Europe is a much more fragmented market, and different kinds of product design can be tried, resulting in potential innovations. Unilever has a deliberate policy of decentralizing R&D. It believes that by locating R&D activities in a number of countries, an international firm can take advantage of its unique ability to do research in a variety of national environments. The probability of success is increased if there is a good liaison between laboratories. Worthington Pump's Italian subsidiary in 1975 earned $200,000 in royalties from its American parent because of developments originating in the local R&D operation. This is an explicit and notable illustration of the contribution of foreign R&D in one company (Gruber, 1967).

An international division of labor in R&D can sometimes mean faster and more effective results than centralized R&D. Examples of this division of labor are Honeywell and Kodak. Honeywell introduced a new five-model computer line in 1974. Development began in the early 1970s with competitive pressures for an early output. The French company was assigned one of the five models for development, and the Italian company another. French and American operations shared responsibility for the critical Model 64. The programming languages and software were shared by the company's British and U.S. operations. Technical coordination was from Minneapolis. The international division of labor enabled Honeywell to meet its goals for introducing the new line.

For its instant camera, Kodak required a fast film using a high-speed emulsion four times as responsive to light as any then known. An international team began working on this in 1973. It involved 1,000 employees in Europe and the United States for one year. The final product used an emulsion developed in England, refined in Rochester, and made commercial with the help of French expertise in emulsion control. This marked another successful collaboration in international R&D (Tsurumi, 1979).

Local R&D will be better attuned to local market needs and desires than R&D centralized in a distant and different market. This is especially true with purely technical aspects. This applies more to consumer than to industrial goals, but industrial goods are not exempt either. For instance, Otis Elevator conducted R&D on small elevators in Europe because there is no real market for them in the United States. An example in consumer goods is Beecham's in Brazil. The local subsidiary felt there was a local demand for a deodorant with a strictly feminine image. The Brazilian staff developed the product and made extensive local tests of the deodorant and perfume elements. From these tests the Brazilian company developed and introduced the product. Within one year it was already vying for the number one position in the market. In automobiles, Ford in Brazil provides an example. For many years, Ford had reasonable success in that country by adapting cars originally made in the United States. Yet Ford's biggest winner was the Corcel, a car produced by local R&D in Brazil (Pierson, 1978).

It is likely that R&D obtained through acquisition will be contrived by the acquiring firm. Most acquisitions are not made to obtain R&D facilities, but once the R&D is acquired there are strong reasons for keeping it. These reasons include morale in the subsidiary, government and public relations, and new skills and personnel acquired. Often the acquired R&D is in a product area new to the firm; for example, in Italy Dow Chemical acquired LePetit in pharmaceuticals, and likewise Gillette acquired DuPont in France where Cricket lighters had been developed (Pierson, 1978).

For U.S. firms the attractiveness of expanding abroad can increase with changes in application of U.S. tax law. Assume an American firm does all of its R&D in the United States but has half of its sales abroad. If the firm can get credit on its U.S. taxes for only the proportion of R&D uncovered, this would give the firm incentive to move some or all of that uncovered part abroad where it, too, could enjoy a tax savings. This is an oversimplified illustration of a complex topic, but it does indicate the potential influence of tax considerations on R&D locations (Fischer and Behrman, 1979; Tsurumi, 1979; Gruber, 1967).

It is possible that some multinationals have not yet addressed the question of whether to conduct R & D abroad. Many others, however, have had to face the issue either when it was raised by their subsidiaries or foreign governments, or when they acquired a foreign firm with R&D. Rather than responding to such events on an ad hoc basis, the firm can improve its decision-making by incorporating R&D location policy into its overall strategy for international business development. Historically, much of the internalization of a firm's marketing, production, and especially R&D has been relatively unplanned, resulting in mismanagement of technology transfer and creating conflicts between donors and recipients. All three activities should be part of the firm's global strategic planning to provide best returns for both parties involved in the transaction.

REFERENCES

Anderson, Bruce A. (1979). "Acquiring and Selling Technology-Marketing Techniques." *Research Management* 22 (May): 26-28.

Blumenthal, Tuvia (1979). "A Note on the Relationship Between Domestic Research and Development and Imports of Technology." *Economic Development and Cultural Change* 27 (January): 303-306.

Edfelt, Ralph (1980). "International Competition and U.S. Public Policy." *California Management Review* 23 (Fall): 5-10.

Finnegan, Marcus B. (1979). "R&D for Developing Countries: II—The Code of Conduct Issue." *Research Management* 22 (May): 39-41.

Fischer, William A., and Jack N. Behrman (1979). "The Coordination of Foreign R&D Activities by Transnational Corporations." *Journal of International Business Studies* 10 (Winter): 28-35.

Green, Robert T., and James Lutz (1980a). "Changing National Concentrations of High Technology Exports." *Columbia Journal of World Business* 15 (Spring): 52-60.

Green, Robert T., and James Lutz (1980b). "U.S. High Technology Import/Export Performance in Three Industries." *Journal of International Business Studies* 11 (Fall): 112-117.

Gruber, William (1967). "The R&D Factor in International Trade and International Investment of U.S. Industries." *Journal of Political Economy* 75 (February): 20-36.

Hill, John S., and Robert R. Still (1980). "Cultural Effects of Technology Transfer by MNC's in Lesser Developed Countries." *Columbia Journal of World Business* 15 (Summer): 40-51.

Johnson, Harry G. (1970). "The MNC's as a Development Agent." *Columbia Journal of World Business* (May/June): 25-30.

Lewis, Henry R. (1980). "The Impact of Industrial Innovation on the Economic and Social Welfare of the U.S." *Research Management* 23 (November): 10-13.

Pierson, Robert M. (1978). "R&D by Multinationals for Overseas Markets." *Research Management* 21 (July): 19-22.

Research Management (1979). "Acquiring and Marketing Technology—Industrial Research Institute Position Statement on Licensing of Technology" (May): 32-33.

Salomon, Jean Jacques (1981). "Technology and Economic Policy in a Changing World." *Research Management* 23 (January): 36-41.

Sangster, Raymond C. (1979). "R&D for Developing Countries. I—The Role of Industrial R&D." *Research Management* 22 (May): 34-38.

Teece, David J. (1976). *The MNC and the Resource Cost of International Technology Transfer.* Cambridge, Mass.: Ballinger.

Tsurumi, Yoshi (1979). "Two Models of Corporation and International Transfer of Technology." *Columbia Journal of World Business* 14 (Summer): 43-50.

Wallender, Harvey W., III (1980). "Developing Country Orientations Toward Foreign Technology in the Eighties: Implications for New Negotiation Approaches." *Columbia Journal of World Business* 15 (Summer): 20-27.

14

Transferring Technology to Generate Effective Entrepreneurs in Less Developed Countries

A. C. SAMLI AND MARTIN L. GIMPL

Economic development that results in higher levels of real income, greater employment, and a higher quality of life is typically the stated objective of all countries whether they are developed, developing, or undeveloped. Plans are made and vigorously promoted to achieve these objectives. These plans for economic development may be couched in economic terms, but the real aim is the encouragement of new businesses and the expansion of existing businesses into the areas of higher productivity and greater effectiveness.

Developing a new business or expanding an existing one depends on the effective use of technology, physical resources, and money. This development also requires an agent—the entrepreneur. A business cannot start itself merely by identifying needed areas of development and by making the provisions for adequate capital and technical skills. These skills, capital, and other resources of business must be brought together, matched against the established opportunity range, and directed properly so that the new venture will be a success. The entrepreneur is the catalyst who brings these elements together and provides a meaning and direction for them.

Without inputs from the entrepreneur it is impossible to fulfill the economic development goals. Thus, it may be posited that in their strides for economic development, the developing countries are in great need of entrepreneurs. According to Harpham: "One of the hallmarks of an underdeveloped country is that it doesn't understand that you can make things and develop skills. Instead it looks for some organization outside its own borders that is going to come and reap the whole magic for it."[1]

This chapter posits that the skills (or the technology) for developing and utilizing entrepreneurs are transferable. Less developed countries (LDCs) are not likely to develop this technology on their own; therefore, it is necessary to understand how entrepreneurship is developed and promoted, and how such know-how can be transferred. In order to accomplish these goals, this chapter presents six major sections: (1) definition of entrepreneurs, (2) the sources of entrepreneurship, (3) what it takes to become an entrepreneur, (4) the process of entrepreneurship, (5) promotion of entrepreneurs, and, finally, (6) tools for transferring skills to develop entrepreneurs.

DEFINING ENTREPRENEURS

The French economist Cantillon is said to have introduced the term *entrepreneur*. His definition was "the agent who purchased the means of production for combination into marketable products."[2] J. B. Say[3] expanded Cantillon's ideas. He conceptualized the entrepreneur as the organizer of the business firm. Many years later Dewing viewed an entrepreneur as a promoter who transformed ideas into profitable business.[4] As such, that person would have imagination, initiative, judgment, and restraint. Schumpeter saw an entrepreneur as an administrator with the ability to carry new combinations of practices in running a business.[5] These combinations include introducing new goods and new methods of production, opening new markets, finding a new source of raw materials, and carrying out a new organization of any industry. Since that time there have been many definitions of an entrepreneur, but there is a lack of consensus as to what the concept exactly means. In this chapter, therefore, we attempt to describe the concept instead of defining it.

An entrepreneur is a highly motivated and trained person who tries to perform well regardless of the nature of the job. He or she is an *opportunity seeker* who looks for ways to improve performance. In the process, the entrepreneur also tries to improve his or her socioeconomic status. The entrepreneur is a *decision-maker*. He or she is the person who decides on what resources, and skills, and how much capital is needed to take advantage of certain opportunities in the marketplace. Finally, an entrepreneur is an *achiever* who takes pride in high-level performance. Some authors maintain that entrepreneurs need to achieve. Their achievement lies not only in generating the ideas for a new business venture, but also in making it operational.

SOURCES OF ENTREPRENEURSHIP

One source of the technology, resources, and entrepreneurial skills is the multinational corporation (MNC). MNCs are capable of identifying markets and then providing the technology and resources to satisfy the markets.

Another source of the high-productivity, growth-producing technology and entrepreneurial skills is the local technically trained entrepreneur. Encouraging local engineers, scientists, and others with applicable expertise to become entrepreneurs is preferable to MNCs for expansion of business.

To see why a country should favor the promotion of local entrepreneurs over MNCs, let us first look at MNCs as a source of new business. Industrial growth may be promoted by attracting MNCs to a country or region. The MNC will bring with it the productivity-improving technology, the management, and the marketing technology necessary to get a new venture started. MNCs are likely to be attracted overseas by (1) cheaper or more abundant resources, for example, minerals, forests, and power (2) cheaper labor; (3) more liberal tax and investment laws; and (4) access to a market available only to home-based businesses (import substitution). In discussing regional development within a country, any "out of town" company may be viewed as an MNC.

What, if any, are the objections to relying on MNCs for creating new business and thereby improving productivity and quality of life?

1. MNCs do not locate any of their top management in the host country: management located there by the MNC is either there for a short training period or deal-ended. The management located there is not privy to any important decision-making of the MNC.

2. MNCs primarily use only parent company nations as managers in top positions; the nationals of LDCs do not reach the top levels. Engineers may become managers of production or of a technical function but not managing directors.

3. When the product life cycle of the locally produced product is over, the location of new generation facilities is an open question again. Since none of the power or important decision-making capacity is located in the host country, growth of a self-sustaining type is impossible with MNCs.

4. MNCs do not train people in entrepreneurial skills. R&D is carried out by the parent company so that first-rate technology is held back and exploited first in the parent company.

5. MNCs often invest little of their own capital. MNCs in many LDCs seem to finance their local operations by local borrowing and debt issues. The MNCs provide and retain all the equity and raise all the debt finance in the host country.

6. Dividend payments overseas are a drain on our overseas reserves and are seldom reinvested in the host country.

7. Through the mechanism of transfer pricing, tax can be effectively avoided.

In general, government loses control over economic policy when a large amount of business is in the control of MNCs that have access to overseas financial markets and are able to act outside economic policy.

The alternative to growth through MNCs is the technically trained entrepreneur. The local entrepreneur can participate in new busines formation through existing companies (internal entrepreneurs) or by starting his or her own company (external entrepreneurs). Because existing companies are reluctant to accept radical new ideas, the entrepreneur must usually find his or her own new venture. Existing firms will gladly adopt productivity-improving technology that will cause small, gradual, and predictable changes that are consistent with its present products and markets, but the adoption and economic realization of radically new products, processing techniques, marketing strategies, and management strategies require the hand of a highly competent entrepreneur. Promoting productivity improvement through entrepreneurial activity is the difference between 1 to 2 percent improvements in productivity and 100 to 1,000 percent improvements.

Local entrepreneurs are the only group that can be counted on to promote economic growth consistent with local goals and local opinion as to what constitutes a better quality of life. Some comparisons that can be made between growth based upon local entrepreneurs and MNCs are as follows:

1. Entrepreneurial growth can be expected to be self-sustaining and a source for continued growth when the product life cycle ends. Second-generation products will be designed, and marketing and production will be controlled by the host country interests. Second-generation products developed by MNCs based in the host country may or may not be produced there.

2. Technical entrepreneurship, in particular, relies on the supply of highly technically trained manpower. This source is underutilized in many LDCs. MNCs that develop their own technology overseas do not need many of the host country's technically trained people. Their best inventors, scientists, and engineers are underemployed while they import technology.

3. High-technology-based industries started by local entrepreneurs can be expected to be highly oriented to the export market as compared with most MNCs which are oriented to import substitution production.

4. LDC entrepreneurs can be expected to keep the power and decision-making base in their own country. Decisions may be made for the good of the host country, and wayward ventures may be brought into line by public pressure and government action. Policing MNCs is a difficult and sometimes impossible task.

WHAT IT TAKES TO BECOME AN ENTREPRENEUR

Requirements (not necessarily in order) for a new venture include the following: (1) an opportunity must be located and identified; (2) the person must have the necessary behavioral (psychological) background; and (3) a final push or precipitating event is needed to get the venture into being. Each of these factors is briefly examined below.

Opportunities

In looking for opportunities, the entrepreneur must evaluate both potential markets and potential products or services. A good opportunity exists when one finds a large fast-growing market and matches it with a product or service that one can produce better than anyone else for one's market segment. The entrepreneur can begin the search by looking first at products or services and, when there is a unique product or service, then looking for a niche in the market. This is termed an inside-out approach and is often followed by technically oriented entrepreneurs and firms. Many opportunities are missed with this type of product-service-first thinking. Better for locating opportunities is outside-in thinking, where the entrepreneur first looks for market opportunities and then thinks if the company can service the market segment located. Thinking of markets first and deciding what the consumer wants do not come naturally to technically trained persons. They prefer to decide on a product first. However, deciding first on a product and then looking for a market for it can lead entrepreneurs down roads where there is little payoff.

Locating an opportunity for a new venture is a result of creative thinking —something a university education seems to hinder rather than enhance. Locating a good opportunity requires the ability to successfully forecast the sociological, technological, and economic future.

A factor that limits the set of opportunities that will be entertained by a prospective entrepreneur is the *social self-image*. An individual's social self-image is the view of what roles that person finds socially acceptable. During the formative years the prospective entrepreneur forms an opinion as to what type of work is acceptable.

The following episode may illustrate the concept of social self-image:

When Joe was in his final year at engineering school studying metallurgy one of his classmates, Dave, with no academic problems dropped out to go into the scrap metal business, saying he had had enough of university. To the rest of the students, careers in the steel industry, nuclear industry, aerospace industry were at the top of almost everyone's list of prestige, and conditions were such that the choice was theirs. Although training in metallurgy would give someone a big advantage in the scrap metal business, the scrap business conjured up images of "Steptoe and Son" and in prestige would rate with dustmen or used car salesmen. Joe chose the nuclear industry. Some ten years later Joe saw the advantages of entrepreneurship and started a powdered metal part business. He had a visit from Dave whom he had not seen since he left university. Dave drove a Mercedes with a radio telephone, showed Joe the pictures of his corporate plane, and acquainted him with the scrap metal business in which he was now one of the top dealers. They entered into an agreement that day that Joe would sell the scrap from his new venture to Dave's company. In the ten years since Dave had left his engineering classmates behind he had done much better financially than any of them. The rest of them had a social self-image of themselves that precluded the scrap business and many other worthwhile pursuits. Engineers are capable of entering just about any business; they don't only have to design reinforced concrete beams, transmission lines, or assembly lines.

What types of opportunities should technically trained people entertain in their search for a new venture? In considering an opportunity, a choice will have to be made in terms of product strategy. The strategies available include:

1. A first-in-the-field or product leader strategy.

2. A follow-the-leader strategy whereby a market leader is imitated.

3. Application-engineering where market niches are sought by modifying and combining products for a particular segment.

4. Me-too products, a strategy whereby products that are existent are made.

For new ventures, only first-in-the-field and application-engineering strategies should be encouraged. There will be many ideas using follow-the-leader and me-too strategies, but they should be resisted. These last two strategies will require much more capital to get started and will probably never be internationally competitive. Me-too and follow-the-leader ventures are the first to surface in developing economies. One has only to look around at developed countries and see that steel plants, tire factories, automobile assembly plants, or an import-substitution-based industry are needed to save foreign exchange or soak up excess labor. In fact, these ventures will never be able to exist without vast amounts of protection in terms of quantitative and qualitative restrictions on imports. They will continue to be a drain on the economy. However, ventures based on first-in-the-field and application-engineering strategies should eventually have export potential and will not need protection.

A good opportunity must have a large potential; it is no good wasting good technical entrepreneurial talent on a one-man band or a "mom and pop" operation. The venture must have the potential of becoming something more than the entrepreneur. This rules out consultancies and one-man research firms where, when the staff goes home, the business goes home.

Behavioral Characteristics

The personality characteristics for successful entrepreneurship include a high need for achievement and an internal locus of control.[6] Persons with a high need for achievement prefer activity over passivity; like concrete and prompt information on how well they are performing; set goals that are intermediate in risk—not too high, not too low—and take calculated risks that tend to maximize success; are able to defer gratification; and tend to view people as means rather than as ends. Thus, the person with a high need for achievement tends not to accept people for their own sake, but for their potential personal benefit.

Having an internal locus of control means controlling one's own destiny and taking responsibility for one's actions. Entrepreneurs feel that their successes and failures are the results of their actions and not those of bankers or of luck. They believe that good fortune was there because of their foresight, and failures were due to their lack of planning. They take full responsibility for their actions.

Both need for achievement and internal locus of control are learned behavior. David C. McClelland has taken people with a low need for achievement and, by putting them in with a group of people with a high need for achievement for a period of as little as six weeks, transformed them into people with high need for achievement.[7] By associating with people with internal locus of control and high need for achievement, you can develop their personality traits.

In areas of the world and in societies with a high incidence of entrepreneurship, prospective entrepreneurs can easily find role models for other successful entrepreneurs. It is easy for an electronics engineer in the San Francisco Bay area, or Minneapolis-St. Paul, or Boston to identify successful entrepreneurs with backgrounds like themselves. The Jewish person living outside of Israel or a Chinese living outside China is more likely to have a close relation who has been an entrepreneur. There are higher incidences of entrepreneurship in these two groups than in the regular population of that society.

Credible examples are needed for prospective entrepreneurs so as to encourage need for achievement and a personal responsibility for one's actions. Once the individual has the required personality and has identified an opportunity, a final push is needed to put the venture on the road.

Precipitating Events

For people to become entrepreneurs, some type of precipitating event is needed to push them over the edge. They may have been thinking about an opportunity and have the right type of personality but, if they are happy in their present situations, they are unlikely to take the plunge.

The prospects must first become dissatisfied with their present lot. This can be anything from a lack of opportunity through a downturn in business conditions to being sacked. Working for a top position for ten years, only to see the boss's idiot son taking over, has triggered many entrepreneurial careers. Schapero quotes one entrepreneur: "I looked at the boss and said, if that dumb son-of-a-bitch can start a company, I sure can."[8]

Most entrepreneurs are displaced persons who have been dislodged from some nice, familiar niche, and have tilted off course. Some are political refugees: the Asians who left Uganda for New Zealand; the Cubans who fled to Florida; the East Germans who fled to West Germany; and the French from North Africa who fled to France—all have a high incidence of entrepreneurship.

THE PROCESS OF ENTREPRENEURSHIP

A brief discussion of the entrepreneurial process is in order here. This process is illustrated in Figure 14.1.

The entrepreneur who detects the presence of an opportunity is typically the one who conceptualizes the whole new venture. This conceptualization

Figure 14.1
The Entrepreneurial Process

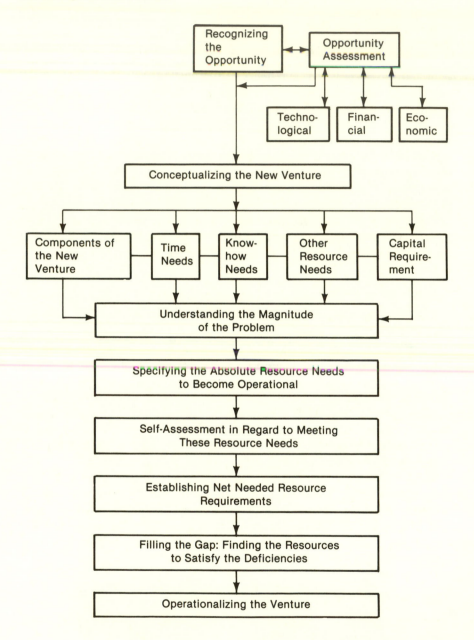

activity would imply that the entrepreneur has utilized certain analytical abilities. The conceptualization leads to dissection of the new venture concept, which would lead to determining its key components.

Without understanding the components of the proposed venture, it is difficult to assess one's ability to solve it. Hence, the entrepreneur thinks in terms of time, effort, know-how, and other resource requirements to tackle the problem. Once the magnitude of the new venture is understood, the entrepreneur is in a position to specify all the needs to tackle the new venture. The next step, typically, is to assess one's self. The entrepreneur, at this point, objectively tries to take a good look at the personal resources. This activity determines the *net needs* or the deficits that must be accommodated if the project is to materialize. At this point the entrepreneur either finds the gap too great to be eliminated or develops ways to bring all the needed resources together. Once all of the necessary resources are brought together the entrepreneur is ready to begin the new venture.

This model is not the only normative model. Even though each situation is slightly different and each entrepreneur has a somewhat different modus operandi, the model presented here is a generalized version of a large variety of approaches.

The entrepreneurial process is discussed in this section particularly because of its importance. Unless the role, skills, and the operational behavior of entrepreneurs are understood, it is not possible to promote entrepreneurship in a country.

PROMOTING ENTREPRENEURS

So far we have argued that entrepreneurs are vital to growth plans. What can be done to encourage and promote them so that more worthwhile ventures will be started? Figure 14.2 illustrates a support system that promotes entrepreneurs.

Figure 14.2
A Model of an Entrepreneurship Support System

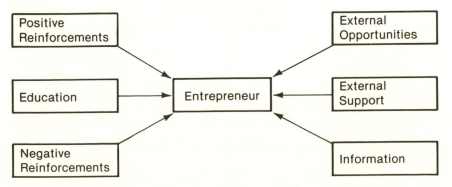

Positive Reinforcements

Positive reinforcements indicate an environment surrounded with examples of entrepreneurial success stories. The prospective entrepreneur may either find special stimulation from seeing others' successful ventures or be inspired by exposure to the entrepreneurial efforts of someone in the immediate family. The efforts or advice of role models other than the immediate family may also be effective. The important factor here is the proper persuasion and encouragement for the prospective entrepreneur from a credible source. This "credible source" may vary from culture to culture or even within various subcultures. While, for instance, the immediate family may be a most important persuader in the Arab culture, in the United States it may be the peer or a member of a reference group who may provide the most valuable positive reinforcement for the prospective entrepreneur. American blacks, for instance, will not be open to suggestions unless there is already an existing role model without a credibility gap. Thus, a positive reinforcement for this subculture is having seen somebody who has succeeded in a similar venture who is of the same race.

Other types of positive reinforcement exist on the basis of cultural values. In some cultures, for instance, becoming one's own boss is important, and in others following the family tradition of owning a small business is more prevalent. Provided that there are practical examples and guidance, these types of values set the foundation for positive reinforcement.

Education

Education has several roles to play in supporting and encouraging entrepreneurs. First, the education system has a role in making entrepreneurship a credible alternative career. University and other tertiary training are almost universally aimed at preparing students to work for someone else. Careers in industry and in the state civil service are about the only ones that students are exposed to. Entrepreneurship does not enter any of the students' role models for a successful career. Surprisingly, very few well-educated people in developing countries become entrepreneurs.

To change this pattern, the tertiary educational institutions must demonstrate to the student the alternative to working for the establishment —being an entrepreneur.

It is important to realize that students leaving university are usually not ready to start new ventures. Generally, about ten years of seasoning is needed, during which contacts are made and the person acquires the requisite technical, financial, and managerial expertise to gain the necessary confidence. The seeds of entrepreneurship, however, must be planted during the formative years at university. The lag between university and entrepreneurship also emphasizes the need for extensive work in adult education in entrepreneurship.

Because of the importance of technical entrepreneurs in starting ventures that have potential for exports and very large sales and employment, it is imperative that engineering and agricultural students be exposed to entrepreneurship as an alternative career while they are at school.

The second role of education is in the mechanism of venture formation. How to recognize an opportunity and form a business plan to take advantage of it is the basis of many entrepreneurship courses. Teaching students how to form a business plan could be the basis for both the full-time program and the adult education-extension studies division.

Negative Reinforcements

Schapero[9] and Liles[10] have noted that entrepreneurs need final pushes or "precipitating events" before they take the plunge. They also note that displaced persons have a very high incidence of entrepreneurship.

To achieve higher incidences of entrepreneurship, negative reinforcement or a stick may be carefully applied as far as a social and political policy permits.

Young technocrats entering government service should not have tenure. A policy that would force all government-employed technical researchers and scientists to leave after, say, five years should increase the rate of entrepreneurship or emigration among this group.

Permitting well-trained political refugees to gain permanent residence but denying them access to employment in the establishment could also promote entrepreneurship.

External Opportunities

Numerous factors within the economy or the business sector provide the opportunity for the prospective entrepreneur on which to capitalize. Four such factors are discussed here: (1) national development programs, (2) natural infrastructures, (3) artificially created infrastructures, and (4) small business development programs.

National and/or Regional Development Programs

These programs create changes in the economy and eventually in the society. These changes provide opportunities for prospective entrepreneurs. If, for instance, the Turkish government decides to include a large high-technology sector in the five-year development plan, numerous entrepreneurs can start their own small businesses and be very successful. An entrepreneur can start a small establishment to produce complementary products; another may start a small firm producing certain parts for computers; a third may develop a software firm; and yet a fourth may start a small consulting firm as to how to utilize high-tech products in various industries.

Natural Infrastructures

Many countries and regions have natural infrastructures that are suitable for entrepreneurs. In the southeastern region of Yugoslavia, where silver and silversmiths are plentiful, an entrepreneur may develop a factory and international souvenir business based on silversmithing. In Japan, where the automotive industry is highly advanced, major auto companies use hundreds of small establishments for some of the parts for their automobiles. Yet, these small establishments are run by entrepreneurs who have foreseen a market opportunity and have established a niche for themselves in the marketplace.

Artificially Created Infrastructures

Aside from national development plans and their impact on the infrastructure, there are other conscious and deliberate attempts to develop infrastructures in a country or in regions. These infrastructures in time emerge on the basis of the direction that the national and regional economies take. These changes in the infrastructures immediately lead to new entrepreneurial opportunities. When the watchmaking industry emerged in Switzerland, it provided opportunities to many entrepreneurs who somehow saw an opportunity and got hooked up with that industry. Similarly, in Japan and in China, some regions are required to devote themselves primarily to certain industries. In one part of Sinkiang Province in China, a number of villages are assigned to the sunflower industry. Each village is to meet a quota. In such a situation, an entrepreneur who can develop better processing equipment or who can improve the total process can certainly be rewarded amply in the system and be successful.

Small Business Development Programs

A positive social attitude toward small business development programs almost always leads to developing a favorable attitude toward entrepreneurship as well. A pro-small business mentality, from a socioeconomic-political perspective, includes providing opportunities for small businesses by giving them financial help, managerial advice, and tax incentives. The Small Business Administration in the United States functions on this basis. It not only assists businesses to get started, but also helps out those that need the help. Similarly, local economic development agencies in the United States assist small businesses to get started.

External Support

The external support system for entrepreneurship must include at least three factors: venture capital, specific factual support, and one-on-one directional support.

Venture Capital. Venture capital is supplied by both the entrepreneur and external individuals as well as institutions.

In one American study, 40% of the technically oriented firms were started prmarily with founders' capital; in a Canadian study 35% of the firms were initially financed by the founders. The exent to which founders can save sufficient capital depends upon salary and taxation levels. Observers believe that entrepreneurship in the United Kingdom and Canada is seriously hampered by the difficulty in saving "seed capital" In the American electronics industry, stock options, which are often intended to bind executives to firms, sometimes make it financially feasible for them to become entrepreneurs.[11]

The willingness of institutions and individual investors to invest in new technologically based firms varies significantly. In the LDCs where entrepreneurial activity needs to be supported more readily than the rest of the industrialized world, this willingness is even less. This being the case, both governments and funding institutions must take the availability of the venture capital problem seriously.

The rewards to venture financing are chiefly large capital gains. New ventures need a source of equity and not high interest debt. A common way of financing start-ups is to advance the money in equity or in the form of low-interest debt, with options or warrants to convert the debt into equity shares. To achieve its capital gain, the venture capital investor must sell his or her shares. This means that the new venture must have a goal of (1) a public offering, (2) provision for the entrepreneur to buy out the venture capital firm at some pre-agreed-upon price and time, or (3) a merger with a firm for cash or publicly traded shares. The venture capital firm can be expected to participate in management by appointing a director and extracting an agreement to liquidate its holdings by one of the above methods.

Venture capital firms usually specialize in one or two industries in which the principals of the venture capital company are experts. They become familiar with markets, technology, and existing industry in their area of interest. Money is made available to new companies that meet their criteria for success in these industries.

Private individuals, banks, and insurance companies can and should be involved in new venture financing. In LDCs it is imperative for the state to take an active role in the venture capital market, probably through the national development bank. The development bank must be willing to participate in equity offerings and not just be a lender of last resort.

Pressure can be placed on insurance companies to put some of their investment portfolio into new venture finance. Real estate ventures have long been the province of insurance companies, causing many downtown areas to be overbuilt in high-rise office buildings. If the insurance companies can be encouraged to participate in other new ventures, the growth can be faster and better balanced.

Specific Factual Support. A prospective entrepreneur needs some very specific information about the availability of the opportunity, about how to put together the various factors so that the new venture will materialize, and about the technical aspects of the project, for example, production, processes, special technology, and markets. All of this informaton must be made available to the prospective entrepreneur.

An organization (usually a state-run small business agency) needs to be able to provide guides to prospective markets (internal and export), finance, and technology. Information on how to organize a new venture and prepare a business plan is also needed.

One-on-One Directional Support. In areas or countries where specific role models or private guidance are not readily available, particularly in the LDCs, it is necessary to have specific one-on-one direction. A knowledgeable and credible guide must provide direction and advice particularly at the beginning stages of the venture. Without this support, the effects are likely to be wasted since an entrepreneur does not usually possess some of the finer points in managing a small business. State-run small business agencies are useful vehicles for providing this support on a subsidized basis.

Information

Entrepreneurs must have specific as well as general information. Their needs for specific information will remain acute, not only at the beginning of the venture but also throughout its lifetime. Venture-specific information, combined with external support activities, is likely to create an ideal situation for entrepreneurship to emerge and thrive.

A large variety of specific information must be obtained and made available if the new venture is to be successful. Table 14.1 illustrates the types of information needed by the entrepreneur.

TOOLS FOR TRANSFERRING ENTREPRENEURSHIP SUCCESSFULLY

Thus far, the discussion has been restricted to the entrepreneurial process, skills, and the support system that is essential if entrepreneurship is to flourish. While in developed Western countries entrepreneurs emerge without much effort from government sources, in most underdeveloped countries without government help there can be only little progress. The entrepreneurial talent may be suppressed because of the cultural climate, where individuals are brought up to listen and follow orders and instructions, rather than being encouraged to use their own initiative. They may not be conditioned to think for themselves and to act as individual decisionmakers. Unless they are instructed to utilize their entrepreneurial skills (if any) it is quite likely that they will not. Thus, deliberately singling out and training entrepreneurs becomes more important in these countries than in their developed counterparts. Thus, it is particularly important to explore

Table 14.1
Types of Information Needed by the Entrepreneur

Market Information	Size
	Change
	Location
	Demographics
	Behavior patterns
Physical Facility	Location
	Size
	Proximity to market
	Proximity to supplies
	Layout
Technical	Procedures
	Equipment
	Blueprints
	Power needs
Accounting	Bookkeeping
	Organization of accounts
	Pro forma operating statement
	Pro forma balance sheet
Financial	Sources of funds
	Financial needs
	Cash flow analysis
	Best organizational structure
Operational	Marketing program
	Personnel
	Managerial structure
Export Potential	Possible markets
	Specific alternatives in entering the market
	International promotion
	International documentation, shipping, and so on

how the know-how to develop entrepreneurs in developed countries can be used in LDCs.

Since in most LDCs knowledge of economic and technological changes in the society at the individual level is lacking, an individual entrepreneur is not likely to make a careful selection and evaluation of the venture. This job has to be performed by an outside agency. Not only selection of the ventures but also their careful assessment must be performed at the early stage (Figure 14.3) before these ideas are shared with prospective entrepreneurs. Indeed, in Turkey on numerous occasions the government started the enter-

Figure 14.3
Developing New Ventures in the Third World Countries

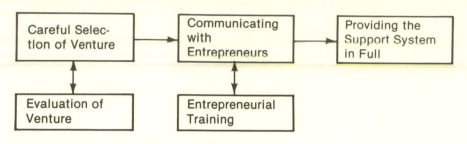

prise and sold it to the private sector. Similarly, the New Zealand government developed the primary steel industry and sold it to the private sector.

When the idea is shared with the prospective entrepreneur, very specific and exacting training must be provided (Figure 14.3). After this particular stage, the procedure becomes much the same as the way it has been discussed in this chapter. The support system must be provided in full, and continual interaction must be developed between the support system and the new entrepreneur.

It must be emphasized that generating new ventures in underdeveloped countries will require a very concerted effort by some external agency such as the national or local government. The support systems have a more serious role to play than those in the industrialized world, until the venture becomes a reality. Even after this point, the support system should not abandon the new entrepreneur and should make itself available for some guidance and advice.

SUMMARY AND CONCLUSIONS

Transferring the technology that will be utilized to generate effective entrepreneurs in LDCs is an extremely critical activity in the development of these countries. Entrepreneurs are particularly needed in these countries, and prevailing conditions are not fully conducive for their development.

This chapter explores the sources of entrepreneurs and concludes that it is economically sounder for entrepreneurs to be developed within the country rather than being imported into the country by multinational companies. The chapter also describes entrepreneurship and analyzes specific features of entrepreneurs and the entrepreneurial process.

A model is presented describing how entrepreneurs are promoted in developed countries. Six key areas are discussed in this context: (1) positive reinforcement, (2) negative reinforcement, (3) education, (4) external opportunities, (5) external support, and (6) information.

Finally, the chapter discusses how the tools and skills used in the developed countries can be transplanted to LDCs. It is argued that the government should perform a special assessment of the new venture, and at times the selection of the specific entrepreneurs, since the private sector has neither the access to information nor the technical skills.

NOTES

1. P. Harpham in William Gasson, "NZ's Choice: Hightech, or a Third World Economy," *Better Business* (June 1983): 22.

2. Cantillon, cited in Joseph A. Schumpeter, "Economic Theory and Entrepreneurial History," *Change and the Entrepreneur* (Cambridge: Harvard University Press, 1948).

3. J. B. Say, also cited in Schumpeter, "Economic Theory."

4. Arthur Stone Dewing, *The Financial Policy of Companies* (New York: Ronald Press, 1914), pp. 215-254.

5. Joseph A. Schumpeter, *The Theory of Economic Development* (Cambridge: Harvard University Press, 1934).

6. Albert A. Schapero, "The Displaced, Uncomfortable, Entrepreneur," *Psychology Today* (November 1975): 83.

7. D. C. McClelland, "Achievement Motivation Can Be Developed," *Harvard Business Review* (November-December 1965): 55-66.

8. Schapero, "The Displaced," p. 83.

9. Ibid.

10. Patrick Liles, "Who Are the Entrepreneurs?" *MSU Business Topics* (Winter 1974): 1-14.

11. Arnold C. Cooper, "Technical Entrepreneurship: What Do We Know?" *Research and Development Management* (February 1973): 59-64.

15

Conceptual and Measurement Problems in International Technology Transfer: A Critical Analysis

ASIM ERDILEK AND ALAN RAPOPORT

International technology transfer (ITT) has been a subject of considerable interest to several diverse groups, including government policymakers, international civil servants, business executives, and business as well as academic researchers. This broad interest has spawned numerous discussions and studies on various aspects of the subject. Despite all this attention, the concept of ITT remains vague, controversial, and inadequately operationalized. Moreover, satisfactory measurement of ITT is frequently hindered by the lack of appropriate data and the diversity as well as the complexity of the channels through which technology is transferred.

In this chapter we analyze critically the concept and measurement of ITT. We begin by discussing some of the reasons why many people perceive ITT as an increasingly important phenomenon and public policy issue. Next, we consider possible definitions of ITT, as well as some of the problems associated with arriving at a generally acceptable and operationally useful definition. After reviewing the alternative channels through which technology can be transferred, we focus on three different approaches to conceptualizing and measuring ITT. We assess some of their strengths and weaknesses but make no attempt to arrive at a synthesis. Finally, we summarize our analysis and state its basic conclusions.

THE GROWING IMPORTANCE OF INTERNATIONAL TECHNOLOGY TRANSFER

ITT has been occurring since almost the dawn of civilization. It has, therefore, evoked considerable interest and discussion for a very long period of time. There is a popular perception, however, that its importance has been increasing substantially more recently. Public officials in many countries express serious concern about the causes and effects of ITT (in terms of either inflows or outflows of technology). Their concerns have led to considerable study and debate, at both the national and international levels, on whether governments, individually or in collaboration, should and can control ITT, in ways that will minimize its negative effects and encourage its positive ones.

Several broad indicators suggest that both the speed and the spread of ITT have been increasing rapidly during the last two decades or so. The world appears to have become much more integrated and interdependent as more and more nations have entered the world trading system and as international trade as a percentage of gross national product has risen for many, especially the industrialized countries. Furthermore, direct foreign investment (DFI) activity has increased substantially. Along with the increases in international trade and investment, there has been a remarkable expansion in the stock of knowledge, coupled with vast improvements in global communication and transportation facilities that have permitted knowledge to diffuse more rapidly throughout much of the world.

Higher educational levels and technical capabilities in less developed countries (LDCs) have expanded these countries' capacities to absorb new technology. The greater capability to both transmit and receive information has reduced the costs of transferring technology, leading to the possibility of more and faster transfers. Furthermore, the process of technological development itself has become much more internationalized than ever before with the expansion of DFI, along with the growing role of the multinational corporations (MNCs), as well as the spread of joint R&D ventures, cooperative research arrangements, co-production agreements, and the like among different countries.

It is generally accepted that the flow of technology across national boundaries has increased rapidly. Unfortunately, however, our ability to identify and measure the diversified processes that constitute ITT remains rather limited. Therefore, it is difficult to document and substantiate what actually is occurring in this area. International trade indicators point to a growing relative share of trade in high-technology products, at least for the industrial countries. Likewise, DFI activity indicators show growing shares of MNCs in world manufacturing production and trade. But no equally satisfactory indicators are yet available for ITT.

Whether or not ITT is growing in importance in some quantitative sense, it is being subjected to intense scrutiny by public policymakers, those involved in it directly, and those interested in studying its various dimensions. Public officials at both the national and international levels are primarily interested in how ITT affects domestic economic development, international competitiveness, and national security. They are concerned about the need for and the efficacy of national controls on either outflows or inflows of technology. Besides the many national governments assessing their role in ITT, several international institutions, including General

Agreement of Tariffs and Trade (GATT), United Nations Conference on Trade and Development (UNCTAD), the Organization for Economic Co-operation and Development (OECD), and the United Nations, have set up commissions and study groups to investigate various aspects of the subject.

The private economic agents, firms as well as individuals, who are directly involved in ITT as either suppliers or recipients of technology are obviously also interested in a better understanding of the subject. Their individual activities concern the selection of technologies as international transferors or transferees, the choice of the channel(s) of transfer, the pricing of the transactions, and the choice of the payment mechanism(s). Besides being occupied with ITT itself, they have to keep up and cope with the attempts of national governments to exert increased control over ITT.

The scientific study of ITT is prompted by both the policy considerations that have been discussed above and a desire to better understand the process itself. The aspects of ITT that are of primary interest appear to fall into three broad categories: understanding the process itself, especially its determinants; effects on transferors and transferees; and factors affecting its control. Although we can debate whether these issues are any more important now than they have been in the past, they are presently receiving considerable attention. A clearer formulation of the concept and better measurement of ITT should help in examining and resolving some of these important issues.

THE PROBLEMS IN CONCEPTUALIZING
INTERNATIONAL TECHNOLOGY TRANSFER

We have already discussed the phenomenon of ITT too long without having attempted to define it. Unfortunately, ITT is not an easy process to define, particularly in an operational manner. Of the three words associated with the process, "international" is the easiest one to define operationally. Technology transfer across national boundaries is generally accepted as international technology transfer. As long as nation-states are well defined, there is no problem in determining whether or not a particular technology transfer is international. Denoting a particular transfer as international by using this definition, however, does not by itself provide any information about the nationality of either the (original) supplier or the (ultimate) recipient of the technology in question. Such information may be of critical importance with respect to several public policy issues, particularly those in which the ultimate possession of the technology is an important consideration.

"Technology" is a more complex concept. It generally refers to a class of knowledge about a specific product or production technique. The technical skills necessary to utilize a product or a production technique may also have to be included in the definition of technology. This latter issue arises because technology is usually not a form of knowledge that is easy either to reproduce or use. The recipient of technology must have adequate education or experience to at least recognize that the knowledge being transmitted is useful. The other interesting aspect of technology is its public good status. When knowledge is made available to another party, that knowledge usually remains available to the transmitting party. However, although one's use of technology does not diminish another's use of it, the benefits derived from using a particular technology can be and are generally affected by the number of parties having access to it.

"Transfer" is the most controversial of the three words. There is considerable debate about the factors that determine whether a transfer of technology has actually occurred. Some participants in this debate contend that technology is not really transferred unless the knowledge that has been transferred is actually used by the transferee. Others argue that what the transferee does or can do with the knowledge he or she receives should not be a factor in determining whether a transfer has occurred, although they recognize that the mastery of that knowledge is a critical factor in examining the effect of any given transfer. The fact that technology is knowledge rather than some tangible product makes the concept of transfer a difficult one to define operationally. When a product crosses a national boundary, it is no longer in its original location. Whether or not it is used, it can be said to have been transferred. However, in transferring knowledge, the transferor is not giving up the knowledge, but is essentially sharing it with others. If the recipient does not understand what he receives, can it still be called knowledge? We do not think so.

THE CHANNELS OF INTERNATIONAL TECHNOLOGY TRANSFER

The conceptualization and measurement of ITT are further complicated by the diverse channels through which it can occur. It can occur through both formal and informal channels. Many of these channels often work in concert. Some channels involve voluntary and intentional ITT; others do not. The principal channels of ITT are licensing; direct foreign investment; sale of turnkey plants; joint ventures, cooperative research arrangements, and co-production agreements; export of high-technology products and capital goods; reverse engineering; exchange of scientific and technical personnel; science and technology conferences, trade shows, and exhibits; education and training of foreigners; commercial visits; open literature (journals, magazines, technical books, and articles); industrial espionage; end-user or third country diversions; and government assistance programs.

ITT through most of these channels is very difficult to detect and monitor. Formal channels (the first five above) usually involve the market mechanism and assign an explicit value to ITT. It is not known whether the bulk of ITT occurs through the formal channels or through the informal ones that are much more difficult to detect and monitor. If actual transfers cannot be clearly recognized, it is difficult, if not impossible, to determine the more important transfer channels. The criticial first step in analyzing ITT is to distinguish among its different occurrences. Even for those transfers that can be clearly recognized, it is difficult to place a value on the transaction, especially if the transfer channel is an informal one. Even when an explicit value is available, it may not reflect the "true" value of the technology being transferred.

THREE APPROACHES TO CONCEPTUALIZING AND MEASURING INTERNATIONAL TECHNOLOGY TRANSFER

In the rest of this chapter "technology" refers to *industrial* technology. It means the accumulated knowledge and know-how required for either manufacturing a final product or processing intermediate inputs. That accumulated knowledge and know-how includes product designs, production techniques, and related managerial systems. Technology "transfer" means the transmission, revision (adaptation), and implantation (absorption) of such accumulated knowledge and know-how that are actually put to productive use. In short, transfer is active, deliberate, and effective diffusion engineered by either the transferor or the transferee (but not necessarily by both of them).

Our definition of technology stresses its *specificity* in terms of both its inputs and outputs (as in Pavitt, 1983). Furthermore, it is taken to be a primarily *private* good whose transfer from one production unit to another, even within the same firm, has a real resource cost. In short, technology is a highly specific private good with positive costs of production to its initial owner (Mansfield, 1968), and positive costs of transfer to its transferee and/or transferor (Teece, 1977).

In this section, we present a critical analysis of the conceptual and measurement problems in ITT according to *our* definitions of technology and its transfer. Obviously, the conceptual problems precede the measurement problems since, conceptually, fuzzy entities do not lend themselves to precise and useful measurement.

In categorizing the conceptual and measurement problems, we can focus on the (1) determinants, (2) channels, and (3) effects of ITT. The resource costs and benefits of the transfer can then be analyzed in terms of its determinants, channels, and effects.

What makes the conceptualization (that is, the construction of generally useful concepts, and their use in formulating empirically testable and generally valid hypotheses) exceptionally difficult is the specificity of technology in terms of its highly differentiated inputs and outputs. "The sources, nature and mechanisms for international transfer of technology vary considerably from sector to sector" (Pavitt, 1983, p. 9).

Furthermore, although technology is a primarily private good, it is not easily priced and traded through arm's-length transactions in interfirm markets either domestically or internationally. This is due to the inherent asymmetry in the distribution of the information about the technology between its owner and potential buyers, and the well-known fundamental paradox resulting from its correction (Teece, 1981). Much international technology transfer is "internalized" within MNCs as owners of technology bypass the external markets in order to maximize their expected net benefits from the transfer. Even when a technology *can* be transferred via an arm's-length transaction in an interfirm market, neither its sale nor its purchase is a necessary or sufficient condition for its transfer. Not all technologies transferred are paid for directly and explicitly, for example, in cash. Conversely, not all technologies paid for directly and explicitly are transferred (effectively), that is, put to productive use on an ongoing basis by the transferees.

We now focus on three different approaches to conceptualizing and measuring ITT:

1. The *macro*economic (M) approach which restricts its coverage to transfers that generate monetary *payments* and *receipts* and which relies on *balance of payments* (BOP), often highly aggregated data for their measurement (the M-BOP approach).

2. The *micro*economic (m) approach which restricts its coverage to selected specific firms and/or sectors in terms of case studies (CSs) and which relies on firm-specific, often primary data, that go beyond monetary payments and receipts (the m-CS approach).

3. The *micro*economic (m) approach which restricts its coverage to patentable technological information as a proxy for technology and relies on patent citation (PC) data for measuring the international transfer of such information (the m-PC approach).

The Macroeconomic Balance of Payments Approach

This approach conceptualizes ITT as a commercial, mutually agreed on transaction between either "affiliated" or "unaffiliated" enterprises, based in the United States and abroad. The U.S. Department of Commerce (DOC) definition of direct foreign investment (DFI) in terms of at least 10 percent of ownership (in voting securities) distinguishes between affiliated (DFI-related) and unaffiliated (either portfolio investment-related or unrelated) enterprises. The 10 percent cutoff is, of course, merely a statistical convention. Whether 10 percent or more ownership is sufficient for at least some managerial control can be determined in terms of specific cases only. This would be true of any other cutoff figure not close to 100 percent. We should note, however, that different countries use different cutoff figures. This renders the comparability of DFI and ITT data of different countries, especially the OECD countries, difficult, if not impossible.

The U.S. DOC breaks down *total gross receipts* from ITT into the following hierarchical categories:

I. "Fees and royalties" covers *all* transactions, yielding the grand total.

    A. "Royalties and license fees" covers the receipts from transferring *rights* to intellectual property, including patents, technical and managerial know-how, and trademarks.

    B. "Service charges and rentals" covers (1) "Services rendered," (2) "R&D assessment," and (3) "Rentals for tangible property," which include the receipts from providing *services* in order to effectuate ITT.

    C. "Film and tape rentals."

The conceptual basis of this categorization seems to be the proper distinction between the *rights* to intellectual property transferred to the technology buyers and the *services* rendered to them to effectuate the ITT (Contractor, 1983). In other words, the mere transfer of rights to technology is an incomplete account of ITT; its transmission, revision, and implantation require the services of the transferor.

There are several problems with the U.S. DOC's categorization:

1. It restricts both the rights transferred and the services rendered to those paid for directly and explicitly in cash. Those not paid for directly and explicitly, which are expected to be important in ITT between *affiliated* enterprises, are omitted.

2. The rights transferred and services rendered, whether paid or unpaid for, by themselves may not result in (effective) ITT. The U.S. DOC framework is limited to the coverage of the gross receipts (monetary benefits) of the technology seller and the gross payments (monetary costs) of the technology buyer. It omits from consideration the nonmonetary benefits and the total (monetary and non-monetary) costs of the seller, as well as the nonmonetary costs and the total benefits of the buyer. Without their inclusion, we cannot analyze satisfactorily the determinants, the choice of channel, and the effects of ITT in terms of the net total benefits of the seller and the buyer from ITT. Furthermore, such net benefits often accrue over time, with different streams of costs and benefits for both the seller and the buyer for any given ITT. But the U.S. DOC framework is not an intertemporal one. Its year-by-year coverage does not distinguish even among the annual gross receipts and payments over time for any given ITT.

3. The U.S. DOC categorization includes items such as "rentals for tangible property" and "film and tape rentals" that are at best remotely related to ITT.

Since they are not separately reported, except at the most aggregate level, their exclusion is impossible in working with the disaggregated DOC data.

4. The U.S. DOC data on licensing come from two different sources, presumably distinguishing between affiliated and unaffiliated transactions. Now, as some reporters of affiliated transactions have also direct and indirect unaffiliated transactions, some reporters of unaffiliated transactions have also direct and indirect affiliated transactions. The exact nature of this overlap, however, is unlear (Contractor, 1983).

5. The U.S. DOC data do not cover all channels of ITT. They omit trade in capital goods, "reverse engineering," migration or exchange of technologists, flows of scientific and technological literature, and industrial espionage. Admittedly, these omitted channels are very difficult to detect, quantify, and measure. In some cases, however, they could be more important than DFI and licensing, the two channels that the U.S. DOC data cover. That is why the microeconomic-case study approach becomes indispensable in such circumstances.

6. The regional and sectoral disaggregations of the publicly available U.S. DOC data are constrained by both the resources available for collecting and processing the data and the confidentiality requirements. This is, strictly speaking, neither a conceptual nor a measurement problem, but its restrictive effect on empirical and policy analyses is a serious one. It can be somewhat ameliorated for an outside researcher, however, if the U.S. DOC performs, for a fee, the researcher's calculations and hypothesis testing, taking advantage of greater internal data disaggregation.

The Microeconomic Case Study Approach

This approach conceptualizes ITT as a highly detailed transaction (not necessarily either commercial or mutually agreed on) between specific real-life, either affiliated or unaffiliated enterprises, based in different countries. Its coverage is limited to a sample of cases. It trades off the general coverge of the population for the rich detail of sample coverage. Often its detailed coverage is at the project, process, and product level. Therefore, it is fully in accord with our emphasis on the specificity of technology which requires a highly disaggregated microeconomic approach.

The fruitful use of this approach requires a certain technical familiarity with the sample of technologies, firms, and industries chosen for study. No such familiarity is required in using the macroeconomic-balance of payments approach. This familiarity increases in importance as the sample coverage narrows but deepens, that is, fewer types and units are covered but in greater detail.

Unlike the M-BOP approach, this approach is capable of accounting for both the monetary and nonmonetary costs and the benefits of both the transferee and the transferor. In other words, it can in principle provide full coverage of the total real resource costs of and benefits from ITT. Moreover, it is capable of encompassing all possible channels of ITT instead of being limited to DFI and licensing only. It can also account for the intertemporal patterns of total net benefits and their sensitivity to choice of different channels of ITT. Therefore, it can yield managerial implications as it clarifies and generalizes the consequences of past decisions by transferees and transferors.

This approach has been successful in bringing economists into direct contact with the real business world and with the intrafirm decision-making processes. As a result, economists, whose training in the United States is mostly neoclassical, have realized that the study of ITT requires new concepts and models besides the neoclassical ones. Thanks to these new concepts and models, technology is no longer believed to be a public good with magical qualities that can be analyzed in terms of relative factor endowments, productivities, and prices only.

The potential power of this approach is limited, however, by several problems:

1. Like the case study approach to conceptualizing and measuring any phenomenon, it is inherently arbitrary in the choice of its cases and data. It seldom resorts to statistically random sampling. It often requires the consent and close cooperation of the transferees and transferors in forming its sample and obtaining its data. Who and what get included in the sample and which type of data are obtained for the sample are frequently determined *ex post*. Whatever *ex post* rationalization is produced by the practitioners of this approach for their ultimate sample and data coverage, some arbitrariness is bound to remain.

2. The practitioners of this approach often begin without an explicit, rigorously formulated model of ITT. They first find out *how* ITT occurs and then try to explain *why* it occurs. They derive their hypotheses from the study of their sample. They experiment with different econometric forms and variable specifications until they are satisfied with their results. Then they conclude that their model is supported by the empirical evidence. Of course, testing a model with the data from which the model has been derived does not provide much support for the general validity of that model. It has to be tested with other, independently obtained data sets with different cross-sectional or time-series coverage. Some practitioners of this approach do, however, recognize and admit the shortcoming: "The model was estimated only on the data which suggested it, so the estimation does not test its validity" (Flaherty, 1982, p. 13).

3. This approach is usually based on primary data collected directly from the respondents in the sample. Questionnaires are often used to obtain comparable data. Who fill out the questionnaires and whether the questionnaire responses are checked and clarified by followup interviews determine the quality and usefulness of the data. It is very time-consuming work to collect questionnaire data and conduct interviews (Erdilek, 1982). Furthermore, for private researchers who have to rely exclusively on the voluntary cooperation of their respondents, the potential inconsistency or untruthfulness of responses remains an unresolved issue. Clever questionnaire design and followup interviews can catch some but not all inconsistent or untruthful responses.

4. Like its counterpart in studying international trade, this approach has been unable to reconcile and synthesize its various ad hoc hypotheses, generated by independent researchers and covering different sectors, countries, and periods. Of course, this is partly, if not largely, due to the inherent specificity of technology and its differentiated diffusion patterns. Part of the problem, however, is the partial equilibrium nature of this approach. It focuses on a truncated, if not completely isolated, component of the ITT pheneomenon. Unfortunately, a mere collection of partial equilibrium analyses does not serve as even a proxy for general equilibrium analysis.

The Microeconomic Patent Citation Approach

This is a very recent approach which may prove to be highly significant within its limited framework. It confines its attention to patentable technological information as a proxy for technology and relies on patent citation data for measuring the international transfer of such information.

It distinguishes between the nationalities of the inventors and the owners (assignees) of patents. It focuses for clarity on "pure U.S. patents" and "pure foreign patents" where "pure" denotes the common (either U.S. or foreign) nationality of the patent inventors and owners. Furthermore, it differentiates between the uninational and multinational (subsidiary status) identities of the corporate assignees (McAllister, Carpenter, and Olivastro, 1983).

The primary objective of this approach is to measure the "foreign technological presence" in a national patent system. The most straightforward indicator of such a presence is the simple percentage share of pure foreign patents in the national patent system. Patent "citation" (referencing) in terms of citations to foreign origin patents within the national patent system and citations to foreign patent systems is a less obvious, but nevertheless crucial, indicator. These citations, taken from the front pages of patents, are classified separately for pure national patents and pure foreign patents within the national system in which they are found.

A strong advantage of this approach is its *full* (population) coverage of the national patent system. Furthermore, it is able to present its indicators by flexible sectoral Standard Industrial Classification (SIC) disaggregation.

Its data base, independently obtained by government agencies, is public and amenable to objective interpretation. With the increasing capacity and decreasing unit user cost of computers, its data base is becoming more easily accessible and processable. Furthermore, the data base enables both cross-sectional and time-series measurements.

The problems with this approach seem to be the following:

1. Its effectiveness depends on the existence of well-developed and interactive national patent systems. Such systems are confined to a small subset of the set of

capitalist developed countries (CDCs). Therefore, ITT between less developed countries (LDCs) and CDCs and ITT among LDCs are largely beyond the reach of the m-PC approach.

2. At present, this approach offers merely a counting and taxonomic device with a simple and limited conceptual basis. It has not yet been integrated into a model with a corporate or national decision-making framework. This approach informs us about the extent of "foreign technological presence" and its change over time, but does not explain them. Consequently, it is of limited use in prediction of future foreign technological presence and in policymaking.

3. Patentable *and* patented technology is certainly not all technology. Much of technology is either unpatentable or deliberately not patented, even if patentable. Therefore, this approach cannot enable us to measure and analyze ITT in unpatented technologies.

4. Not all patents represent technology with either present or future commercial application. Many patents are never commercially exploited in the sense that not all inventions develop into innovations. Patents represent, in general, *potential* technology. Therefore, they can be useful in measuring and analyzing potential ITT, unless we can identify and isolate patents that are actually exploited from the population of all patents.

5. For most CDCs, ITT is increasingly a two-way phenomenon. This approach is limited, however, to measuring ITT *into* a country (the United States in its present application) from the rest of the world. It could be applied, of course, to studying ITT into several different CDCs. But different CDCs have different national patent systems. Consequently, the results obtained for different CDCs would be difficult to compare.

SUMMARY AND CONCLUSIONS

This chapter analyzes the concept and measurement of international technology transfer (ITT). ITT has become an increasingly important phenomenon in both public policymaking and private business planning. However, the concept of ITT remains vague and controversial, and, not surprisingly, the measurement of ITT continues to be imprecise and inadequate.

The problems in conceptualizing ITT stem from the complexity of "technology" itself and the multiplicity of channels of its "transfer." The difficulties in measuring ITT are due partly to the conceptual problems themselves and partly to data imperfections.

This review of the three alternative approaches to conceptualizing and measuring ITT shows that they all suffer from major shortcomings. Much analytical and empirical research is needed to improve the strengths of the individual approaches. There is also a great potential in a synthesis of the three approaches. Before such a synthesis can be achieved, however, their joint use, based on an ad hoc three-tiered approach, should be considered. Such an approach, by virtue of its macro-meso-micro span, can provide public officials and business executives with a more complete account of

ITT. Both the determinants and net benefits of ITT almost always have such a macro-meso-micro range. Even if the specific concern with ITT in individual cases is either primarily macro (as it often is in national public policy) or primarily micro (as it often is in corporate planning), the three-tiered approach could be the optimum one. Of course, the relative emphases placed on the individual approaches in their joint use would vary from case to case.

Without a better understanding of where, why, and how ITT occurs, and what (both public and private) net benefits it yields, policies aimed at improving the international scientific and economic position of the United States may miss their target. Today, more than ever, improvements in science and technology, which themselves have become widely specialized and internationalized, account for either an individual enterprise's or a national economy's ability to remain competitive. ITT, as trade in applicable and applied commercially useful knowledge, is important not only in itself, but also in determining the structure of both international trade in goods and services, and direct foreign investment. Therefore, it requires at least as much research effort as those that have been devoted to studying international trade and investment. We hope that our analysis will draw greater attention to this need.

REFERENCES

Contractor, Farok J. 1983. "The Importance of Licensing Versus Foreign Direct Investment in U.S. Corporate Strategy: An Analysis of Aggregate U.S. Data." Paper presented at the U.S. Social Science Research Council Conference on International Technology Transfer, New York, June 2-3.

Erdilek, Asim. 1982. *Direct Foreign Investment in Turkish Manufacturing: An Analysis of the Conflicting Objectives and Frustrated Expectations of a Host Country.* Tuebingen: J.C.B. Mohr (Paul Siebeck).

Flaherty, M. Therese. 1982. "International Technology Transfer, Global Strategies, and Government Policies in High Technology Industries." Harvard University Graduate School of Business Administration, Working Paper HBS 82-37.

McAllister, Paul R., Mark Carpenter, and Dominic Olivastro. 1983. "Ten Year Trends in U.S. Technological Dependence on Foreign Technology as Indicated by Referencing from U.S. Patents." Final Report prepared for the National Science Foundation, August.

Mansfield, Edwin. 1968. *The Economics of Technological Change.* New York: W. W. Norton.

Pavitt, Keith. 1983. "Technology Transfer Amongst the Industrially Advanced Countries: An Overview." Paper presented at the U.S. Social Science Research Council Conference on International Technology Transfer, New York, June 2-3.

Teece, David J. 1977. "Technology Transfer by Multinational Firms: The Resource

Cost of Transferring Technological Know-How.'' *The Economic Journal* (June 1977): 242-261.

   1981. ''The Market for Knowhow and the Efficient International Transfer of Technology.'' Stanford University Graduate School of Business, Research Paper No. 608, June.

16

Monitoring and Evaluating New Managerial Technologies

MARVIN B. MANDELL

The transfer of production technologies—that is, the procedures and equipment used to transform raw materials into finished goods and services—is of obvious importance for facilitating development. However, it is becoming increasingly apparent that improved managerial technologies (by which we mean the know-how necessary to organize, direct, and coordinate—in short, guide—activities and the use of resources and production technologies to achieve desired ends) are also vital if substantial improvements in the quality of life in developing areas are to occur (USAID, 1981, Wallender, 1979). Indeed, some observers go as far as to suggest that "management is a major, if not the major constraint, to development performance" (USAID, 1981: 15; also see Johnston and Clark, 1982; Wallender, 1979).

Moreover, improved managerial technnologies are intimately tied in with improvements in production technology. In many cases, improvements in managerial technology are necessary for the successful transfer of new production technologies (Wallender, 1979). Labor-intensive production technologies, which in general appear to have the greatest potential for stimulating development progress, pose an especially strong challenge to management capabilities. Such production technologies involve considerably more complexity and uncertainty than "standard" technologies (Norman, 1981; Allal, et al., 1977). Thus, projects utilizing these types of production technologies are likely to exacerbate the deficiencies in existing management capabilities. Consequently, the successful employment of "appropriate" production technologies is critically dependent on the transfer of managerial technologies (Hesseling, 1982). As Allal and associates (1977: 195) state: "If [labor-intensive] methods are to be used on a larger scale . . . a great deal of effort will have to go into . . . setting up suitable administrative and managerial systems."

Applied social science can substantially contribute to the successful transfer of managerial technologies by facilitating the adoption of new managerial technologies by user organizations. This chapter examines the nature of the adoption process for managerial technologies and considers the ways in which applied social science can facilitate the adoption of new managerial technologies. Next, an attempt is made to identify, in broad terms, what types of applied research are best suited to these roles. Finally, a strategy is outlined for the design and operation of a system for providing such information.

THE NATURE OF MANAGERIAL TECHNOLOGIES AND THEIR ADOPTION PROCESS

Applied social science can play a substantial role in facilitating the adoption of production technologies as well as in facilitating the adoption of managerial technologies. However, there are significant differences between the nature of managerial technologies and production technologies which, in turn, result in significant differences in the adoption processes for the two classes of technologies. These differences in the nature of the two classes of technologies and the adoption processes associated with them imply considerable differences in both the role that applied social science can play in the two types of adoption processes and the way that applied research should be conducted in conjunction with these processes in order to be as useful as possible.

First, managerial technologies tend to be more reversible and more amenable to "partialization" than production technologies. Reversibility refers to "the degree to which and the ease with which the status quo ante can be reinstated" (Lin and Zaltman, 1973: 107). "Partialization" refers to an incremental mode of implementation in which initially an attempt is made to implement the technology in only a small segment of the intended overall target system ("trial application"). Implementation in this small segment is then followed by an attempt to implement the technology in a somewhat larger segment of the intended overall target system. This incremental process of attempting to implement the technology in an increasingly larger portion continues until it has been implemented in the entire intended target system (Rothman, et al., 1981).[1] These two characteristics imply that, rather than a one-shot adoption ("go/no go") decision, the adoption of a managerial technology involves multiple recurrent decisions concerning continuation (retention) and internal diffusion (Kimberly, 1981; Walton, 1975), each of which is critical in the sense that it can potentially block the overall adoption process. Each of the recurrent decisions, moreover, is likely to be influenced by the perceived "effectiveness" of the technology (Lin and Zaltman, 1973). Therefore, the provision of information concerning the effectiveness of those applications of the technology in question conducted to date in the target system being considered is an important function to be played by applied research in this context. Moreover, it is especially crucial that this information be provided during the course of the adoption process (so that it can be taken into consideration in as many of the recurrent retention and internal diffusion decisions as possible) rather than solely following the completion of this process.

Another important difference between managerial and production technologies is that the managerial are considerably more "squishy" than the production in two senses. Managerial technologies tend to be "loose-bundled," that is, they consist of a core collection of components which adopters can "mix and match" (Rice and Rogers, 1980). In addition, individual components included in a given managerial technology are often flexible and modifiable rather than rigid. This characteristic has both a direct and an indirect implication for the role of applied research in the adoption of managerial technologies. The direct implication is simply that one important way in which applied research can contribute to the adoption of managerial technologies is to provide information concerning how a given managerial technology actually operates in order to help the adopting unit and other potential adopters distill the approach. That is, many managerial innovations, by virtue of their "squishiness," can initially only be formulated and communicated in abstract terms, which greatly inhibits their widespread adoption in a single system or set of target systems (Walton, 1975). Documenting the activities entailed in a "trial application" of the technology in a small portion of an organization (Kimberly, 1981; Walton, 1975; and the discussion of "partialization," above) can help overcome this problem.

The indirect implication of the "squishiness" of managerial technologies for the role of applied research in the adoption of such technologies is based on the role of "reinvention" in such processes. In particular, because managerial technologies are "squishy," reinvention, that is, the alteration of a technology during the adoption process (Rice and Rogers, 1980), can be expected to play an especially prominent role. Reinvention (also termed adaptation) is generally viewed to significantly contribute to the continued use of a new technology in that it results in both a better fit with local needs and conditions and greater commitment to that technology on the part of those involved in modifying it (Glaser and Backer, 1977; Larsen and Agarwala-Rogers, 1977; Rice and Rogers, 1980; Berman, et al., 1975). Calsyn and associates (1977) provide a dissenting view. They contend that, while reinvention occurs quite frequently, it tends to seriously compromise the value of the technology. Rice and Rogers (1980) differentiate planned from reactive reinvention. While they limit reactive reinvention to changes in response to specific problems occurring during implementation, reactive reinventions can occur in response to unforeseen opportunities as well as in response to unforeseen problems. The expected importance of reinvention in the adoption of managerial technologies suggests that an important role of applied research is to facilitate appropriate reinvention during such processes.

To summarize, then, the key roles of applied research in the adoption of managerial technologies are to aid participants in that process (and concerned onlookers):[2]

1. To assess the "effectiveness" of those applications of the managerial technology conducted to date in the target system of concern in order to facilitate sound decisions regarding retention and internal diffusion.

2. To clarify how the managerial technology in question actually operates through specifying the activities included in those applications of the technology conducted to date in the target system of concern.

3. To facilitate appropriate reinvention during the adoption process.

A common feature of these three roles is that they are aimed at facilitating components of the adoption process (retention and internal diffusion decisions and reinvention) which occur subsequent to the initial adoption decision. Moreover, they are accomplished by studying applications of the managerial technology which have taken or are taking place in the target system of concern. In short, these functions suggest that the primary way in which applied research can contribute to the adoption of managerial technologies is through monitoring and evaluation, rather than ex ante analysis.[3]

Conventional approaches to monitoring and evaluation are in certain respects ill-suited to the key roles of applied research in the adoption process outlined above. The major weakness of conventional approaches to evaluation is that, for the most part, they have an overly limited aim, namely, "establishing, with as much certainty as possible, whether or not [a well-defined] intervention is producing its intended effects" (Freeman, Rossi, and Wright, 1979: 103). Thus, such approaches are of little use with respect to distilling a managerial technology and reinvention. Moreover, even with respect to assessing the effectiveness of an application of a managerial technology, traditional approaches to evaluation commonly have the following shortcomings for our purposes:

1. Effectiveness is generally viewed in terms of a simple goal model that ignores a number of important complexities.

2. The provision of information is not necessarily consistent with organizational cycles (McConnel, et al., 1982).

3. Rigor in data collection and analysis is overly emphasized at the expense of feasibility and meaningfulness to users.

4. The importance of nonanalytic inputs into assessing the effectiveness of an intervention is not recognized, and the issue of how to integrate nonanalytic inputs and analytic results is not addressed.

The major weakness of conventional approaches to monitoring for our purposes is that its primary goal is to verify that an intervention which is specified a priori in static blueprint terms is being implemented in a manner that is consistent with its design specifications. Moreover, it ignores the question of whether the intended goals of the intervention will be achieved if it is implemented in accordance with its design specifications. Any weaknesses in the theory underlying the intervention as designed which would cause it to be ineffective are left to be answered through summative evaluation, even though by the time the summative evaluation is completed, it is likely to be too late to revise the intervention appropriately. Finally, traditional forms of monitoring generally fail to provide information that might facilitate reinvention in response to unforeseen opportunities.

In light of the importance of monitoring and evaluation in the adoption of managerial technologies and the weaknesses of conventional approaches to monitoring and evaluation, the main focus in the remainder of this chapter is on the design and operation of systems for monitoring and evaluating new managerial technologies which overcome these deficiencies. The acronym MTMES (Managerial Technology Monitoring and Evaluation System) is used here to refer to such a system.

A STRATEGY FOR THE DESIGN AND OPERATION OF AN MTMES

The specific MTMES most appropriate for facilitating the adoption of a certain managerial technology in a given site will not be exactly the same as the MTMES most appropriate for facilitating the adoption of some other managerial technology in that site. Moreover, the specific MTMES which is most appropriate for facilitating the adoption of a given managerial technology in one site may be different than the MTMES which is most appropriate for facilitating the adoption of that same managerial technology in another site (even if the two sites are within the same overall target system). However, some basic principles for designing and operating an MTMES can be identified. In presenting these principles, the next section introduces some background concepts, terminology, and principles drawn primarily from the literature on evaluation and organizational effectiveness. This is followed by an outline of a process for designing and operating an MTMES.

Background Concepts, Terminology, and Principles

At the heart of an MTMES is a site-specific process model of how the managerial technology is expected to work. Such a model is simply a collection of three types of elements—activities, intermediate outcomes (precursors), and terminal outcomes (goals)[4]—which are arranged into a time-ordered, causal sequence of relationships. Let us consider these three types of elements in some detail.

In general, an outcome is some change in the state or condition of a system deemed desirable to attain. For our purposes, it is useful to distinguish between intermediate outcomes (precursors) and terminal outcomes (goals). A terminal outcome (goal) is a change in state that is desirable in its own right. Examples of terminal outcomes might include increased production, reduced unemployment, and lower infant mortality rates.

An intermediate outcome (precursor) is a change in state which, if it occurs, increases the observer's confidence that some terminal outcome will occur.[5] That is, a precursor is of interest because it is an instrumental condition with respect to some goal. A precursor may be either external to the application of the managerial technology in the sense of occurring independently of the technology (that is, it would have occurred even if the technology had not been applied) or internal to the application of the managerial technology in the sense of being caused by that technology. In the former case, the precursor is of interest only if it affects the likelihood of some other outcome occurring. Certain features of a precursor should be noted. First, a precursor is restricted to a change in condition, in contrast to an activity. Second, a precursor must be expected to occur significantly prior (in time) to its associated goal. Third, a series of precursors may be associated with a single goal as illustrated; similarly, a single precursor may be associated with more than one goal as illustrated (see Figure 16.1).

The final element contained in a process models an activity, represents an effort undertaken by site participants which is intended to change the state (condition) of some system, that is, attain an intermediate or terminal outcome. Examples of activities might include preparing plans, developing analytic techniques, and holding a meeting among certain actors.

As discussed in detail below, assessing the effectiveness of an application of a managerial technology is a particularly thorny task. However, as the

Figure 16.1
Site-Specific Process Model of Managerial Technology

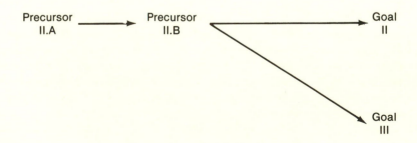

discussion of effectiveness will show, knowledge of the extent to which relevant goals are achieved is at the core of assessing the effectiveness of an application of a managerial technology. Thus, information concerning terminal outcomes has obvious relevance for assessing the effectiveness of an application of a managerial technology.

Somewhat less obviously, information concerning precursors and activities also has an important role to play in assessing the effectiveness of an application of a managerial technology. For one, in many cases information concerning the extent to which certain goals are achieved cannot be obtained until the latter stages, or even after the completion, of a particular adoption process. Yet, in many cases various organizational cycles, most notably retention and internal diffusion decisions (see above), require that the effectiveness of an application of a managerial technology be assessed at earlier points in time. In such situations, information concerning the attainment of intermediate outcomes can often be relied upon as a surrogate in assessing the effectiveness of an application of a managerial technology. In this sense, information concerning precursors can be thought of as a "leading indicator" of the effectiveness (in terms of goals) of an application of a managerial technology. It must be recognized, however, that there may be considerable slippage between precursors and their associated terminal outcomes, especially in cases where the intermediate outcome considered is the first in a long chain of precursors leading to a particular goal.

Information about precursors, along with information on activities, can play another important role in assessments of the effectiveness of an application of a managerial technology. Strictly speaking, to show that relevant goals are achieved is not the same as demonstrating that the application of a managerial technology has been effective. Rather, it must also be demonstrated that the goals were achieved through the application of the managerial technology; that is, that the goals would not have been achieved in the absence of that technology. Traditionally, this is accomplished by also observing whether the goals are achieved in a control group in which the technology of concern is not implemented. This tactic, however, is often not feasible in the current context. A second tactic for determining whether the goals would have been achieved in the absence of the management technology is to develop and apply a simulation model of the system of concern (Larkey, 1977). Again, this is not viewed as feasible in the current context. Constructing a plausible causal chain of events that leads from activities to goals and providing as much empirical validation of this chain as possible (through information on activities and intermediate outcomes) is a third way to cope with the issue of whether the application of the management technology is the cause of relevant goals being achieved. That is, to the extent that one can coherently account for goal achievement in terms of activities and intermediate outcomes that are associated with the application of the managerial technology, rival explanations of goal achievement become less credible.[6] (This logic can be extended to attempts to attribute the occurrence of intermediate outcomes to the application of a managerial technology when those intermediate outcomes are used as surrogates for terminal outcomes as discussed below. In such cases, one would attempt to account for achievement of the intermediate outcome serving as a surrogate for a terminal outcome in terms of earlier intermediate outcomes and activities.)

Another important role of information in intermediate outcomes is facilitating the process of reinvention. Assessments of the extent to which some precursor is attained provide rapid and timely feedback to site participants concerning the efficacy of their activities. Indications that an important precursor has not been attained by the time it had been expected are important signals of the need for reinvention in time to make the application of the managerial technology succeed. Conversely, the occurrence of a previously unanticipated "positive" precursor, if detected, represents an opportunity that might trigger reactive reinventions. Moreover, simply calling attention to precursors is likely to instigate a search for alternative—and perhaps better—paths to a given goal. Explicitly considering previously overlooked paths is likely to facilitate planned reinventions.

In addition to playing an important role in assessing whether the achievement of certain outcomes was due to the application of a managerial technology, information concerning the activities involved in the application of that technology has obvious importance in helping users to distill the approach.

In summary, then, the primary role of information concerning terminal outcomes is to aid in assessing the effectiveness of an application of a managerial technology. Information on precursors has three primary roles, namely:

1. It can serve as a surrogate for information on terminal outcomes, which is particularly important in cases where information concerning goals cannot be obtained in a timely fashion.
2. It can help to determine whether the occurrence of a subsequent intermediate outcome or a terminal outcome was caused by the application of the managerial technology.
3. It can facilitate the process of reinvention.

Finally, information on activities can help potential users both to distill the managerial technology and to determine whether the achievement of certain outcomes was due to the application of that technology.

Complementary Sources of Knowledge Concerning
Activities, Precursors, and Goals

Knowledge about the activities, precursors, and terminal outcomes associated with an application of a managerial technology can be obtained from sources other than the MTMES developed. In particular, "ordinary knowledge" processes and "social learning" (Lindblom and Cohen, 1979) as well as standard reporting systems are important mechanisms for developing such knowledge. Thus, an MTMES should complement and supplement, rather than displace, these other mechanisms. In operational terms, this means that an MTMES should be selective, rather than comprehensive, in terms of the activities, precursors, and terminal outcomes on which it focuses. That is, although a large number of activities, precursors, and goals are relevant in an application of a managerial technology, the MTMES need not and should not attempt to provide information about all of them. Moreover, these alternative knowledge sources are important inputs into the development of an MTMES (see Figure 16.2).

Conceptualizing the Effectiveness of an Application of a Managerial Technology

The effectiveness of an application of a managerial technology should be conceptualized in terms of improvements in the performance of some significant real-world system, such as a firm, an agricultural system, or a health system. Recent work in evaluation and organizational effectiveness, however, suggests that basing assessments of effectiveness on this type of conceptualization is likely to make such assessments considerably more complex and less conclusive than assessments of effectiveness are often claimed to be. In particular, a key implication of this work is that it is unrealistic to expect to be able to obtain a single, universal assessment of the effectiveness of an application of a managerial technology.

The first task that must be accomplished if the above approach is to be operationalized is the specification of the boundaries of the "system of concern." This system may be a project, a set of projects in an organization, a set of organizations, or a part of an organization. Specifying the boundaries of the "system of concern" is analogous to the consideration of externalities in cost-benefit analysis. The question here is how far to extend the boundaries of the system beyond direct, first-order effects. In many cases, researchers limit their focus to easily identifiable first-order effects (for example, change within a single organization), but in many instances it is necessary to consider secondary and tertiary effects, especially when there is reason to believe that the application of the managerial technology has potential for significant effects on units beyond the immediate site in which the technology is being implemented. The difficulty here is in determining just how far to trace indirect effects and what magnitude of indirect effect is likely to be sufficiently consequential to warrant attention. The appropriate boundaries of the "system of concern" depend in large part on one's purposes (Katz and Kahn, 1978). Since different actors are likely to have different purposes, no single set of system boundaries is likely to be appropriate.

Figure 16.2
Complementary Sources of Knowledge

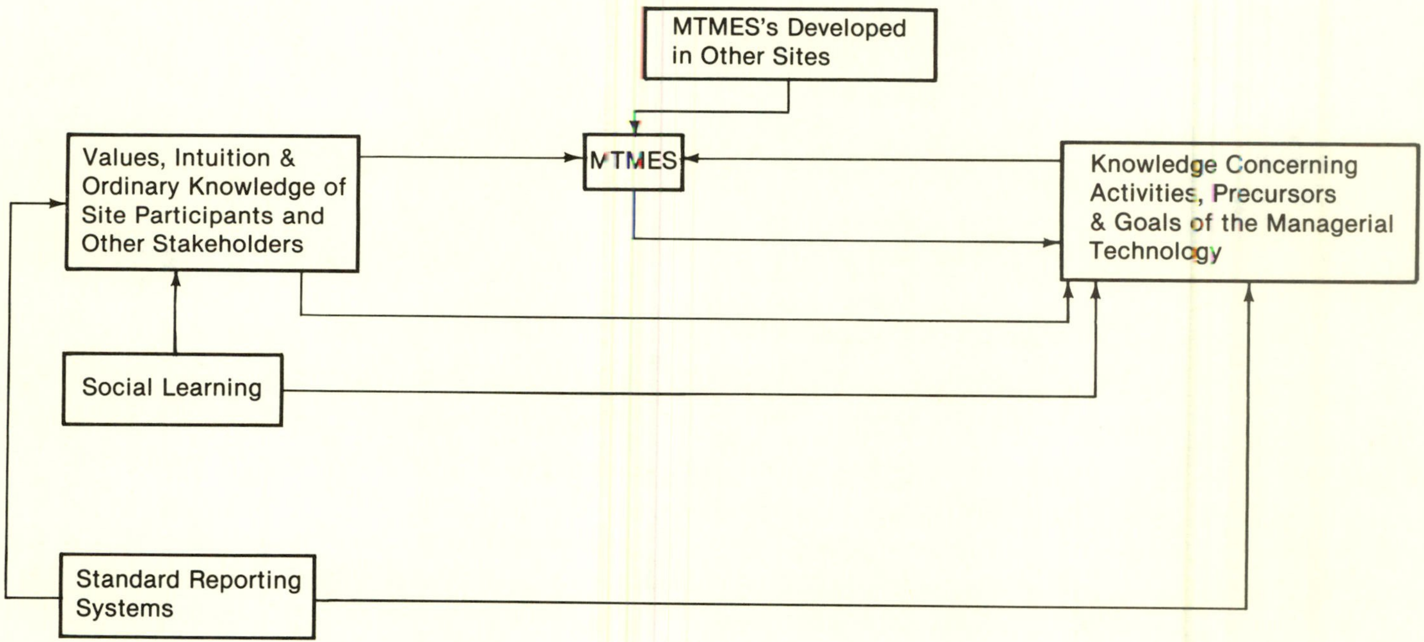

Even thornier than the specifications of the boundaries of the system of concern is the problem of determining whether a given system is effective. Hall (1982) proposes that organizational effectiveness[7] be viewed in terms of a "contradiction model." This model is an attempt to encompass the insights provided by previous models of organizational effectiveness, such as the goal model, the systems-resource model, the participant-satisfaction model, and the social-function model. The key features of Hall's contradiction model are as follows:

1. *Organizations have multiple and conflicting constituencies.* In Hall's usage, a constituency refers to a group of people affected by an organization. A constituency need not be organized or even aware that it is affected by an organization. Moreover, a constituency can be either internal or external to the organization.

2. *Organizations have multiple and conflicting goals.* This multiplicity exists on three levels. First, a single constituency at a given point in time is likely to hold multiple and conflicting goals for the organization. Second, the goal set of a single constituency may shift over time. Third, different constituencies are likely to hold different, though overlapping, goal sets. Thus, if effectiveness is viewed as the attainment of most or all of an organization's goals, an organization cannot be effective, since certain goals can only be attained at the expense of the accomplishment of other goals.

3. *Organizations have multiple and conflicting time frames.* In many instances an action that maximizes the attainment of a certain goal in the short run will not maximize the attainment of that goal in the long run, and vice versa. Different time frames are likely to be important to different constituencies. For example, Hannan and Freeman (1977) note that higher levels of an organization often take a longer time perspective than lower levels.

These three features imply that "*no organization is effective.* Instead, organizations can be viewed as effective (or ineffective) to some degree in terms of specific . . . goals, constituents, and time frames" (Hall, 1982: 302; emphasis in original).

A Process for the Design and Operation of an MTMES

Figure 16.3 depicts a process for designing and operating an MTMES which is based on the foregoing principles. The first three steps in this process are intended to produce one or more tentative site-specific process models of how the managerial technology is expected to work. The next step identifies the information which the MTMES will provide at various points in time. The final step is the actual collection, processing, interpreting, and reporting of the data.

The process represented in Figure 16.3 is iterative. That is, after proceeding through the process initially, it is necessary to return to certain points in the process from time to time and revise the MTMES. However, not all

Figure 16.3
A Process for the Design and Operation of an MTMES

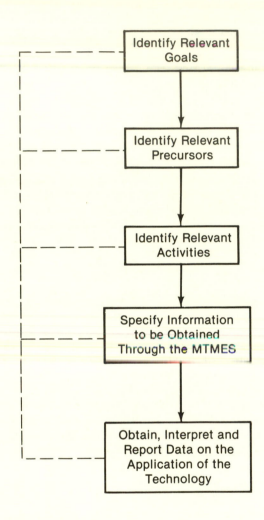

steps should necessarily be repeated during all iterations. For example, it might be desirable to return to steps 3 and 4 on a quarterly basis, to step 2 on a semiannual basis, and to step 1 on an annual basis.

Thus, the MTMES developed in a particular site will constantly evolve in two respects. First, the set of activities, precursors, and goals included in the site-specific process model of the managerial technology is likely to be revised periodically in response to the identification of previously unforeseen precursors (opportunities), the detection of unachieved precursors, shifts in goals, and changes in the "action plan." The information produced by the MTMES is, of course, expected to play a major role in these revisions, but other forces are likely to play a role as well. Second, even if the process model remained fixed, it might be determined, say, that during the early stages of the application of the managerial technology, the MTMES should collect information regarding certain activities and precursors, while during later stages a different set of activities should be focused on and efforts to collect information concerning some precursors should be replaced by efforts to collect information regarding selected goals.

A central principle of an MTMES is that by involving various users (especially site participants and potential target system adopters) at various points in this process, the utility of an MTMES can be greatly enhanced. User involvement improves the fit between the users' information needs and the information provided by the MTMES. In addition, it creates a sense of ownership of the system on the part of users which, in turn, is presumed to increase the likelihood of their using its outputs. Nonetheless, certain possible obstacles and drawbacks of user involvement should be kept in mind. (For a discussion of these obstacles and drawbacks, along with some means of avoiding them or overcoming them, see Mandell, forthcoming.)

Identifying Terminal Outcomes

The set of terminal outcomes identified will ideally include all goals that various constituencies believe to be relevant. The contradiction model of organizational (system) effectiveness discussed above suggests that the list of such goals will be large and diverse. Stakeholder surveys (Lawrence and Cook, 1982) are likely to be a useful tool for identifying relevant goals. The first step in such a survey is to develop a list of stakeholders. A "snowball" approach is likely to be appropriate here. That is, an initial list of stakeholders, perhaps consisting of those with a (known) formal connection to the system of concern and those identified by site participants as being relevant stakeholders, would be generated. Each member of this initial list would then be asked to identify other actors whom they perceived to be stakeholders in the application of the managerial technology. These "second-round" nominees would then be asked, in turn, to identify others whom they perceived also to be stakeholders, and so on. Each stakeholder, either through an interview or a written questionnaire, would be asked to identify goals which they believed to be important components of the effectiveness of the system of concern in the application of the managerial technology. Certain variants of this basic form of stakeholder survey might be appropriate in some situations. First, the list of "actual" stakeholders might be limited to those who are identified by at least some minimum number of others as being a stakeholder. Second, once the list of stakeholders is finalized, the interview/questionnaire component might take the form of a modified Delphi process. That is, after the initial set of questionnaires/ interviews was completed, a feedback report consisting of an edited list of all goals specified would be distributed to each respondent; the respondents might then be given the opportunity to add goals to the list. They might, in addition, be asked to rate (say on a five-point scale) the importance of each goal to them.

Identifying Relevant Precursors

For each goal identified, one or more plausible chains of precursors leading to that goal should be constructed. In addition to the linkages between precursors and goals, linkages among precursors need to be speci- fied. Consensus on each chain is not necessary at this point; indeed, in many respects it is preferable that alternative plausible chains be identified. In particular, identifying alternative plausible chains of precursors, which is directly analogous to "theoretical triangulation" (Denzin, 1970), can reduce the likelihood of overlooking important precursors, that is, failing to detect significant opportunities and problems. For one, an MTMES cannot be "programmed" to collect information concerning the occurrence/ non- occurrence of a precursor unless it is explicitly identified. This is not to say that the occurrence/nonoccurrence of a precursor can only be sensed if an MTMES is "programmed" to scan for that event; alternative sources of information (most notably, informal serendipitous observation) might also enable site participants to detect whether that precursor occurs. The point is that the likelihood of accurately detecting the occurrence/nonoccurrence of a precursor is increased if an MTMES is "programmed" to scan for that event. Moreover, the power of serendipitous observation to accurately detect whether a precursor occurs is increased when a possible precursor is a priori explicitly identified, since explicitly identifying a precursor is likely to make it more salient to observers.

Awareness of plausible chains of precursors constructed in MTMESs developed at other sites, even if the relevant goals are different, may provide useful insights and "sparks" to participants in this task. Various forms of structured group processes, for example, nominal group technique (Delbecq, et al., 1975) and "brainstorming" (Osborn, 1957; Porter, et al., 1980) may also be useful for this task.

Defining Activities

In step 3 the tentative site-specific process model(s) of the application of the managerial technology is completed by identifying relevant activities included in the application of the managerial technology and their linkages to various precursors and goals. A key issue is whether or not to attempt to identify an exhaustive list of activities included in the application of the managerial technology. Experience in studies of managerial job behavior, which we believe to be directly analogous to the task of determining activities included in an application of a managerial technology, suggests that an exhaustive approach is weak in terms of its ability to distinguish *important* aspects of managerial behavior (Campbell, et al., 1970). Thus, it appears that, in light of the need to help users distill the managerial technology of concern, a more purposive, selective approach is more appropriate.

One possibly appropriate technique, which has been used successfully in studies of managerial behavior to pinpoint the more important elements of job behavior, is the Critical Incidents Method (Flanagan, 1954; Campbell, et al., 1970). The initial step in this method is to identify a large number of "critical incidents," which in the current context are activities crucial for achieving a certain outcome (goal or precursor). Traditionally, critical incidents are identified from retrospective behavioral accounts obtained from those close to the system being studied (for example, managers). In the current context, the body of relevant past experience available at the time the site-specific process model is formulated is not likely to be large enough to allow a sufficiently large number of critical incidents to be identified. Thus, for an MTMES it will be necessary to replace or at least supplement lists of "critical incidents" obtained through retrospective behavioral accounts with "critical incidents" identified by having site participants specify a priori the activities they believe will be especially critical for the achievement of specified outcomes (precursors and goals). Again, "brainstorming" and the nominal group technique might be useful tools for this task. After a large number of critical incidents are identified, they are abstracted to form categories of activities that are represented in the process model and also form potential foci of MTMES-based observations.

Specifying Information to Be Obtained Through the MTMES

The next step shown in Figure 16.3 entails the determination of the information to be obtained through the MTMES. This step consists of three related components, namely:

1. Determining which goals, precursors, and categories of activities the MTMES will provide information about.
2. Specifying the time for collecting information on each of these elements.
3. Specifying the data collection technique(s) to be used to obtain information about each of these elements (for example, survey, interview, direct observation).

The previous three steps are likely to result in a long and diverse list of goals, precursors, and categories of activities about which an MTMES *might* be called on to provide information. However, it will rarely be feasible to rely on the MTMES to provide information regarding all of these elements. Fortunately, the existence of information sources other than the

MTMES to provide relevant information generally eliminates the necessity of relying on the MTMES to provide information regarding all of the elements included in the process model(s) specified. Thus, it will be necessary to screen the list of goals, precursors, and categories of activities that exist at the end of step 3. In doing so, a number of criteria might be taken into consideration, including:

1. The perceived importance of the element.
2. The extent to which applied research can provide credible information concerning that element and the cost of doing so.
3. The extent to which alternative sources of information concerning that element are available and the credibility of the alternative sources of information.

Researchers and site participants should generally collaborate in performing this task.

It is not necessary for any given goal, all of its associated precursors, and all related activity categories to be either included in or excluded from the MTMES as a class. That is, even if no information concerning a given goal is sought through the MTMES, information concerning some precursors and/or activity categories associated with that goal might still be included in the MTMES and vice versa.

Specifying time limits for collecting information on each element selected for observation through the MTMES involves more than simply deciding on start-up and termination points. It is also necessary to decide how frequently, and at what times, information concerning a given element is to be obtained. Of particular concern in this regard is that, since both precursors and goals are defined in terms of change of state, for each outcome (goal or precursor) considered in the MTMES, a choice must be made as to whether the MTMES is to be relied on to provide information concerning the attribute of the system associated with the outcome prior to the change in state (prior state), after the change in state (ex-post state), or both. Observations of some attribute of the prior state of a system are often referred to as "baseline" measurements. Our notion of an MTMES contains important implications concerning baseline measurements which may run counter to conventional wisdom. First, "comprehensive" baseline measurements (that is, a baseline measurement associated with each and every goal and precursor) are not necessary. Rather, since we see an MTMES as focusing on only a subset of all activities, precursors, and goals of concern, at most baseline measurements for the focal precursors and goals are needed. Moreover, for some focal outcomes, sufficient information concerning the prior state of that aspect of the system may be available from sources other than the MTMES, thereby eliminating the need for baseline measurements corresponding to that outcome. Finally, it is not necessary for all baseline measurements to be taken at the initiation of an application of a managerial technology, nor must all baseline measurements be taken at the same point in time. Rather, it is only necessary that the baseline observations of the attribute of the system associated with a given outcome be taken prior to the occurrence of the event of interest. The time each event is expected to occur should be specified in the process model of the application of the managerial technology. Indeed, the later the baseline measurement is taken, the less the likelihood that extraneous events (history, maturation; see Freeman, Rossi, and Wright, 1979; Cook and Campbell, 1979) will confound assessments of the impact of managerial technology.

It is also important to emphasize that users (even within a single subset specified above) are likely to have different interests and, hence, place different values on various types of information. This highlights the importance of "stakeholder analysis" (Lawrence and Cook, 1982; Mitroff, et al., 1979; Goodman and Pennings, 1980) within this step. The issue here is the determination of interested parties and, in turn, in most instances, assessment of their interests and information needs. An MTMES, as opposed to basic research, is intended to have instrumental value, but instrumental to whom?

Obtain, Interpret, and Report Data on the
Application of the Managerial Technology

The final step in the process sketched in Figure 16.3 is the actual production of MTMES outputs (information). It is important to emphasize that non-MTMES inputs, such as "ordinary knowledge" (Lindblom and Cohen, 1979) and values, play a key role in this step in two respects. First, in unstructured, complex situations, such as those in which an MTMES will be employed, applied research can only provide insight into relevant concerns; it cannot yield solutions or "self-evidence prescriptions" (Elmore, 1975; also see Blumstein, 1979, and Brill, 1979). That is, MTMES-based data cannot be interpreted in a straightforward, technical manner since, as P. P. Rieker (1980) notes, "the data never point to one and only one course of action, recommendation, or conclusion." Rather, a number of alternative implications may follow from a given set of MTMES-based data. In making the leap from such data to valid "acton recommendations," such elements as values, other forms of knowledge, assumptions one is willing to make, and risks one is willing to take necessarily play a vital role (Rieker, 1980).

Second, as noted above, insights into the occurrence of relevant outcomes (goals and precursors) and activities included in an application of a managerial technology can be obtained from information sources other than the MTMES. These alternative sources include casual and serendipitous observation and routine reporting systems. Where the insights obtained from these alternative sources are especially notable—for example, because they are surprising or indicate the need to revise the process model formulated (which may, in turn, indicate the need or opportunity for reinvention or suggest new foci of data collection)—they should be incorporated in MTMES reports. However, selectivity in terms of reporting non-MTMES-based insights in order to avoid information overload should be stressed.

A second point to be emphasized here is that the way in which information concerning the application of a managerial technology is reported strongly influences the credibility, and hence the use, of MTMES data. In particular, the characteristics of both the media and the format used to transmit this information should be tailored to the needs and capabilities of the user (see Braskamp, et al., 1982; House and Coleman, 1980). Relevant issues here include:

- Should the information be reported in writing, verbally, or both?
- To what extent should data be used to support conclusions and recommendations?
- How long should the report be?

SUMMARY AND CONCLUSIONS

This chapter is based on two key tenets. First, the transfer of managerial technologies is an essential element in improving the quality of life in developing areas. Second, applied social science can play a significant role in aiding this process. Looking at the nature of managerial technologies and the adoption process associated with them, we conclude that monitoring and evaluation, rather than ex ante analysis, is the most appropriate form of applied social science for facilitating this process. However, conventional approaches to monitoring and evaluation do not appear to be well suited to the key anticipated roles of applied research in the adoption of new managerial techologies. Therefore, a foundation for designing and operating monitoring and evaluation systems that are likely to be appropriate for these roles has been described.

NOTES

This chapter has benefited greatly from frequent discussions with Barry Bozeman. I would also like to acknowledge financial support provided by the Development Project Management Center, U.S. Department of Agriculture, to investigate some of the issues discussed here. Of course, statements contained herein do not necessarily represent the official position or policies of the U.S. Department of Agriculture.

1. We will use the term *site* to refer to that portion of the overall intended target system in which an attempt to implement a managerial technology is occurring at a given point in time. Thus, "partialization" entails successive attempts to implement a managerial technology in an increasingly larger site.

2. "Concerned onlookers" might include external funders and those expected to be involved in implementing the technology in other target systems.

3. There is an additional reason to emphasize monitoring and evaluation rather than a priori analysis. Managerial technologies not only tend to be squishy in the two senses discussed above, but also involve highly complex and ambiguous cause-effect relationships. Thus, valid and precise a priori analysis of managerial technologies is likely to be very costly or infeasible.

4. The terminology here is adapted from Mohr (1973) and Deniston, et al. (1968).

5. In some cases, of course, a given outcome may be both a precursor and a goal.

6. A similar argument in a different context is presented in Downs (1981).

7. Hall's discussion and the discussion presented here are phrased in terms of organizational effectiveness. However, both discussions apply directly to the more general concept of system effectiveness.

REFERENCES

Allal, M., G. A. Edmonds, and M. I. Hussain (1977). "Development and Promotion of Appropriate Road Construction Technology." *International Labor Review* 116: 183-195.

Behrman, J., and H. Wallender (1976). *Transfers of Manufacturing Technology Within Multinational Enterprises*. Cambridge, Mass.: Ballinger.

Berman, P., P. W. Greenwood, and M. McLaughlin (1975). *Federal Programs Supporting Educational Change, Vol. 4: A Summary of the Findings in Review*. Santa Monica, Calif.: Rand Corporation.

Blumstein, A. (1979). "Operations Research in the Public Sector: Frustration, Failings and Future." In K. B. Haley (ed.), *Operational Research '78*. Amsterdam: North Holland.

Braskamp, L. A., R. D. Brown, and D. L. Newman (1982). "Studying Evaluation Utilization Through Simulation." *Evaluation Review* 6: 114-126.

Brill, E. D., Jr. (1979). "The Use of Optimization Models in Public-Sector Planning." *Management Science* 25: 413-422.

Calsyn, R. J., L. G. Tornatzky, and S. Dittmar (1977). "Incomplete Adoption of an Innovation: The Case of Goal Attainment." *Evaluation* 4: 127-130.

Campbell, J. P., M. D. Dunette, Lawler III, and K. E. Weick, Jr. (1970). *Managerial Behavior, Performance, and Effectiveness*. New York: McGraw-Hill.

Cook, T. D., and D. T. Campbell (1979). *Quasi-Experimentation: Design and Analysis Issues for Field Settings*. Chicago: Rand McNally.

Delbecq, A. L., A. H. Van de Ven, and D. H. Gustafson (1975). *Group Techniques for Program Planning*. Glenview, Ill.: Scott, Foresman and Company.

Deniston, O. L., I. M. Rosenstock, and V. A. Getting (1968). "Evaluation of Program Effectiveness." *Public Health Reports* 83: 323-335.

Denzin, N. K. (1970). *The Research Act: A Theoretical Introduction to Sociological Methods*. Chicago: Aldine.

Downs, G. W. (1981). "Monitoring the Health Planning System: Data, Measurement and Inference Problems." In Committee on Health Planning Goals and Standards (ed.), *Health Planning in the United States*, Vol. 2. Washington, D.C.: National Academy Press.

Elmore, R. F. (1975). "Design of the Follow Through Experiment." In A. M. Rivlin and P. M. Timpane (eds.), *Planned Variation in Education.* Washington, D.C.: Brookings Institution.

Flanagan, J. C. (1954). "The Critical Incident Technique." *Psychological Bulletin* 51: 327-358.

Freeman, H. E., P. H. Rossi, and S. R. Wright (1979). *Evaluating Social Projects in Developing Countries.* Paris: OECD.

Glaser, E. M., and T. E. Backer (1977). "Innovation Redefined: Durability and Local Adaptation." *Evaluation* 4: 131-135.

Goodman, P., and J. Pennings (1980). "Critical Issues in Assessing Organizational Effectiveness." In E. E. Lawler, D. Nadler, and C. Comman (eds.), *Organizational Assessment.* New York: John Wiley and Sons.

Hall, R. H. (1982). *Organizations: Structure and Process.* 3d. ed. Englewood Cliffs, N.J.: Prentice-Hall.

Hannan, M. T., and J. Freeman (1977). "Obstacles to Comparative Studies." In P. S. Goodman and J. M. Pennings (eds.), *New Perspectives on Organizational Effectiveness.* San Francisco: Jossey-Bass.

Hesseling, P. (1982). *Effective Organization Research for Development.* Oxford: Pergamon Press.

House, P., and J. Coleman (1980). "Realities of Public Policy Analysis." In S. S. Nagel (ed.), *Improving Policy Analysis.* Beverly Hills, Calif.: Sage.

Johnston, B. F., and W. C. Clark (1982). *Redesigning Rural Development: A Strategic Perspetive.* Baltimore: Johns Hopkins University Press.

Katz, D., and R. L. Kahn (1978). *The Social Psychology of Organizations.* 2d ed. New York: John Wiley and Sons.

Kimberly, J. R. (1981). "Managerial Innovations." In P. C. Nystrom and W. H. Starbuck (eds.), *Handbook of Organizational Design.* Vol. 1. New York: Oxford University Press.

Larkey, P. D. (1977). "Process Models of Governmental Resource Allocation and Program Evaluation." *Policy Sciences* 8: 269-301.

Larsen, J. K., and R. Agarwala-Rogers (1977). "Reinvention of Innovative Ideas: Modified? Adopted? None of the Above?" *Evaluation* 4: 136-140.

Lawrence, J.E.S., and T. J. Cook (1982). "Designing Program Evaluations with the Help of Stakeholders." *Journal of Policy Analysis and Management* 2: 120-123.

Lin, N., and G. Zaltman (1973). "Dimensions of Innovations." In G. Zaltman (ed.), *Processes and Phenomena of Social Change.* New York: John Wiley and Sons.

Lindblom, C. E., and D. K. Cohen (1979). *Usable Knowledge.* New Haven: Yale University Press.

McConnel, W. A., T. D. Nguyen, and S. Barto (1982). "Enhancing Program Review for Evaluation and Management." *Evaluation and Program Planning* 5: 37-44.

Mandell, M. B. (Forthcoming). "Client Involvement in the Design and Selection of Evolution Studies." *Knowledge* 5.

Mitroff, I. I., J. R. Emshoff, and R. H. Kilmann (1979). "Assumptional Analysis: A Methodology for Strategic Problem Solving." In L. E. Datta and R. Perloff (eds.), *Improving Evaluations.* Beverly Hills, Calif.: Sage.

Mohr, L. B. (1973). "The Concept of Organizational Goal." *American Political Science Review* 67: 470-481.

Norman, C. (1981). *The God That Limps: Science and Technology in the Eighties.* New York: W. W. Norton.

Osborn, A. F. (1957). *Applied Imagination.* New York: Scribner's.

Porter, A. L., F. A. Rossini, S. R. Carpenter, and A. T. Roper (1980). *A Guidebook for Technology Assessment and Impact Analysis.* New York: North Holland.

Rice, R. E., and E. M. Rogers (1980). "Reinvention in the Innovation Process." *Knowledge* 1: 499-514.

Rieker, P. P. (1980). "Evaluation Research: The Design-to-Use Process." *Knowledge* 1: 215-235.

Rothman, J., J. L. Ehrlich, and J. G. Teresa (1981). *Changing Organizations and Community Programs.* Beverly Hills, Calif.: Sage.

U.S. Agency for International Development (USAID) (1981). *Management Development Strategy Paper: AID's Response to the Implementation Needs of 1980's.* Working Paper of the Management Development Working Group.

Wallender, H. W. (1979). *Technology Transfer and Management in the Developing Countries.* Cambridge, Mass.: Ballinger.

Walton, R. E. (1975). "The Diffusion of New York Structures: Explaining Why Success Didn't Take." *Organizational Dynamics* 3, No. 3: 3-22.

Selected Bibliography

Almond, Gabriel A., and Sidney Verba (1963). *The Civic Culture*. Princeton, N.J.: Princeton University Press.

Atkinson, John S. (1966). "Notes on the Generality of the Theory of Achievement Motivation." In A *Theory of Achievement Motivation*, edited by John W. Atkinson and Norman T. Feather. Huntington, N.Y.: Robert E. Krieger Publishing.

Bauer, P. T. (1967). *West Africa Trade: A Study of Competition, Oligopoly, and Monopoly in a Changing Economy*. New York: Augustus M. Kelley.

Behrman, J., and H. Wallender (1976). *Transfers of Manufacturing Technology Within Multinational Enterprises*. Cambridge, Mass.: Ballinger.

Belshaw, Cyril S. (1965). *Traditional Exchange and Modern Markets*. Englewood Cliffs, N.J.: Prentice-Hall.

Cassen, Robert, et al. (1982). *Rich Country Interests and Third World Development*. London: Crown Helm.

Cilingiroglu, A. *Transfer of Technology for Pharmaceutical Chemicals*. Paris: OECD, 1975 and *Acquisition of Technology from Multinational Corporations by Developing Countries*. United Nations Publication, Geneva, 1974.

Dewing, Arthur Stone (1914). *The Financial Policy of Companies*. New York: Ronald Press.

Friedman, Milton (1957). *A Theory of the Consumption Function*. Princeton, N.J.: Princeton University Press.

Gruber, William H. (1969). *Factors in the Transfer of Technology*. Edited by William H. Gruber and Donald G. Marquis. Cambridge, Mass.: MIT Press.

Norman, C. (1981). *The God That Limps: Science and Technology in the Eighties*. New York: W. W. Norton.

Porter, A. L., F. A. Rossini, S. R. Carpenter, and A. T. Roper (1980). *A Guidebook for Technology Assessment and Impact Analysis*. New York: North Holland.

Rothman, J., J. L. Ehrlich, and J. G. Teresa (1981). *Changing Organizations and Community Programs*. Beverly Hills, Calif.: Sage.

Seurat, Silvère. *Technology Transfer: Realistic Approach*. Houston: Gulf Publishing Co., 1979.

Wallender, H. W. (1979) *Technology Transfer and Management in the Developing Countries*. Cambridge, Mass.: Ballinger.

ARTICLES

Berliger, J. S. "Managing the Soviet Economy: Alternative Models." *Problems of Communism* (January-February 1983): 40-56.

Cooper, Julian. "Western Technology and Soviet Economic Power." Paper delivered at the 1983 Millennium Conference: Technology Transfer and East-West Relations in the 1980s. London School of Economics, May 1983.

Doz, Yves L. "Strategic Management in Multinational Companies." *Sloan Management Review* (Winter 1980): 27-46.

Gimpl, M. L. "The Role of Multinational Corporations and Local Entrepreneurs in Economic Development." *Economic Bulletin* (1975).

Hendon, Donald W. "Toward a Theory of Consumerism." *Business Horizons* (August 1975): 16-23.

Holiday, George D. "The Role of Western Technology in the Soviet Economy." *Issues in East-West Commercial Relations*. A Compendium of Papers submitted to the Joint Economic Committee, U.S. Congress, January 12, 1979, p. 82.

Liles, Patrick. "Who Are the Entrepreneurs?" *MSU Business Topics* (Winter 1974): 1-14.

McClelland, D. C. "Achievement Motivation Can Be Developed." *Harvard Business Review* (November-December 1965).

Nye, Joseph S., Jr. "Technology Transfer Policies." *Issues in East-West Commercial Relations*. A compendium of papers submitted to the Joint Economic Committee, U.S. Congress, January 12, 1979, p. 16.

Pegan, John R. "Basic Business in a Changing World." *Les Nouvelles* 17, No. 1 (March 1982): 51.

Rieker, P. P. "Evaluation Research: The Design-to-Use Process." *Knowledge* 1 (1980): 499-514.

U.S. Agency for International Development (1981). *Management Development Strategy Paper: AID's Response to the Implementation Needs of 1980's*. Working Paper of the Management Development Working Group.

Walton, R. E. "The Diffusion of New York Structures: Explaining Why Success Didn't Take." *Organizational Dynamics* 3, No. 3 (1975): 3-22.

Yavas, Ugur. "The Turkish Marketing Scene: A First Hand Report." *Journal of International Marketing and Marketing Research* (October 1981): 83-95.

Index

About the Contributors

KENNETH D. BAHN is Assistant Professor of Marketing at Virginia Polytechnic Institute and State University. His areas of interest and publication are consumer behavior and buyer behavior.

S. TAMER CAVUSGIL is Professor of Marketing and Director of the Center for Business and Economic Research at Bradley University. He has published extensively in the areas of international marketing, international technology transfer, and export management.

SANDY B. CONNERS is a Ph.D. Candidate in Marketing at Virginia Polytechnic Institute and State University. Her research interest areas are distribution channels and feed distribution.

ASIM ERDILEK is Associate Professor of Economics at Case Western Reserve University. His areas of research interests are international trade theory and practice.

MARTIN L. GIMPL is Senior Lecturer at the Canterbury University, Christchurch, New Zealand. He has done research and has published in the areas of entrepreneurship, forecasting, and business strategy.

BRUCE D. HIENEMAN is an Instructor in Finance at Northeast Missouri State University, Kirksville, Missouri.

ERDENER KAYNAK is Professor of Marketing and Chairman of Department of Business Administration, Mount Saint Vincent University. He has published extensively on international food distribution systems, international comparative marketing systems, and Third World marketing practices.

RUSTAN KOSENKO is a Ph.D. Candidate at Virginia Polytechnic Institute and State University. He is Assistant Professor at MacMaster University, Canada. His research and publication interests are in the areas of industrial marketing, pricing, and international technology transfer.

MARILYN L. LIEBRENZ is Associate Professor of Business Administration at George Washington University. Her research interests are in international marketing strategy, technology transfer, and international competitiveness.

MARVIN B. MANDELL is Assistant Professor in Policy Sciences Graduate Program at the University of Maryland-Baltimore County. His research interest areas are techniques of quantitative analyses and the use of analytically based information in decision making.

STANLEY J. PALIWODA is a Lecturer at University of Manchester. He has published in the areas of technology transfer and international marketing. He is a specialist in European and marketing systems.

ALAN RAPOPORT is an Economist at National Science Foundation, Policy Research and Analysis Division. His research areas are international economics and economics of science and technology.

A. COSKUN SAMLI is Professor of Marketing at Virginia Polytechnic Institute and State University. He has done extensive research and publishing in the areas of international marketing, marketing and economic development, and technology transfer.

M. JOSEPH SIRGY is Assistant Professor of Marketing at Virginia Polytechnic Institute and State University and a Social/Organizational/Marketing Psychologist. He has done extensive research and publishing in consumer psychology and applications of general systems theory to marketing.

JANE H. WALTER is Assistant Professor of Human Development and Services at North Carolina Agricultural and Technological State University. She has done research and publishing in cross cultural counseling and women in development.

UGUR YAVAS is Associate Professor of Marketing at the University of Dhahran in Saudi Arabia. He has published extensively in many areas of marketing. His recent research interests are in international marketing and marketing research.

About the Editor

A. COSKUN SAMLI is Professor of Marketing and International Business at Virginia Polytechnic Institute and State University, Blacksburg, Virginia. He is the author of well over fifty journal articles on international business and marketing and most recently wrote *Marketing and Distribution Systems in Eastern Europe.*